Genocide in the Carpathians

Stanford Studies on Central and Eastern Europe
Edited by Norman Naimark and Larry Wolff

Genocide in the Carpathians
War, Social Breakdown, and Mass Violence, 1914–1945

Raz Segal

Stanford University Press
Stanford, California

Stanford University Press
Stanford, California

©2016 by the Board of Trustees of the Leland Stanford Junior University. All rights reserved.

This book has been published with the assistance of the Yoran Schnitzer Foundation and the Stephen Roth Institute for the Study of Contemporary Antisemitism and Racism at Tel Aviv University.

No part of this book may be reproduced or transmitted in any form or by any means, electronic or mechanical, including photocopying and recording, or in any information storage or retrieval system without the prior written permission of Stanford University Press.

Printed in the United States of America on acid-free, archival-quality paper

Library of Congress Cataloging-in-Publication Data

Names: Segal, Raz, author.
Title: Genocide in the Carpathians : war, social breakdown, and mass
   violence, 1914-1945 / Raz Segal.
Other titles: Stanford studies on Central and Eastern Europe.
Description: Stanford, California : Stanford University Press, 2016. |
   Series: Stanford studies on Central and Eastern Europe | Includes
   bibliographical references and index.
Identifiers: LCCN 2016010624 (print) | LCCN 2016011000 (ebook) |
   ISBN 9780804796668 (cloth) | ISBN 9780804798976 (electronic) |
   ISBN 9781503613607 (paper)
Subjects: LCSH: Genocide--Ruthenia (Czechoslovakia)--History--20th century. |
   Ruthenia (Czechoslovakia)--Ethnic relations--Political aspects. | World
   War, 1939-1945--Atrocities--Ruthenia (Czechoslovakia) | State-sponsored
   terrorism--Hungary--History--20th century. | Holocaust, Jewish
   (1939-1945)--Ruthenia (Czechoslovakia) | Hungary--Relations--Ruthenia
   (Czechoslovakia) | Ruthenia (Czechoslovakia)--Relations--Hungary.
Classification: LCC DK508.9.Z35 S44 2016 (print) | LCC DK508.9.Z35 (ebook) |
   DDC 947.7/9084--dc23
LC record available at http://lccn.loc.gov/2016010624

Typeset by Bruce Lundquist in 11/13.5 Adobe Garamond

Contents

List of Illustrations	vii
Preface and Acknowledgments	ix
Introduction	1
1 Subcarpathian Rus' Until World War I: A Culture Across Ethnic and Religious Boundaries	19
2 The World Beyond the Mountains: Embittered and Embattled Modernists in Interwar Czechoslovakia	33
3 A Little World War: Carpatho-Ukraine	51
4 A Big World War: "Greater Hungary" and Genocide in the Carpathians	65
5 Site of Hatreds: Destruction in Subcarpathian Rus'	89
Conclusions, Comparisons, Implications	113
Notes	129
Selected Bibliography	193
Index	205

Illustrations

Maps

1 The Subcarpathian Rus' counties in northeastern Hungary (Ung, Ugocsa, Bereg, Máramaros), early twentieth century — 2
2 Hungary in the twentieth century — 4
3 Carpatho-Ukraine, 1938–1939 — 53

Figures

1 Postcard depicting a street in Munkács, 1909 — 22
2 The empty field in the place of the old Jewish cemetery in Mukachevo, Ukraine, 2012 — 114

Preface and Acknowledgments

THIS BOOK represents a journey that lasted more than a decade. It took me to unexpected places—personally, emotionally, geographically, and professionally—though separating these spheres obviously works better on paper than in practice. As I traveled these intersecting paths, some of my initial baggage remained behind. Home, in the sense of attachments to certain people and places, changed, as some people and places left my life and new encounters slowly grew to form unwavering anchors. I therefore write the first words of gratitude to my partner during the last six years, Anat Plocker, whose love, care, insights, and advice proved crucial as I made my way across the stormy waters of research and writing.

Yehuda Bauer was the first to push me to explore the Jewish communities of the Carpathian region, and in the decade that followed since then, I enjoyed and benefited from countless discussions with him about my ideas and interpretations. Yet what began as a research project on the life and destruction of Jewish communities in one region during World War II within the paradigms of Jewish studies and Holocaust history quickly assumed additional dimensions. As I broadened the lens, I saw that studying the first half of the twentieth century in the Carpathian region offers a chance to examine, reexamine, think, and rethink central issues, processes, and linkages in modern European history.

This professional shift happened slowly, over the course of a few difficult years, both personally and professionally, and it would have certainly failed without the guidance, enormous support, and friendship of Debórah Dwork, the founding director of the Strassler Center for Holocaust and Genocide Studies at Clark University. Especially in moments when I felt the most anxious and lost, her advice filled me with renewed confidence and helped me find my path and my voice. Her unwavering dedication, energy, and commitment to the mission of the Strassler Center now inspire me immensely as I think about the future of Holocaust and genocide scholarship and my work within it. These few lines could never capture my sense of gratitude to Debórah, who has made it possible for me to envision my place in the field.

Landing in an unfamiliar place always prompts in me a blend of anxiety and anticipation. When I arrived in Budapest in the summer of 2010 for a year of archival research, my decadelong relationship had just collapsed, and a sense of uncertainty seemed as if it would last forever. Anxiety clearly dominated. The tremendous help I received from George Roth and his family as I arrived in the city thus truly lifted me up. George was born in the Carpathian region, in the town of Mukachevo, right after World War II, and when he heard about my work and me, he asked that I contact him when I landed in Budapest. I did, and he immediately made me feel at home. Quite literally: he and his wife offered me an apartment they owned right at the center of the city, and they spent a whole day driving me around and helping with the practicalities of settling into a new place. Throughout my year in Hungary they kept their door open for me, for which I cannot thank them enough. In Budapest, too, László Csősz, a colleague who became a good friend, has always shared with me his exceptional knowledge and expertise in the history of Hungary, as well as providing me with a place to sleep in short research trips before 2010.

I benefited from the dedicated work of archivists and librarians at Yad Vashem in Jerusalem; the Memorial Museum of Hungarian Speaking Jewry in Safed; the State Archives of the Transcarpathian Province in Berehovo; the Hungarian National Archives, the Archive of the Institute of Political History, the National Széchényi Library, and the Central European University in Budapest; the Joint Distribution Committee Archives and the YIVO Institute for Jewish Research in New York; and the United States Holocaust Memorial Museum in Washington, D.C.

It took me one long year to gain access to the State Archives of the Transcarpathian Province in Berehovo, and I would have surely remained on its doorstep if not for Rabbi Mendel Teichman, who then served as the region's rabbi in Uzhhorod. His help and connections opened crucial doors for me, and his family welcomed me warmly and generously every time I appeared in their home. Rabbi Teichman also introduced me to Robert Drob, who guided me patiently and kindly every time I traveled to the region, explained how I should best proceed in order to put my hands on the files in the archive, and went to great lengths to ensure that I felt comfortable in his hometown. The gratitude I owe to Rabbi Teichman and Robert deserves emphasis, as I could not have written the last two chapters of this book without the material I found in Berehovo.

Several people allowed me to consult private material in their possession. Meir Frankel of the Munkács community in Brooklyn generously invited me to his home to sift through a room full of reports, correspondence, newspapers, and photographs that he has gathered. And Thomas Mermall, a survivor from Poroskő, gave me a copy of the diary his father had kept while they hid together in the forests of the Carpathian Mountains between April and October 1944. I met Thomas when he came with his wife to listen to a lecture I delivered at the YIVO Institute for Jewish Research in New York in 2010. As it happened, I concluded my lecture with his story, based on an English translation of part of the diary that I had just found at the United States Holocaust Memorial Museum. In the following two years I enjoyed several meetings and discussions with Thomas, before his untimely death in September of 2011.

Research for this book involved reading in Hungarian, Yiddish, German, and Hebrew, as well as English. I spent two intensive summers in Hungary struggling with Hungarian, particularly in the Debrecen Summer School, followed by a year in which I lived in Budapest. Yet I would have never made it through the piles of documents that I accumulated during my research in Budapest and Berehovo without the dedicated help of Kata Bohus, a good friend and an excellent scholar of the history of Hungary after 1945. Kata also introduced me to Korlan Smagulova in Budapest, who translated from Russian and transcribed some of the testimonies of Roma that I found in the Shoah Foundation collection. Samuel Barnai translated and transcribed the rest.

The research for this book and the time it took for my ideas to ferment and, then, for me to put them into words required extensive financial resources, which I received from the Strassler Center for Holocaust and Genocide Studies at Clark University, the Fulbright Scholar Program, and the Natalia and Mendel Racolin Memorial Fellowship at the YIVO Institute for Jewish Research in New York. Two grants from the Hungarian Scholarship Board allowed me to learn Hungarian at the Debrecen Summer

School. A grant from Targum Shlishi, a Raquel and Aryeh Rubin Foundation, another grant from the Dr. Moshe and Prof. Margarete Fezzy Fund for the Study of Bohemian Jewry, and a personal gift from Yitzhak Livnat, a survivor from Nagyszőllős, made my financial situation a bit less dire just at the right moments. A generous fellowship from the Harry Frank Guggenheim Foundation supported me when I wrote major parts of the pages that follow. Finally, a Lady Davis Fellowship at the Avraham Harman Institute of Contemporary Jewry in the Hebrew University of Jerusalem and a Thomas Arthur Arnold Fellowship at the Zvi Yavetz School of Historical Studies in Tel Aviv University provided both vibrant intellectual settings and financial support as I revised, added, deleted, added again, and so on.

Many people in addition to those I have already mentioned became part of my journey. I shared my life for about a decade until 2009 with Shirly Bahar, a gifted scholar of Israel's society and culture, and our numerous conversations about her work and mine have contributed immensely to this book. Paul Robert Magocsi, the foremost expert on the history of the Carpathian region and Carpatho-Ruthenians, the majority population, has supported my work since we first met in his office at the University of Toronto in 2007. A leading scholar in Ukrainian studies, Magocsi guided me as I ventured into this field, introduced me to its central figures, and made sure that I could add my voice to debates and discussions that proved valuable as I shaped my arguments about relations between Jews and Carpatho-Ruthenians. Others read all or parts of the manuscript in some version and generously offered indispensable insights, help, and encouragement, as well as their friendship, for which I could not thank them enough. These include Yehonatan Alsheh, Betsy Anthony, Omer Bartov, Donald Bloxham, Evgeny Finkel, Alexis Herr, Thomas Kühne, Tom Lawson, Natalya Lazar, Mark Levene, Jody Manning, Dirk Moses, Antony Polonsky, Ilana Rosen, and Uğur Ümit Üngör. I am also grateful for the reviews of the anonymous readers, who gave me an opportunity to sharpen my arguments, correct some errors, and make sure to admit my fault for any of the oversights and partial interpretations that necessarily remain.

Daniel Blatman at the Hebrew University and Scott Ury at Tel Aviv University have offered much advice along the way, also helping me acquire a bit of orientation in the maze of Israeli academia. And I thank Amos Goldberg for hours on end of inspiring discussions that turned, since we first met in 2009, into friendship and a common endeavor to make some room in Israeli universities for the study of genocide and mass violence. I did not know a decade ago that this field of study even exists, and I did not yet know all the people I would meet as I ventured into it, individuals who would make this journey an enriching and exciting experience.

Finally, I am thankful for the support and encouragement I received at Stanford University Press throughout the publishing process. I am particularly appreciative of Norman Naimark, who, together with Larry Wolff, edits the Stanford Studies on Central and Eastern Europe; former executive editor Eric Brandt; assistant editor Friederike Sundaram; publishing director Kate Wahl; and production editor Mariana Raykov. And I am grateful for the terrific job of a number of people who worked with SUP: Joe Abbott, who copyedited the manuscript; Bill Nelson, who redrew the maps; and Daniela Blei, who prepared the index.

As I write these lines, my two-and-a-half-year-old daughter, Elka, is playing on the carpet right next to me. Everything interests her—every color, every shape, every object, and every new person who throws a smile her way. Her big, wondering eyes thus remind me all the time of the endless possibilities in the future. As I now bring this journey to an end and look to the future, I embrace Elka's curiosity, and, just as I stumbled across the Carpathian region a decade ago, I now seek a new encounter to push me to see and think about the world in ways I cannot yet imagine.

Genocide in the Carpathians

Introduction

THE LANDS OF EASTERN EUROPE—often referred to somewhat vaguely as east-central Europe and central Europe[1]—have attracted considerable scholarly attention since the end of World War II. The last twenty years, in particular, have seen the emergence of a large and diverse literature on that area of the world, ranging from social and political histories, to investigations of mass violence, to multidisciplinary analyses of literature and film. The borderlands of eastern Europe, however, have received limited treatment, and they remain under-researched or, as in the case of Subcarpathian Rus', almost completely neglected.[2] One reason for this lacuna may lie in the use of the term *borderland* and the images associated with it, which have elicited both idyllic and demonized interpretations of societies that live in such regions.[3] When used simply in a descriptive manner, however, the term need not raise preconceived notions that impede analytical clarity. The problem, rather, concerns the privilege enjoyed by research in the framework of nation-states, which affords short shrift to locations—both geographic and conceptual—that spill beyond it.[4] *Genocide in the Carpathians* shifts the lens, focusing on the margins of Czechoslovakia and Hungary during the interwar and World War II periods, respectively, both as viewed by the authorities and as experienced by the inhabitants of one region.

Addressing the potential of regional histories, historian Celia Applegate has captured the promises of centering (so to speak) the periphery: "What is at stake . . . is the extent to which a renewed engagement with the regional level of experience—an engagement sensitive to the interactions of

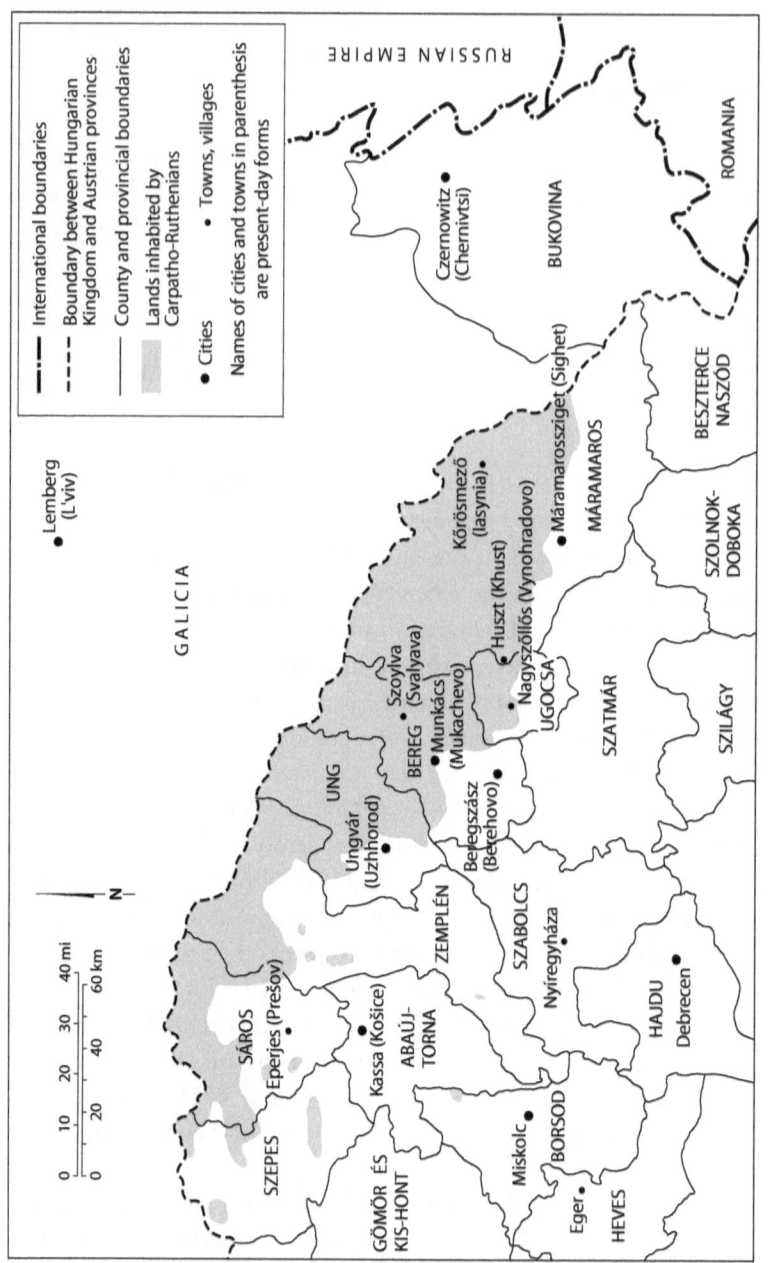

MAP 1. The Subcarpathian Rus' counties in northeastern Hungary (Ung, Ugocsa, Bereg, Máramaros) in the early twentieth century. Based on Paul Robert Magocsi, *The Shaping of a National Identity: Subcarpathian Rus', 1848–1948* (Cambridge, MA: Harvard University Press, 1978), 10. All maps adapted for use with permission from Professor Paul Robert Magocsi.

society, identity, and place—can productively destabilize our perceptions of European history. . . . It remains to be seen how a focus on the regional level of experience can help us once again to think big."⁵ More recently, the political scientist Charles King has identified and advocated for "a micropolitical turn" in the study of social violence, noting how macrolevel concerns about the reasons of violence have overshadowed a host of research questions about social mobilization, its impact on collective identities, and the vicissitudes of mass atrocities.⁶ Holly Case's study of another borderland area in wartime Hungary—Transylvania—deals precisely with these issues. Case shows how Hungary and Romania sought to take advantage of World War II and their roles in Nazi Germany's Axis alliance in order to realize violent political visions of nation and state building that clashed in Transylvania.⁷

Assuming a similar analytical lens, *Genocide in the Carpathians* draws on a diverse set of primary sources in Hungarian, Yiddish, Hebrew, and German, as well as English—correspondence and reports of state authorities, personal documents such as letters and postcards, and postwar testimonies and memoirs—to illuminate the social and political dynamics of multiethnic and multireligious Subcarpathian Rus' from the nineteenth century until immediately after World War II. During that period the region came under the rule of six different regimes and occupiers and was ultimately engulfed by the global conflagration of World War II and its immediate aftermath.

Subcarpathian Rus' consisted of four counties (vármegye)—Ung, Ugocsa, Bereg, and Máramaros—situated in the northeastern corner of the Hungarian Kingdom within the Austro-Hungarian Empire until World War I (map 1). Part of the Eastern Front moved back and forth in the region, and fighting went on until 1920 between Romanian, Hungarian, and Czech forces. Eventually, the territory became the easternmost part of interwar Czechoslovakia. In two stages, in November 1938 and March 1939, the Hungarian army occupied the region and crushed the autonomous Carpatho-Ukraine that existed during those few months within the Second Czecho-Slovak Republic. Another occupying force came in March 1944, as the Wehrmacht strolled into Hungary without so much as firing a single shot. Finally, after the Hungarian authorities and German occupiers joined hands enthusiastically in ghettoizing and deporting the region's Jews to Auschwitz in April, May, and June, the Soviet army took the area in October 1944. Within less than a year, in the summer of 1945, it turned into a part of Soviet Ukraine.

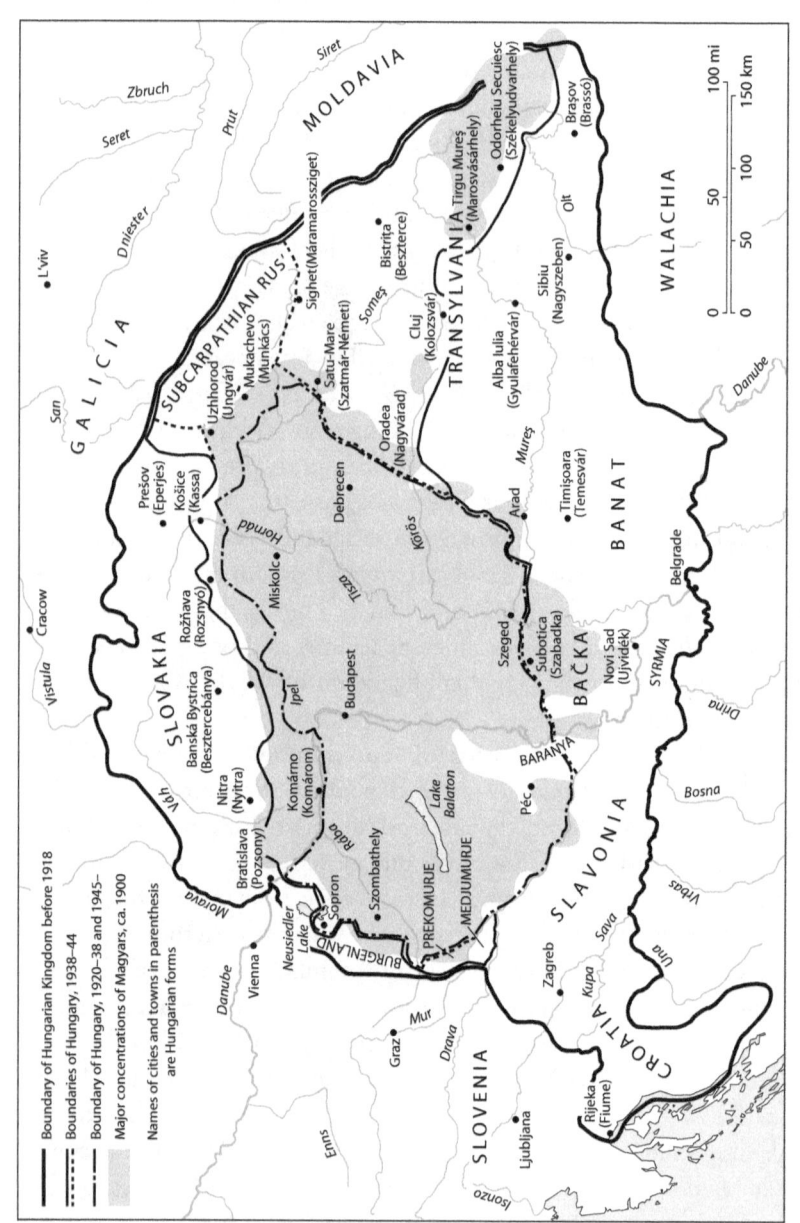

MAP 2. Hungary in the twentieth century. Based on Paul Robert Magocsi, *Historical Atlas of Central Europe* (Seattle: University of Washington Press, 2002), 147.

From 1938 the inhabitants of Subcarpathian Rus'—non-Jews as well as Jews—experienced a range of mass violence planned and implemented by the Hungarian authorities. These episodes included state-sponsored robbery, sporadic violence and uncoordinated expulsions, full-fledged deportations, and mass killings. An ethnonational vision fed this onslaught. The end of World War I and the Trianon Treaty (1920), which took from Hungary two-thirds of its prewar territories and three-fifths of its population, set the stage for the emergence of a revisionist consensus in Hungary and the longing to establish a "Greater Hungary" with a marked Magyar majority.[8] This vision entailed a multilayered attack against non-Magyars, first and foremost in the multiethnic and multireligious borderlands—northeastern Hungary and Subcarpathian Rus', northern Transylvania, and Bácska and Baranya, which Hungary occupied from Czechoslovakia, Romania, and Yugoslavia, respectively, between November 1938 and April 1941 (map 2).[9]

The view of the state from the time of Hungarian rule before World War I sharpened in the turmoil of national defeat and humiliation, assuming exclusivist and violent dimensions. Whereas Budapest perceived minority populations in the borderlands of the Hungarian Kingdom as backward and had tried to "magyarize" them aggressively before World War I, from 1938 onward, as the Hungarian army occupied these regions, the authorities turned increasingly to mass violence in order to shape their societies into integral parts of a Magyar-dominated state. Although different from colonialism and imperialism in a number of ways, the idea of a "Greater Hungary" derived from the colonial binaries of civilization and backwardness that marked the cultural boundaries of Europe. Asserting primacy and eliminating difference in the borderlands of "Greater Hungary" involved "civilizing" projects and efforts at assimilation. Various considerations and opportunities rendered large-scale deportations and mass murder a desirable option at certain points in time, and changing circumstances induced processes of de-escalation to less lethal forms of mass violence and oppression. While the state rather than a settler population designed and carried out mass violence and other measures, the regime aimed, in a way similar to colonial violence, to facilitate the expansion of "Greater Hungary" through cultural and social destruction.[10]

Indeed, the designs, plans, and policies of Hungary reveal significant continuities that stretch before and after March 1944—when Nazi Germany invaded Hungary—shifting the focus from the typical treatment of the Holocaust in Hungary in the frame of the German "final solution" to the Hungarian drive to remake society and the state. Understanding the specific victimization of the Jews in Subcarpathian Rus' thus rests on an exploration of modern Hungarian history and an appreciation of the links between different layers of violence and measures that the government aimed at groups under its control.

The multilayered mass violence that descended on the inhabitants of the towns and villages in the mountains and on the slopes of the Carpathians changed their social fabric. *Genocide in the Carpathians* traces and explains the relations between Jews and their Carpatho-Ruthenian neighbors, the majority population in the region, as both groups faced a violent state.[11] The persecution and destruction of the Jewish communities in Subcarpathian Rus' is thus viewed through the lens of intergroup relations under the impact of external political and military processes.

Subcarpathian Rus': Historical Background

Subcarpathian Rus',[12] today the Transcarpathian (Zakarpats'ka) oblast in western Ukraine, is an eastern European borderland inhabited by a multiethnic and multireligious population (more multi in the past, but still so today), with a history replete with examples that show how peripheral societies face and respond to rapid national, military, economic, and social changes. The region stretches from the Carpathian Mountains (the Polonyna Beskyds and Hutsul Alps) to the south, with its main towns (Uzhhorod, Mukachevo, Berehovo, Vynohradovo, and Khust) at the foothills, where the Hungarian plain begins. Carpatho-Ruthenians, the majority population in Subcarpathian Rus' (about 445,000 people in 1930, or 63 percent), have stoked debate about their ethnic and national identification. Four competing interpretations have vied for supremacy since the second half of the nineteenth century: Russian, Ukrainian, Carpatho-Ruthenian, and Hungarian.[13] Religion also divides Carpatho-Ruthenians; struggles between the Greek Catholic (Uniate) Church and the Orthodox Church punctuate the history of the region.[14]

The ethnic mosaic of the region prior to World War II consisted, in addition, of Magyars (ethnic Hungarians, 115,000, 15 percent) and Jews (100,000, 13 percent), as well as small numbers of Czechs, Slovaks, Romanians, Germans (*Karpatendeutschen*), and Roma.[15] Romanians dominated in the southeastern part of the Hungarian county of Máramaros (Rumanian Maramureş), most of which, south of the Tisza River, became part of

Romania after World War I. Local Germans, who had immigrated to the region from the early eighteenth century on, lived mainly in the vicinity of Munkács and Huszt and in the mountainous areas of Máramaros.[16] And almost completely overlooked by scholars, groups of Roma have inhabited the region since the fifteenth century.[17]

Coexistence marked interethnic relations well into the interwar period, particularly between Jews and Carpatho-Ruthenians. This situation, because of the seclusion of the region until after World War I and the strength of local identities that transcended ethnic and religious divides, changed as Subcarpathian Rus' opened to the world around it. Archival and oral history sources suggest that no significant anti-Jewish sentiments existed among Carpatho-Ruthenians until the 1920s, when the new officials from Prague who arrived as agents of Czech state building governed in a way that induced the perception of Jews as disloyal to their longtime neighbors. As we will see, concerns about loyalty and disloyalty, tied to ethnic groups and to their imagined threat to the social order and the state, became dominant markers that decided the fate of people under Hungarian occupation.

Research Approaches

The multiethnic and multireligious character of society in Subcarpathian Rus' sits at the heart of this book.[18] My analysis locates the persecution and annihilation of Jews in Subcarpathian Rus' in the context of plans and policies of the Hungarian state to obliterate diversity and create a Magyar majority through various state measures and, whenever national and international opportunities allowed, mass deportations. As we will see, these schemes targeted Carpatho-Ruthenians and Roma in addition to Jews. Such contextualization challenges much of the existing scholarship on the Holocaust in Hungary and focuses attention on multilayered mass violence, where interrelated attacks take place in the same territory. Focusing in this way on processes rather than outcomes elucidates the destruction of Jewish communities in Subcarpathian Rus' during World War II as rooted *primarily* in Hungarian contexts and circumstances that intersected with German plans and industrial mass killing in Auschwitz.

Combining and integrating several points of view fleshes out those Hungarian contexts. Because of the problems of reading the histories of Jews in Europe as culminating deterministically in the Holocaust or, alternatively, with the Holocaust bracketed out of them, *Genocide in the Carpathians* explicitly bridges the history of Jews in Subcarpathian Rus' before and during World War II.[19] It also treats the modern history of Jews in Europe as an integral part of modern European history. While this frame may seem obvious, existing scholarship on the region consists of parallel rather than intertwined accounts.[20] The study of the Holocaust underscores this kind of divide, as only recently and with much controversy have scholars begun to draw lines from the genocide of Jews in Europe to mass violence in modern Europe before, during, and after World War II.[21]

My narrative, then, looks at links and connections rather than comparisons, which have given rise to conceptual and methodological problems associated with the hierarchies created by the terms *Holocaust*, *genocide*, and *ethnic cleansing*.[22] Thinking about the Holocaust as unique, using whatever word or rhetorical device, has overshadowed other processes and events in human history. Such scales have also marginalized an integrated picture of World War II, which challenges the strict isolation and separation of these categories and, in the case of Hungary, points to new interpretative frameworks concerning the destruction of Jewish communities and the mass murder of more than half a million Jews.

Numerous stories of individuals, families, communities, villages, and towns portray the intra- and intergroup dynamics within this history in Subcarpathian Rus'. Foregrounding them, *Genocide in the Carpathians* confronts all too common assumptions about social relations in eastern Europe, particularly between Jews and their neighbors. It discusses the ways in which common feelings among Jews and Carpatho-Ruthenians of a shared society gave way to hostility and conflict, tearing the social fabric apart even as both groups came under attack from outside.

Methodologies

Survivors' Accounts

Deciphering the ways in which social interactions changed with shifting political, social, and military situations, as tens of thousands of Jews and non-Jews in the region faced foreign occupation and increasingly harsh state measures and violence, calls for engagement with survivors' accounts. In addition to the window these sources open on to personal experiences, they illuminate the political atmosphere of persecution and mass murder, the actions of killers, and the responses of onlookers.

The methodological pitfalls posed by the use of postwar testimonies in writing Holocaust history have received much attention, especially concerning the incorporation of patterns of collective memory, rumors, and intentional as well as unintentional mistakes into survivors' descriptions and narratives. Yet prompted by earlier work of literary scholars and by current studies in anthropology, particularly on the significance of "raw memories" and "subaltern subjectivities," a growing consensus among historians treats testimonies as indispensable.[23] Key studies in recent years on the Holocaust *and* on other cases of mass violence have furthermore relied on survivors' accounts specifically to gain insight into intergroup dynamics.[24] *Genocide in the Carpathians* thus turns to several collections of postwar testimonies of Holocaust survivors (recorded at different times, in a number of places, and in several languages), as well as personal accounts of non-Jews—such as testimonies of Roma who lived in the region during World War II and suffered persecution at the hands of the Hungarian authorities[25]—in order to shed light on the changing nature of social relations in Subcarpathian Rus' in the first half of the twentieth century.[26]

Recasting Terms: Antisemitism *and* Bystanders

Fine-grained scrutiny of the relations between Jews and Carpatho-Ruthenians raises new questions on the meanings of two key terms: *antisemitism* and *bystanders*. These concepts are so commonly invoked that scholars rarely define them. The historian David Engel has posited that the general and all-encompassing usages of the word *antisemitism* have rendered it a rather blunt concept that betrays a lack of analytical attention to historical contingency.[27] In his study of discrimination and violence against minorities in medieval Europe, historian David Nirenberg made a similar point, asserting that "quests for the origins of European intolerance have much in common. All take the long view, seeking to establish a continuity between the hatreds of long ago and those of the here and now. This focus on the *longue durée* means that events are read less within their local contexts than according to a teleology leading, more or less explicitly, to the Holocaust."[28] Treating anti-Jewish persecution and violence in local contexts pushes us to identify, describe, and explain the connections between these events and processes and others that happened at the same time and place, including other instances of mass violence. Yet although widening the lens to include such links would follow standard professional practice, histories of antisemitism have remained largely severed from such relevant contexts, reflecting the central role of the term in formulating both the history of Jews and the Holocaust within and beyond that history as unique. Saul Friedländer's *Nazi Germany and the Jews, 1939–1945* (2007), a central and widely celebrated contribution in Holocaust scholarship of the last decade, exemplifies the perspective that separates the Holocaust from key events that affected non-Jews during World War II.[29] In his introduction Friedländer summarizes (not entirely accurately) important scholarly trends only to marginalize them and place them beyond his purview:

> The persecution and extermination of the Jews of Europe was but a secondary consequence of major German policies pursued toward entirely different goals. Among these, the ones most often mentioned include a new economic and demographic equilibrium in occupied Europe by murdering surplus populations, ethnic reshuffling and decimation to facilitate German colonization in the East, and the systematic plunder of the Jews in order to facilitate the waging of the war without putting too heavy a material burden on German society or, more precisely, on Hitler's national-racial state. Notwithstanding the vistas sporadically opened by such studies, their general thrust is manifestly incompatible with the central postulates underlying my own interpretation.[30]

Friedländer's "central postulates," as he explains in the next sentence, consist of the "ideological-cultural factors as the prime movers of Nazi policies in regard to the Jewish issue."[31] Thus, Friedländer's much vaunted "integrated history"—a narrative that seeks to combine the viewpoints of perpetrators, victims, and the surrounding world—integrates rather selectively. By asserting that the examination of the messy and complex world of mass atrocities during World War II holds merely sporadic merit, Friedländer in effect limited the explanatory potential of his major analytical concept, "redemptive anti-Semitism."[32]

Indeed, the old controversies in Holocaust historiography between intentionalists and functionalists and the more recent debates about the Holocaust in the frame of Nazi colonial mass violence show, beyond the lingering disagreements, that the term *antisemitism* may easily blur complex realities, in which anti-Jewish ideas, positions, and policies intermingled with other interests and evolved into actions in pursuit of multiple goals.[33] A number of scholars have demonstrated how exploring multidimensional pictures in German-occupied areas in Poland and the Soviet Union *sheds new light* on the Holocaust.[34] This perspective also charts a new research path in the study of Hungary during World War II and, more broadly, of the Axis and German-occupied states in southeast Europe. In-depth research on Romania and the Ustaša regime in Croatia, for example, moves us beyond the traditional focus in Holocaust scholarship on the role of Nazi Germany[35] or the area that historian Timothy Snyder has labeled "the Bloodlands"[36] and holds much potential for new ways to think about, understand, and connect World War II to other wars and mass atrocities in modern Europe.[37]

Like *antisemitism*, the term *bystanders* deserves critical attention. Although many comprehensive accounts of the Holocaust have focused on either perpetrators or victims, few have treated in detail the standpoint of bystanders under direct German or Axis rule.[38] The existing scholarship also tends to use *bystanders* as a static category, similar to the prevalent treatment of perpetrators and victims;[39] as with the way that *antisemitism* appears in many studies, *specific* conditions rarely figure in the discussion. Furthermore, although social psychologist Ervin Staub analyzed bystanders in genocide as active agents in *The Roots of Evil* (published in 1989),[40] it took more than a decade for his ideas to spur additional explorations. Historian Tim Cole and, more recently, political scientist Ernesto Verdeja have shown the way by emphasizing the dynamic quality of the bystander position.[41]

Examination of the contexts that framed the *interactions* between Jews and Carpatho-Ruthenians provides a fresh perspective on bystanders both as a research category and as active people, notwithstanding the dangers and constraints of mass violence in Subcarpathian Rus'. More specifically, we learn of the *particular* nature of the anti-Jewish enmity that emerged among Carpatho-Ruthenians before and during World War II and why, in most cases, it failed to turn into physical aggression. Contrary to much received wisdom, *Genocide in the Carpathians* suggests that animosities not rooted in well-established public discourses carry little potential to become violent. The debate around Jan Gross's work on the Jedwabne pogrom in German-occupied Poland (summer 1941) has given rise to scholarship that emphasizes communal violence against Jews in eastern Europe during World War II. Yet a broad European—even only eastern European— perspective suggests that such violence happened much less frequently than we imagine.[42] Jews in Subcarpathian Rus' and in the other wartime border territories of Hungary suffered the violent demise of their worlds and lives with very little communal violence, if at all. This raises questions about social crises in which many people see and hear state violence without taking part directly in the carnage.

Emotion-Based Approach to Mass Violence

Emotions play an indispensable role in human affairs, especially when it comes to the formation of group identities and related behavior patterns in times of turmoil. Yet, as historian Joanna Bourke has argued, emotions as an analytical subject have been overshadowed as a result of an "emphasis on rationality following the belief that arguments about change over time can be constructed only through the analysis of ideology or economic structures. . . . Focusing on human rationality seemed a more respectful way of interpreting people's behavior in the past."[43] While some scholars certainly adhere to such reasoning, political scientist Roger Petersen has pointed out that "no one denies that emotions exist, but few have tried to systematically link them to ethnic conflict."[44]

Indeed, social psychologists Daniel Bar-Tal, Eran Halperin, and Joseph de Rivera have stressed that "emotions constitute a central element of the human repertoire and that the study of their functioning is a prerequisite for the understanding of individual and collective behaviors." However, "research on the role played by emotional climate and other collective emotions in conflicts and conflict resolution is only at its primary stages."[45] Social psychologists Colin Leach and Larissa Tiedens have explained, more generally, that weaving "together emotional experiences and expression with social relationships, the emotional is seen as very social and the social as very emotional."[46] Recognizing the significance of emotions in the history we seek to understand, Alon Confino has observed that "the persecution and extermination of the Jews was fueled by emotions, and all interpretations that avoid, deny, or ignore this are bound to miss a fundamental human element embedded in the event."[47] As my critique of the terms *antisemitism* and *bystanders* drills down exactly on the human element, asking how Jews and Carpatho-Ruthenians lived together and drifted apart, work on the history and sociology of emotions affords a new lens to interpret these social dynamics.

Building on historian Barbara Rosenwein's programmatic essay on emotions in history[48] and on Roger Petersen's study of emotions in eastern Europe throughout the twentieth century,[49] *Genocide in the Carpathians* discusses the meanings that Jews and Carpatho-Ruthenians attached to identities, social encounters, and shared memories, as they tried to make sense of political and social changes. More specifically, anti-Jewish animosity emerged among Carpatho-Ruthenians for the first time in the 1920s and 1930s, framed by a sense of crisis engendered by the policies of the Czechoslovak state. The government in Prague would not grant Carpatho-Ruthenians autonomy, as stipulated in the agreements it signed after World War I. As we will see, the real and perceived role of Jews in maintaining this decision bred much resentment. This emotion, in turn, functioned as an affective disposition through which many Carpatho-Ruthenians interpreted events and responded to them as both they and their Jewish neighbors faced mass violence under Hungarian occupation.[50]

While many accounts implicitly or explicitly associate antisemitism with hatred and, by implication, a potential for violence, the social fabric in Subcarpathian Rus' before and during World War II disintegrated without violence between neighbors. Evoking hatred also often marginalizes the relational aspect and the particular histories that framed contact between people. Yet what Jews felt toward non-Jews and how they engaged with them—and vice versa—figure as essential elements in this study, as it focuses on the political processes through which social relations generated emotions that, in turn, realigned ties across society.[51] Scholarship on emotions thus helps to move us beyond the generalizations and limitations imposed by the terms *antisemitism* and *bystanders* in describing and explaining the motivations, choices, and forms of behavior of Carpatho-Ruthenians *and* Jews as these had changed from one world war to the next.

Subcarpathian Rus' in the Twentieth Century: An Integrated History

Genocide in the Carpathians assumes a broad view and constructs a narrative of the intertwined pasts of the groups that *together* composed the society and culture that came under pressure and attack by several central and regional state authorities as they strove to realize visions of nation and state building. The integrated approach in this study, therefore, draws on scholarship in several fields—the histories of Hungary and Czechoslovakia, Holocaust history and genocide research, the history of Jews, and Ukrainian studies. This frame casts a wide net to show how the changes and tribulations that punctuated the history of Subcarpathian Rus' in the first half of the twentieth century tell us much about central issues in the history of modern Europe.

Paul Robert Magocsi's monumental work *The Shaping of a National Identity: Subcarpathian Rus', 1848–1948* (1978)—still a rare contribution in

Ukrainian studies on the region[52]—traces the emergence and trajectories of national movements and related issues of language among Carpatho-Ruthenians. It addresses mostly the period prior to World War II, focusing on the perceptions and actions of state authorities and Carpatho-Ruthenian leaders with very little consideration of how they affected social relations in the region. *Genocide in the Carpathians* builds on this analysis by exploring the interactions within the region's multiethnic and multireligious society rather than just one group, for significant aspects of the formation of national identities in the region emerged out of these social dynamics.

The interwar period, in particular, when Czechoslovakia ruled Subcarpathian Rus', proved crucial to the crystallization of national movements, in part as a response to state-building policies envisioned in Prague that changed the nature of relations between Jews and Carpatho-Ruthenians. This work thus foregrounds a region overlooked by recent scholarship on interwar Czechoslovakia, contributing to the shift of emphasis from that state as an exceptional democracy in central and eastern Europe at the time to the characteristics it shared with its increasingly more authoritarian neighbors, including discriminatory measures against minorities.[53]

If thinking of nationalism among Carpatho-Ruthenians with little reference to other groups tells a partial story, concentrating exclusively on Jews proves equally problematic. While the few scholarly works that deal with Jews in the region provide important viewpoints to consider, as well as fascinating material, they hardly discuss the experiences of Jews in light of the varied composition of the region's population and its history as a whole.[54]

Insufficient grounding in broad historical contexts particularly impedes examination of the annihilation of Jews and Jewish communities in Subcarpathian Rus' in the spring and summer of 1944. Randolph Braham's two-volume magnum opus *The Politics of Genocide* will most probably remain the single most important reading for students of the destruction of Jews in Hungary.[55] Yet it pays only scant attention to the crucial links between policies and actions against Jews and assaults aimed at other groups in the frame of the political vision of "Greater Hungary" before and after March 1944. While the work of historians Christian Gerlach and Götz Aly on Hungary places more emphasis on the role of the Hungarian state, they still train their lens on the period after the German invasion of Hungary and, for the most part, disregard the historical trajectory of Subcarpathian Rus'.[56]

Two elements mark the literature on the Holocaust in Hungary. First, it addresses mostly Budapest and the provinces within the Trianon borders, reflecting thereby a more general tendency in scholarship on the history of Jews in Hungary.[57] Tim Cole's *Traces of the Holocaust*, an influential contribution in the field, is a social history with eye-opening insights. It deals, however, almost exclusively with areas within the pre-1938 borders of Hungary—that is, before the occupation of the wartime border territories between November 1938 and April 1941—but in the post-March 1944 period, even though around half of the approximately half-million victims of the Holocaust in Hungary had lived in the borderlands.[58] Encompassing a larger span of time, Paul Hanebrink's *In Defense of Christian Hungary*, another central work, provides a masterful examination of the persecution and destruction of Jews in modern Hungary as part of a Christian anti-Jewish project.[59] But Subcarpathian Rus' and the other borderlands of "Greater Hungary" appear in the text only sporadically. Hence, while the book certainly discusses Christian Hungary as a western Christian project, it pays no attention to the ways in which this political endeavor excluded not only Jews but also Orthodox and Slavic Christians, namely Romanians, Serbs, and Carpatho-Ruthenians, albeit in different ways.

Scholarship on the Holocaust in Hungary, furthermore, ascribes mass violence in Hungary mostly to German influence and, after March 1944, German policies, while portraying pre-1944 mass atrocities as anomalies to a general atmosphere that provided Jews with safety, even as they faced stigmatization and a whole host of restrictions and discriminatory measures.[60] Almost all the (limited) scholarship on the mass deportations of summer 1941—a central episode of mass violence discussed extensively in Chapter 4—adheres to this line of interpretation.[61] Building on recent research on other borderlands in wartime Hungary, this study not only shifts the focus from the center to the borderlands but also reverses this argument, laying bare how the destruction of Subcarpathian Rus' Jews flowed from the vision of "Greater Hungary" and the designs and initiatives of Hungarian authorities with regard to the treatment of Jews *and* other groups.[62]

Moving beyond accounts formed exclusively around national or ethnic groups and the limiting construct of the nation-state, *Genocide in the Carpathians* incorporates the perspectives and sources produced by the authorities of the states that governed the region and the people who lived there in the era of two global wars and shifting borders. It explores the intricate web of relations and interactions among the groups in the region, and the linkages between state policies and mass violence aimed at them both separately and collectively.

Chapters 1 through 3 follow the lives of Jews and Carpatho-Ruthenians until World War II. Jews and Carpatho-Ruthenians maintained porous collective boundaries in the nineteenth century and led lives that, in many ways, flowed into each other and constituted together a society and culture that was larger than the sum of its parts. This situation pertained to occupational choices, residential patterns, and, significantly, to popular religious worldviews anchored in beliefs about supernatural powers. These shared experiences came under pressure when the region became part of Czechoslovakia after World War I. The interests and policies of the government in Prague proved detrimental to the collective aspirations of Carpatho-Ruthenians, who, in turn, believed that Jews preferred to support a foreign power rather than their neighbors, mostly by sending their children to Czech rather than Carpatho-Ruthenian schools. This political constellation gave rise to anti-Jewish resentments, exacerbated by local Ukrainophile activists and Ukrainian nationalists who crossed into the region from the other side of the Carpathian Mountains.

While nationalists deepened the emerging conflict in interwar Subcarpathian Rus' along ethnic lines, political and religious tensions fractured the social setting within groups. The Jewish communities in Subcarpathian Rus' saw some of the most bitter and aggressive conflicts between Orthodox and ultra-Orthodox Judaism at the time. In an effort to gain and secure communal power, both camps, along with Zionists Left and Right, threw themselves into the fray of a highly contentious scene in itself of local, regional, and national politics in Czechoslovakia. A parallel struggle pitted Greek Catholic against Orthodox Christian Carpatho-Ruthenians, which also intermeshed with political clashes between Carpatho-Ruthenian Ukrainophile and Russophile nationalists and between each faction and the state. This situation of social segmentation heightened the problems associated with choosing allies and maintaining or breaking loyalties, thus rendering all the more intense the evolving fissure between Jews and Carpatho-Ruthenians.

This intergroup tension played a part in the small-scale anti-Jewish violence that erupted during the Ukrainophile-dominated autonomous Carpatho-Ukraine in late 1938 and early 1939, though foreign Ukrainian nationalists figured prominently among the organizers and perpetrators. As the Hungarian army invaded the region and destroyed Carpatho-Ukraine, it engaged in several days of mass killings of Carpatho-Ruthenians—mainly local Ukrainophile militiamen but also noncombatants. Jews witnessed these killings; even if some of them wished to help their neighbors, they feared the consequences—and rightly so. Many Jews, however, saw the Hungarian soldiers as rescuers, even though the new rulers wasted no time in making their aggressive intentions against *all* non-Magyars in the region painfully clear, with Jews singled out as especially foreign, disloyal, and dangerous. A society immersed in tensions and conflict faced this concerted attack of the Hungarian occupation that would last five years.

Chapters 4 and 5 elaborate on how the Hungarian authorities sought to transform the region's society to fit their vision of "Greater Hungary." This translated into systematic discrimination and persecution that, in moments of opportunity, morphed into mass violence against Jews, Roma, and Carpatho-Ruthenians. These chapters assume an analytical lens that looks at the *links* between the layers of violence against different groups rather than the more common tendency to think about the fate of Jews *in comparison* to that of another group. Jews figured at the top of the Hungarian authorities' list of victims and faced a sustained attack on a larger scale than Roma and Carpatho-Ruthenians. Yet the analysis of the connecting threads in this multilayered system of violence illuminates the persecution and deportation of the Jews in a new way by considering Hungarian policies *as a whole*.

Looking at the broad picture rather than just a segment—such as the common tendency in Holocaust scholarship to view the period after the German invasion of Hungary in March 1944 and the destruction of Jewish life there as a separate time and event—reveals the continuities that marked the activities of the Hungarian occupiers before and after Adolf Eichmann arrived in Budapest to make the necessary arrangements for a swift genocide. The Hungarian campaign for ethnonational "homogenization" since 1938 thus becomes a necessary element in the account of the ghettoization and mass deportations of Subcarpathian Rus' Jews in the spring and summer of 1944. This broader perspective also underlines how the general term *antisemitism* actually blurs the Hungarian state's anti-Jewish policies and actions by concealing the drive to renounce the claims of belonging of non-Magyars in Subcarpathian Rus'—non-Jews as well as Jews—an essential goal in the planned transformation of the region's society and its integration into "Greater Hungary."

Finally, chapters 4 and 5 chart the demise of the relations between Jews and Carpatho-Ruthenians, which meant that, for the most part, they faced persecution and state violence apart. Yet anti-Jewish resentments failed to push the shared past completely out of people's memories, and we therefore encounter almost no cooperation of Carpatho-Ruthenians with the Hungarian occupiers against Jews. We also see no anti-Jewish communal violence during the war and none after the war, when Jewish survivors returned to the region in search of property and family. This pattern of Carpatho-Ruthenian behavior offers another opportunity to engage critically with the concept of *antisemitism*, now concerning social relations rather than the view of the state and with regard to another general term: *bystanders*. Scrutinizing the meanings of these concepts in the history of Subcarpathian Rus' paves the way for our understanding of the social breakdown caused first because of policies of state building that extended from Prague to the region for almost twenty years after World War I, followed by the onslaught of the Hungarian occupation during World War II that aimed to transform the Carpathians into the northeastern reaches of an ethnonational "Greater Hungary."

Subcarpathian Rus' is a small place. But, to return to the words of historian Celia Applegate, it is small places that help us to "think big." Focusing on Subcarpathian Rus' indeed turns our attention to a central problem in the history of modern Europe—changes in the sense of belonging and in conceptions and perceptions of citizenship as articulated both by state authorities and between neighbors, and whether, how, and why these ideas, emotions, and interactions assumed violent and destructive dimensions. This perspective and these questions contribute to our understanding of the Holocaust as a nexus of multidimensional processes of mass violence. Some of these unfolded independently of the German drive for continent-wide genocide but, at certain junctures, helped turn the "final solution" into a truly international campaign of mass murder. Furthermore, dominant images of foreignness and disloyalty to the Hungarian state linked the attacks against Jews with the assaults on other groups. Highlighting in this way political as well as ideological elements illuminates the impetus to eliminate Jews and Jewish communities not only in Subcarpathian Rus' but also across Axis states in southeast Europe. Grounding the events and processes that we call the Holocaust in European contexts places them within discussions of modern genocides around the globe not as exceptional or paradigmatic points of reference but as integral parts of the political and social systems of the modern and late modern world.

1

Subcarpathian Rus' Until World War I
A Culture Across Ethnic and Religious Boundaries

THE SEEDS OF THE HISTORICAL DYNAMICS that unfolded in Subcarpathian Rus' during the interwar years and World War II lay embedded in the pre–World War I era. What characterized the borderland society of Subcarpathian Rus' before it began to unravel? What roles and positions did Jews occupy? And what was typical of their relations with other groups in the region? The brutal years of World War I that brought this period to a close offer important insights that can help us to understand the later acute crisis that culminated in social disintegration and destruction of Jewish life. Most important, the ways in which external forces introduced violence into the area would continue to color the lives of Jews and non-Jews from one global war to the next.

The experience of estrangement in relation to external elements such as the Hungarian state figured prominently in the history of Jews in Subcarpathian Rus'. It also marked the history of the majority population, Carpatho-Ruthenians. Between them, however, these two groups found much common ground. The factors that accounted for such relations stand at the center of this chapter.

The Nineteenth Century

Jews had begun to settle in Subcarpathian Rus' in the middle of the seventeenth century, and a substantial Jewish presence developed in the first half of the nineteenth century.[1] Between 1830 and 1880 the Jewish population in the region increased dramatically, in tandem with the rapid growth of the population as a whole.² The flow of Galician Jewish immigrants into Subcarpathian Rus', prompted by the partitions of Poland at the end of the eighteenth century, led to the establishment and steady growth of new communities throughout the nineteenth century. The Yiddish-speaking, highly religious character of Galician Jews, particularly Hasidism, thus became a dominant feature of Jewish life in Subcarpathian Rus'.

In most cases local magnates encouraged Jewish settlement. The Schönborn family invited the first Jews to Munkács (Mukachevo), which would become the center of Jewish life in the region. In 1741 these Jews established the first synagogue for their community of around eighty people.³ By the beginning of the twentieth century, nine more synagogues served more than sixty-five hundred souls.⁴ On the eve of World War I Jews numbered almost half of the town's population.⁵ Jewish communities in other towns followed similar patterns of increase.⁶

The region remained a remote area, with few resources, almost no industry, and a mostly poor and illiterate population until World War I.⁷ Only two natural resources sustained the local economy: timber and salt, the latter found mainly in the mine in Aknaszlatina (Solotvyno) in the far eastern part of the region. The salt deposits in Subcarpathian Rus' yielded more than one hundred million kilograms in 1912, which was worth almost twenty million kronen (around four million US dollars at the time).⁸ Otherwise, lack of development marked the area. In 1910 only fifty industrial businesses with more than twenty employees existed.⁹

The poverty of most Jews in Subcarpathian Rus' enhanced their conservative outlook on life and traditional thinking. They looked to their local rabbis for authority in every aspect of life. Such power bestowed control, which rested in the rabbis' hands and was manifested institutionally through their domination of communal bodies and *yeshivot*,¹⁰ as well as in the daily routine of Jewish life. Large families rendered the struggle to make a living especially difficult, but the influence of religious figures ensured the persistence of such traditional practices, and the isolated environment of the region throughout the nineteenth century reinforced this cycle. The social structure and hierarchies thus barely changed until World War I.

These internal characteristics suited the interests of the Hungarian rulers, who regarded the area as a colony.¹¹ The elites that governed the Hungarian Kingdom from 1867 onward had consistently sought to establish Magyar demographic dominance in the areas they controlled. Until World War I they chose aggressive "magyarization" as a means to create a Magyar majority in a kingdom with substantial non-Magyar populations. This policy focused on measures aimed at education and religious institutions—the main places where people acquire their sense of identity.[12] These attempts in Subcarpathian Rus' failed for the most part, notwithstanding their success among Carpatho-Ruthenian Greek Catholic priests. While many priests adopted Hungarian in the liturgy, their parishioners eschewed it in daily life. Living in remote localities throughout the region, the vast majority of Carpatho-Ruthenians continued to speak local dialects and remained distant from Hungarian culture.[13] Most Jews in Subcarpathian Rus', who also lived in the small towns and villages throughout the region, continued to adhere to their way of life as well, even as many of those who settled in the towns at the foot of the Carpathian Mountains learned Hungarian.[14]

Seeking ethnic dominance, Hungarian leaders feared Russian influences in the region, including Orthodoxy. This phobia of Slavic culture, heightened by the interest of Russian scholars and politicians in Subcarpathian Rus' in the late nineteenth century and early twentieth, culminated in a series of trials between 1904 and 1914. The most infamous of these took place in Máramarossziget (1913–1914) against ninety-four Carpatho-Ruthenian farmers who had converted to Orthodoxy and were accused of treacherous ties with Russia.[15] Sharpened by the failure of "magyarization," these trepidations would return to shape state policies with fatal consequences when Hungary ruled the region during World War II.[16]

Hungarian authorities were not alone in their arrogant and contemptuous treatment of the local culture of Subcarpathian Rus'. Most Jews in Hungary referred to Jews in Subcarpathian Rus' using words with degrading connotations, such as *Ostjuden* or *Galitzianer*; indeed, extremely religious and inward-looking, the region's Jews stood at the opposite end of the spectrum from the enthusiastically acculturated community in Budapest, as well as in other places in Hungary.[17] Thus, an article in the first edition (1884) of the *Magyar Zsidó Szemle* (*Hungarian Jewish Review*), a journal established by key figures in Hungarian Jewish life in Budapest, complained bitterly that the "backwardness" of Jews in Subcarpathian Rus' lowered the general cultural level of Hungarian Jewry.[18] Examples from everyday life include a postcard from 1909 showing Orthodox Jews in Munkács; the card was sent by a Jewish woman to her daughter in Budapest. The mother's words reflect her thinly veiled disdain: "The day before yesterday I was here [in Munkács], a place bustling with activities of residents of this kind" (fig. 1).[19]

FIGURE 1. Postcard depicting a street in Munkács, 1909, sent by a Jewish woman to her daughter in Budapest. Source: Private collection of Yitzhak Livnat, Israel.

Uniformity, however, hardly characterized Jews in Munkács or elsewhere in the region. Rivalries and friction defined relations between Hasidic rebbes. Rabbi Yekutiel Yehuda Greenwald, son of Rabbi Moshe Greenwald of Huszt (Khust), described these tensions, which at times led to blows between followers of different rebbes.[20] Non-Hasidic Orthodox rabbis sometimes clashed with Hasidic leaders, but all of them united against the Neolog (Reform) movement in Hungary. The Neolog movement emerged in the 1860s as part of emancipation and acculturation processes and gave rise to a need to rethink and make sense of Judaism, its boundaries, and the political structures of the Jewish world. The only Neolog congregation in Subcarpathian Rus' came into existence in 1869 in Ungvár (Uzhhorod), withstanding the wrath of its critics until its dissolution in 1906.[21] By World War I schism had become routine in Jewish communities in the region.[22] It would persist, as Jews faced trying times in the interwar years and during World War II. Nevertheless, Jews in Subcarpathian Rus' shared a sense of belonging to Judaism as a religious and cultural heritage, even as it held diverse meanings. Yet another sense of a shared society prevailed in contacts between Jews and their Carpatho-Ruthenian neighbors.

Jews and Carpatho-Ruthenians

A diverse scholarship in the last decade, particularly on national indifference, has challenged analysis based on ethnic and national categories, which in effect recycles and reinforces ethnic and national discourses and ideologies.[23] Jews hardly figure in these studies, however, and scholars of Jewish life in modern Europe, for their part, still tend to view Jews as fundamentally different and separate from the societies in which they lived, often treating non-Jews as members of fixed and distinct groups as well.[24] As historians Israel Bartal and Scott Ury have recently argued, "Either under the influence of Marxist concepts regarding the dialectical nature of society and the inevitable historical process, or because of the rise of national divisions in eastern Europe, the Middle East, and other centers of Jewish life, relations between Jews and members of other groups in eastern Europe are often represented as the history of competition, contestation, and ultimately conflict between two 'always-already' oppositional camps that share little save a mutual need for division."[25] Indeed, such positions take a deterministic and ahistorical approach: they view interethnic relations in modern Europe through the framework of the ethnocentric nation-state, a political arrangement that emerged only after World War I. Assuming that this outcome necessarily grew from the historical circumstances and, then, using it to deal with very different times before World War I leaves virtually no room for alternative explanations.[26] Treating the nineteenth century not backward from World War I but on its own terms reveals a different picture.

Such an examination of Subcarpathian Rus' shows that, although Jews and Carpatho-Ruthenians constituted different groups, they lacked strict collective boundaries and led lives that flowed into each other. Landscape accounted for much of this situation, generating close interethnic relations. The heavily forested and secluded Carpathian Mountains provided a fertile setting for the popular mysticism that framed the worldviews and daily rhythms of both Jews and Carpatho-Ruthenians even after World War I. From contemporary accounts we learn that many Jews believed in the supernatural capabilities of those they called "miracle rabbis."[27] That several decades later some Jews still recounted with considerable awe these beliefs, such as the alleged power of Rabbi Yosef Tzvi Dushinsky of Huszt to cause the death of a rival by simply raising his stick, attests to their strength.[28] Indeed, many Jews viewed Hasidic leaders as authorities on every aspect of life. When a cholera epidemic broke out in 1831, a group of Hasidim in Munkács received instructions from their rebbe in Żydaczów not to consult physicians but rather "recite all of Psalms every week . . . recite ketoret [the biblical portion concerning burning of incense in the Tabernacle] before 'May it be Thy will,' and examine the mezuzahs to insure that they are ritually fit."[29] Folk remedies, a related approach to treating sickness, still seemed appropriate to many a century later, notwithstanding the work of Jewish physicians and pharmacists in the town.[30]

Many Carpatho-Ruthenians also preferred magical solutions over medicine. Pëtr Bogatyrëv, an important figure in Russian scholarship on folklore and ethnography in the early twentieth century, made several research expeditions to Subcarpathian Rus' during the 1920s and 1930s, keeping a diary of his observations.[31] In one village, for example, he discovered that Jews and Carpatho-Ruthenians shared mistrust, fear, and hostility toward medicine. Yet, "after a Jewish child was cured following diphtheria vaccination," members of both groups began to overcome these feelings together.[32] Bogatyrëv also documented many "examples of [belief in] supernatural apparitions discovered during my research travels in Subcarpathian Rus'."[33] These include stories in which Jews as well as Carpatho-Ruthenians appear as people with special powers, possibly influenced by the "miracle rabbis" mentioned above.[34] Here, too, in popular mythical tales Jews and their neighbors intermingled. Indeed, as Eugen Schoenfeld, originally from Munkács, remembered, "To a great extent, for most Jews in my city, and I may say among all who lived in Carpathia, customs, religion, and superstition were so greatly intertwined that they became one and the same."[35]

If Jews and Carpatho-Ruthenians shared a belief in the miraculous, they also shared much of the quotidian. The terrain contributed to similar occupational trends in both groups. Many of the employed Subcarpathian Rus' Jews engaged in cutting, transporting, and selling timber—a common livelihood because of the forests that covered the Carpathian Mountains.[36] Others worked in petty trade, small-scale crafts, or operated as day laborers, carters, religious functionaries, and innkeepers. In the larger towns Jews dominated among traders and bankers, and a very small minority practiced medicine and law. But significantly, many Jews worked in agriculture—the occupation of most Carpatho-Ruthenians.[37] According to an article in 1841, it was not uncommon "to see a Jew work a leased land or a vineyard with his bare hands."[38] The rabbinic *responsa* literature[39] from Subcarpathian Rus' reflects this situation as well; much of it deals with issues pertaining to land cultivation and livestock.⁴⁰ This similarity strengthened the ties between Carpatho-Ruthenians and Jews. Indeed, the two groups shared a great deal, which facilitated coexistence. Not surprisingly, many Jews spoke the local dialects of Carpatho-Ruthenian, and many Carpatho-Ruthenians were quite comfortable with Yiddish.

The accounts of Holocaust survivors from the region support these observations. They constitute a large collection—written and oral, published and private, ranging from the immediate postwar period until the early twenty-first century, and authored or provided by people who lived in different places after World War II and spoke several languages. Yet in many cases they refer explicitly to the elements of this interethnic existence in similar ways and terms. Since they recount the situation in the interwar years, when interethnic relations in the region began to deteriorate, their testimonies offer a basis for us to make inferences about the period before World War I. The dynamics of relations between Jews and Carpatho-Ruthenians are addressed in detail in the next chapter; my focus here is on ties between the groups drawing on Jews' descriptions of the physical spaces they shared.

In the small towns and villages, populated predominantly by Jews and Carpatho-Ruthenians and where most of the region's population lived,⁴¹ they typically shared the same streets. Samuel Muller, for example, born in 1912 in Alsókálinfalva (Kalyny), depicted relations between Jews and non-Jews with exactly the same words that he chose to explain the atmosphere between the two Hasidic groups in his small town: "no hard feelings," adding that "we [Jews and non-Jews] mixed, and we lived together."⁴² Naftali Deutsch from interwar Velké Komjaty (Velikiye Komyaty) offered a similar description: "there was no Jewish quarter. . . . In terms of lifestyle, occupation, and appearances, Jews differed little from the non-Jews amongst whom they lived."⁴³ Such situations obtained in other places as well.⁴⁴

Similar residential patterns characterized the larger towns, too, where Jews formed a significant part of the population by the interwar period.⁴⁵ The mixture of Jews and Carpatho-Ruthenians there also included Magyars and Czechs. Abraham Klein remembered that in interwar Mukačevo his family shared a building surrounding a courtyard with "Russians [i.e., Carpatho-Ruthenians], Czechs, Hungarians [i.e., Magyars]. . . . We speak the same language. . . . We had no problem with each other, real friendly."⁴⁶ Many interviewers who collected testimonies for Yad Vashem asked survivors whether they recall separate areas where only Jews lived. The reply of Benjamin Weinberger, referring to his hometown of Užhorod (the Czech name of Ungvár) where he was born in 1927, is typical: "Not really. In the house where we lived there were many non-Jews, mixed."[47]

These examples show that Jews tended to live near non-Jews throughout the region. Jews and Carpatho-Ruthenians also shared traditional family structures, with many children;[48] thus, most of them experienced the same kind of material hardships. The difficult economic conditions spurred many Jews and non-Jews to seek better chances in other places, and the connection of Munkács to the expanding railway system in Europe in the second half of the nineteenth century eased their way. By the time World War I began, an estimated 150,000 Carpatho-Ruthenians had emigrated from the region, the vast majority settling permanently elsewhere, most in the northeastern parts of the United States.[49] An unknown number of Jews embarked on these journeys as well.[50] Emigration, mainly to North America, thus also colored the lives of many Carpatho-Ruthenians and Jews in similar ways.

This analysis suggests that most Carpatho-Ruthenians held no substantial or widespread anti-Jewish positions before World War I. The seclusion of the region not only maintained a traditional society strongly permeated with mystical beliefs that animated the lives of both Jews and Christians; it also promised isolation from national movements until after World War I. As nationalists, along with other modern currents, crept into Subcarpathian Rus' after World War I, their activities slowly soured relations between Carpatho-Ruthenians and Jews. So long as most remained unaffected by such influences, however, the two groups maintained positive relations. Also, the coexistence of two quite similar groups that, nevertheless, adhered to traditional structures and refrained from assimilating into each other ensured that modern forms of anti-Jewish hostility that arose in tandem with assimilation, such as in Germany, could not develop. Contemporary documents, such as a secret police report for the authorities in Vienna in 1890, reflect this reality: "The [Carpatho-Ruthenian] peasants are dependent on the Jew at every stage of their lives. He serves as their customer, counselor, agent and factotum, in the full sense of the word. And if we wanted to banish them the peasants would be the first to demand their return. Although the Jews exploit to the full the advantages accruing from this status . . . , it would be a mistake to speak of the prevalence of antisemitism in the sense of racial hatred."[51]

This assertion goes against the grain of received wisdom about relations between Jews and non-Jews in eastern Europe, marked by the common use of the word *antisemitism*. In many scholarly accounts, however, it remains unclear whether the term *antisemitism* denotes a foregone conclusion or, as argued in this study, suggests research questions. It is clear, however, that the Holocaust rendered a state of affairs such as in Subcarpathian Rus' unimaginable for postwar generations; only recently have scholars rediscovered Jews as integral to the societies in which they lived. Thus, the general deterministic outlook on (negative) relations among groups that arose in the aftermath of World War I bolstered a particular stance about (negative) relations between Jews and non-Jews that sprang from the genocide of Jews during World War II. Challenging these conceptions allows for new questions about Europe before and during Nazi rule and influence.

The Great Shock of the Great War

World War I created an enormous crisis in Subcarpathian Rus'. The worst battles in the history of the Great War turned the Carpathian range in the winter of 1915 into the largest graveyard on Earth, with almost two million military casualties on all sides. Unprecedented want and suffering descended on the civilian population, too, and refugees fled the violence of conquering armies in eastern Europe, running especially from Galicia.

Owing to the strategic importance of the Uzhok mountain pass, northeast of Ungvár, and the Lupkov and Dukla passes to the northwest, particularly ferocious battles raged around Subcarpathian Rus'.[52] During the Carpathian winter war of 1915, the Tsarist army failed to invade the Hungarian plain through the Carpathian Mountains, but the fighting left the region devastated nevertheless. Emissaries and representatives of the Joint Distribution Committee (JDC), an American Jewish philanthropic organization founded during the war,[53] documented the social catastrophe they encountered in the towns and villages of the war-torn area. It was already clear in 1916 that the destruction necessitated the "re-establishment of the [Jewish] congregations in the Carpathians."[54] Two more years of war left the region and its inhabitants in ruins.

These circumstances proved disastrous for the numerous refugees who poured in, moving west and south from the pillage and violence of Tsarist forces. Jews among the refugees turned to local Jews for help, but the latter could provide very little assistance, and in some cases they became refugees as well when Tsarist units penetrated the battle lines. For example, when in the fall of 1914 a rumor spread among Jews in Nagyszőllős (Vynohradovo) that the Austro-Hungarian army might detonate the bridge over the Tisza River near Máramarossziget in order to stop the advance of enemy forces, many of the town's Jews fled.[55] The Austro-Hungarian army eventually managed to repulse the Russian attack in the Carpathian Mountains, but three years later it could no longer hold together an empire exhausted by war and mired in internal conflicts.

The collapse of the Central Powers in the summer and early fall of 1918 brought World War I to an end, but civil wars and mass violence engulfed central and eastern Europe for another two years. The new state of Czechoslovakia emerged in that immediate postwar period and annexed Subcarpathian Rus' but not before conducting successful military and diplomatic campaigns against several ethnic and national rivals. Hungary's republican government of Count Mihály Károlyi claimed the area in November 1918 and established it as an autonomous region under the name Rus'ka Kraïna in the following month. Béla Kun's Hungarian Soviet regime, which toppled the short-lived Hungarian democracy in March 1919, transformed the autonomy into a Soviet entity that lasted forty days. A local Red Guard operated in the compact area around the towns of Munkács and Beregszász (Berehovo), mostly in April, and rioting bands of Hungarian counterrevolutionaries also roamed briefly, while Romanian forces entered from the east and Czech troops from the west. These armies met in Munkács in May, dividing control of the town between them for a short time, the former occupying on its way a strip of land south of the Tisza River, around the town of Máramarossziget, inhabited by a large Romanian population.[56] Romanian forces also terminated the Hutsul Republic, founded by a number of demobilized Carpatho-Ruthenian soldiers in February 1919 around the town of Iasynia in the eastern part of Subcarpathian Rus'.[57] Despite the passing nature of this entity, its protagonists would reappear in the region's history in another transitional crisis, just before World War II.

All these outside intruders introduced anti-Jewish violence, due either to images of Jews as treacherous enemies or to the standard behavior of men at war, who targeted non-Jews as well.[58] Indeed, Baron Zsigmond Perényi, a Hungarian landlord from Nagyszőllős, fled to Budapest, reportedly saying that he preferred a communist regime in Hungary to Romanian occupation.[59] Many Jews had indeed reported violence and pillaging by Romanian soldiers.[60] As we will see, imported violence against Jews in

Subcarpathian Rus' would occur several more times, always with increasing intensity. In this period the violence remained sporadic and ceased once Prague fully established its control in July 1920, and the last Romanian soldiers left the territory.

International maneuvers, intrigues, and agreements eventually cemented the Czech annexation of Subcarpathian Rus'. Carpatho-Ruthenian leaders in North America—among those who had immigrated in the decades preceding World War I—played an important role during this period. The Greek Catholic Union of Rusyn Brotherhood, the central institute of Carpatho-Ruthenians in the United States, faced five political possibilities for the region at the beginning of 1918: independence, autonomy under Hungarian rule, or annexation to Czechoslovakia, Ukraine, or Russia. The Bolshevik revolution in November 1917 crossed the last option off the list, and the uncertain state of the Western Ukrainian Republic in the face of Polish military successes could hardly attract support.[61] Independence seemed imaginary in the face of many powerful forces, and the Greek Catholic hierarchy in the United States expressed a minority opinion in their loyalty to Hungary. A solution within a future Czechoslovakia thus became a very feasible option.

Tomáš G. Masaryk, who would soon become the first president of the new state of Czechoslovakia, and Gregory I. Zhatkovych, the first governor of Subcarpathian Rus' (February 1920–March 1921), had a decisive impact on the process that would turn this possibility into reality. In July of 1918 the Greek Catholic Union joined smaller organizations to form the American National Council of Uhro-Rusyns. In the search for an influential spokesperson this body turned to Zhatkovych, who had been brought to the United States at the age of four and whose father cofounded the Greek Catholic Union. At thirty-two years old Zhatkovych was a successful lawyer in 1918. In the course of the next four months, after a series of meetings and correspondence with Masaryk and President Wilson, Zhatkovych came to adopt the Czechoslovak route, which held a promise of autonomous status for Carpatho-Ruthenians in the emerging state. On 12 November 1918, at a meeting of the American National Council of Uhro-Rusyns in Scranton, Pennsylvania, the Czechoslovak option finally triumphed, and in the following month it was ratified via a plebiscite held among Carpatho-Ruthenians throughout the United States.

Most Carpatho-Ruthenian leaders in the region also came to favor the Czechoslovak option during 1918 and the beginning of 1919. Three main national councils sprang up throughout Subcarpathian Rus'—in Ungvár, Huszt, and Kőrösmező (Iasynia)—and one more gathered at Prešov, which would soon come under Slovak control in Czechoslovakia.[62] They represented the different political directions, including independence. Here, too, union with Czechoslovakia achieved the upper hand, mainly as a result of the work of Antonii Beskyd, the head of the Prešov council. Representatives from Prešov, Ungvár, and Huszt gathered in Ungvár (8 May 1919) as the Central Rusyn National Council, chaired by Avhustyn Voloshyn, and formally accepted regional autonomy under Czechoslovak rule. The pro-Czechoslovak resolution of Carpatho-Ruthenians in the United States, as well as Czech occupying troops in the region since the beginning of 1919, no doubt buttressed this decision.

Following deliberations at the Paris Peace Conference in the first half of 1919, the Treaty of St. Germain-en-Laye on 10 September 1919 turned these decisions into concrete reality, which, by no accident, tallied with the strategic consideration of the victorious powers: the formation of the Little Entente—a prime objective of the Allied countries, particularly France—called for territorial connection among Czechoslovakia, Romania, and the Kingdom of Serbs, Croats, and Slovenes (which officially became Yugoslavia in 1929), and Subcarpathian Rus' facilitated it by linking Czechoslovakia and Romania.[63] The Treaty of St. Germain-en-Laye detailed the autonomous position of Subcarpathian Rus' within the new state in four articles (10–13), which were incorporated into the state's constitution in 1920.[64] They never turned into reality, however, and remained a point of considerable contention between Carpatho-Ruthenian leaders and Prague during the following two decades.

Czech authorities now faced the daunting task of rebuilding a region that, as JDC officials reported, "had been laid waste" by violence, epidemics, and displacement.[65] Following a visit to Subcarpathian Rus', JDC representatives Dr. Julius Goldman and Leon Wechsler wrote (April 1920): "In Uzhorod [sic] the people are ragged and many of them are pale and under-nourished, but they are prosperous compared to the gaunt figures that wander about the streets of Munkaczevo [sic]; and Munkaczevo, we were told, is prosperous in comparison with the mountain villages to the north, where there is actual starvation and transportation is in so primitive a stage that it is almost impossible to bring the necessary food to the outlying districts."[66] Indeed, the population in the small towns and villages experienced "slow starvation" in the summer of 1920, "with no prospect for winter clothing" or shoes, hit by tuberculosis, spotted fever, typhus, trachoma, and dysentery. And "refugees [were] pouring in daily from Poland, Hungary and Russia in a destitute condition."[67]

The havoc in the immediate postwar regional administration, de facto under military control headed by the French general Edmond Hennocque, exacerbated this condition. Zhatkovych spent much of his time in disputes with Czech authorities seeking to advance the promised regional autonomy. Internal disagreements and rivalries with Carpatho-Ruthenian figures, mainly Beskyd, further complicated his position. He resigned the post of governor in March 1921 and returned to the United States.[68]

Subcarpathian Rus'—Podkarpatská Rus' in Czech—thus entered the interwar world in a state of severe turmoil, ravaged by war and conflict, with a destitute and hungry population, growing numbers of refugees, and unstable local authorities struggling among themselves, as well as against the central government in Prague. Indeed, the new state interpreted its postwar commitments vis-à-vis the region in restrictive fashion from the outset, and later, as the next chapter will show, implemented policies that stood in contrast to them. World War I violently cast the people of Subcarpathian Rus' into a new reality, the effects of which would alter their lives beyond recognition and bear fateful consequences in the stormy times that lay ahead.

2

The World Beyond the Mountains
Embittered and Embattled Modernists in Interwar Czechoslovakia

THE IMAGE OF INTERWAR CZECHOSLOVAKIA as an exemplary democracy in an authoritarian neighborhood has eroded in the last decade, as new research has uncovered the ways in which the new state actually conformed to the political and ideological atmosphere of interwar Europe. Detailed examination of the state's guiding principles, system of government, and routine policies, particularly treatment of minorities, has demonstrated the limits of democracy and the practices that increasingly undermined it.[1] Notably, however, very little of this scholarship addresses Subcarpathian Rus', where Czech rule sharply contradicted the myth of Czech democracy.[2] Moreover, Prague's control in the region brought on a crisis between Jews and their neighbors, which intensified in the 1930s as the continent plunged into conflict.

At the root of this interethnic crisis were the new modes in which Jews and Carpatho-Ruthenians began to understand themselves collectively as parts of nations. Several groups offered competing paths in the struggle over the minds and hearts of both publics, particularly of the children and youth. And all of them intersected with older ways and preferences of identification.[3] This modern process is usually described as "the rise of nationalism" and, with regard to relations between Jews and non-Jews, the term *antisemitism* often accompanies the analysis. However, a world of meanings, mentalities, and emotions hides behind every case of nationalism and antisemitism. The history of interwar Subcarpathian Rus' offers a chance to probe this world in one particular social and political setting.

The Wild East of the New State

Much changed in Subcarpathian Rus' as its political center shifted from Budapest to Prague. The image of a backward region remained intact, however, as Czech authorities assumed control, and that image served the Czechoslovak government both as an excuse for not fulfilling international treaties regarding Subcarpathian Rus' and as a basis for policies that, in turn, reinforced the image. As we have seen, the Czechoslovak government agreed to treat Subcarpathian Rus' as an autonomous region. Yet in practice the state simply ignored its international commitment.[4]

Czech leaders regarded Subcarpathian Rus' as uncivilized *terra incognita*, and they rushed their administrators and bureaucrats to manage that "primitive" land. From 1921 to 1935 the number of Czech notaries and assistant notaries climbed from 104 to 164, while the figure for Carpatho-Ruthenians fell from 69 to 43. And 352 Czechs worked in provincial and district head offices in 1935, compared with only 126 Carpatho-Ruthenians.[5] Furthermore, in a move that would recur a few times during the following decades, Czech authorities changed street names to symbolize their control.[6] No wonder that, as literary scholar Elaine Rusinko has argued, "aspects of colonization became ever more apparent as subjects of literary treatment [in the interwar period], and Rusyn writers foregrounded the people's resentment of cultural imperialism."[7] Finally, Administrative Reform Act No. 125 of July 1927, which turned Subcarpathian Rus' into a province equal in status to Bohemia, Moravia, and Slovakia, served a final blow to the issue of autonomy and placed the region under Prague's firm control via the vice-governor, a position always filled by a Czech.[8]

Painful Existence

The majority of people in Subcarpathian Rus' showed little interest in Czech policies as they confronted the hardships that defined daily life in the region. Most villages and towns still lacked basic infrastructure in the 1930s, and many residents lived with no running water and no sewage system.[9] Moshe Moskovitz from Danilovo (Danylovo) recalled a roof of wood tiles that leaked in the rain, covering the one-room dwelling in which his family lived, ate, and slept.[10] Alex Gross from Palanok remembered a house "made by hand from blocks of mud, horse manure, and straw. We had no paved streets. The homes had earthen floors and no running water.

We used outhouses and had a hand-dug water well."[11] The larger towns, such as Mukačevo (Mukachevo), with only limited access to electricity and wells providing most of the water supply, fared little better.[12] Indeed, while Prague invested in building new roads and infrastructure throughout the region, the people who benefited most from them were Czech officials.[13]

New borders created new economic problems. Carpatho-Ruthenian farmers, who had once managed to find seasonal work on the Hungarian plain at harvest time, could no longer supplement their regular income in this way.[14] And Jewish artisans now faced the competition of cheap commodities from the western part of the country.[15] The new frontier between Czechoslovakia and Romania, dividing the former Hungarian Máramaros County, cut villages on one side from centers of commerce in towns on the other, prevented access to agricultural fields, imposed new tariffs, and separated family members.[16] Another national boundary split the former Bereg County between Czechoslovakia and Hungary and divided the vineyards around Kosino (Koson), a major means of employment in the area.[17] The new dividing line between Poland and Czechoslovakia also created problems, as it disrupted the pre–World War I opportunity of selling products from the region in Galicia.[18]

Feeding large families posed challenges before World War I, but Prague's protectionist policy of high tariffs on agricultural imports drove food prices up and numerous families to a constant state of hunger.[19] The rise in food prices as a result of the global economic crisis and an annual population increase of about twenty per thousand surely compounded the difficulties of this terrible situation.[20] Poor nutrition and sanitation conditions caused disease and, at times, epidemics. Meager health services could not cope with the problem, and many accounts report, for example, the death of infants.[21] With the help of the Czechoslovak Red Cross, the Joint Distribution Committee (JDC) established three dispensaries in 1924 in Chust (Khust), Trnovo nad Teresvou (Ternovo), and Volové (Mizhhirya), but these could offer only limited aid.[22]

The timber trade, a central component of the regional economy, suffered badly when Hungary and Czechoslovakia cut trade relations in 1930.[23] Michael Jackson, whose father dealt with timber in Torun (Torun'), remembered the price fall; stock did not move, and mold set in.[24] And the state-driven land reform "proved exceedingly disappointing," according to historian Carlile A. Macartney's report in 1937.[25] This was disappointing for local residents, indeed, but not for the state that used it as a means of

Czech colonization, particularly in multiethnic border areas.[26] Rising unemployment in the region in the 1930s as a result of the world economic crisis—more than 16,500 in 1936 (around 10 percent)—drove many families into a hopeless position.[27]

The JDC tried to help Subcarpathian Rus' Jews confront this dire situation. It began to operate in Czechoslovakia in March 1919, but the first representative in the region, Dr. David Olkon, was not appointed until July 1920.[28] Mukačevo was chosen as the center of JDC activity, mainly because the American Relief Administration and the Czechoslovak Red Cross operated from that town, and the JDC cooperated with them. The region's first governor, Gregory I. Zhatkovych, also "declared his readiness to give the JDC every assistance, both his own and that of his administration."[29] As the JDC faced very difficult transportation conditions, this support eased its operations.[30]

By October of 1920 Dr. Olkon, apparently overwhelmed by the horrible state of the region and with little support from Jews in the state capital, was replaced by Dr. Emanuel Frankel.[31] Over the following eighteen years the JDC founded ten Jewish loan associations in the region. These were urgently needed after the government's deflationary measures in 1922, and they provided several million dollars in assistance.[32] The JDC also allotted sums to found and support vocational schools for youth,[33] and it contributed to the Hebrew Gymnasium in Mukačevo, the flagship Zionist education project in the area.[34] The JDC thus managed to alleviate the plight of the Jews in several ways, but the scale of the difficulties, the economic crisis, local disputes, and corruption left many still suffering.[35]

Political persecution added an additional burden to economic privations. Refugees who had settled in the region after World War I, as well as people who could not prove their legal residence as of 1 January 1910 in a locality that later fell within Czechoslovakia's borders, faced the danger of deportation. Among the latter were Jewish families who had arrived in Subcarpathian Rus' in the nineteenth century and never formally legalized their status.[36] The authorities also used this requirement to make life harder for those Magyars in the region who lacked the needed documentation.[37] The rise of Nazi Germany brought another movement of refugees to Czechoslovakia, non-Jews as well as Jews, some of whom reached Subcarpathian Rus'.[38]

Another group remained vulnerable in the interwar period: Roma. Several Roma testified about both the stability and difficulties that characterized their lives under Czech rule.[39] A Roma school was even established in Užhorod (Uzhhorod) in 1926, though the state probably contributed very little, if at all, to it.[40] Yet Roma still lived on the margins of society, segregated in camps on the outskirts of towns, viewed with suspicion, and subjected to legal surveillance and discrimination.[41]

For Roma, as well as for those without Czechoslovak citizenship—whether refugees or not—the reality of uncertainty, oppression, and prejudice bode ill, especially in central and eastern Europe, where international stability in the 1920s faded into an era of political and economic disruption.

Salvations Old and New

The interwar years in Subcarpathian Rus' saw the rise of a host of people and organizations that promised to remedy the situation of poor farmers and workers, achieve autonomy for Subcarpathian Rus', protect the rights of the Magyar minority and fulfill its hope for the return of Hungarian soldiers, guide Jews into the era of the Messiah, take Jews from the Carpathian Mountains and turn them into Zionists in Palestine with Hebrew on their lips and sparks in their eyes, and make sure that Carpatho-Ruthenians understood that they were Ukrainians or, to the contrary, Russians. All parties held a mix of old and new positions and modes of confrontation, and the resulting canvas of political, religious, and national disputes changed social relations in Subcarpathian Rus' in significant ways.

Political Wars

The interwar period introduced mass politics into Subcarpathian Rus', where both regional affiliates of the large Czechoslovak parties and local groups emerged. The wide spectrum reflected the numerous national, ethnic, religious, political, and economic interests in the region. In Užhorod, for example, nineteen parties participated in the municipal elections in 1931.[42] Throughout the 1920s and 1930s voters could choose from at least ten options when they went to the polls.

Four of the five major parties of Czechoslovakia operated in the region, mostly through alliances with local lists. The powerful Agrarian Party worked through the Carpatho-Ruthenian Agrarian Party and a few Jewish groups; the Social Democrats cooperated with the Jewish Social Democrats and the Jewish Party; and the local Christian-National Party functioned as a branch of the Czech People's Party. The Czechoslovak National Socialists also enjoyed a measure of support in the region.[43]

Demands for autonomy colored the politics of Carpatho-Ruthenian opposition parties. Two succeeded in garnering substantial support: the Autonomist Agricultural Union, established in the early 1920s and led mainly by Ivan Kurtiak, Andrei Brodii, and Iosyf Kamins'kyi; and the Russian National Autonomist Party, founded in 1935 by Shtefan Fentsyk.[44] Two parties formed the Magyar opposition: the Magyar National Party of Endre Korláth and the Magyar Christian Socialist Party of Károly Hokky.[45] Prague viewed activists associated with Magyar irredentism with suspicion, and they became targets of harassment, arrests, and even torture.[46] Not all Magyars in Subcarpathian Rus' supported the Hungarian irredentism espoused by these parties,[47] however; some gave their votes to the Magyar branch of the Social Democrats and to the Communist Party.

Indeed, the Communist Party constituted the most powerful oppositional force in the region, no doubt aided by the widespread poverty and because its appeal transcended national and ethnic divisions.[48] Jews and Carpatho-Ruthenians who had served in the Austro-Hungarian army during World War I and had spent time in Russian POW camps before returning home were the first to expose the population to socialist ideas.[49] In June 1920 the Ruthenian Social Democratic Party held a congress in Užhorod, and less than a year later, in May 1921, it joined the Subcarpathian Rus' affiliate of the newly formed, multiethnic Czechoslovak Communist Party.[50] Jews quickly became very active in the party and in its efforts to persuade the Jewish population that only the Communist Party truly fights for the poor—and most Jews in the region knew the realities of destitution and pauperism all too well.[51]

Several parties claimed to represent specifically Jewish interests, however, and the Jewish Party proved the most substantial and long-lasting among them. Founded as the United Jewish Party in 1922, it became an official branch of the Czechoslovak Jewish Party in 1932; the latter had come into existence as a statewide party only the year before, in January 1931.[52] Several other Jewish parties effectively diminished the strength of the Jewish Party: the Jewish Democratic Party in 1924,[53] the Jewish Economic Party in 1925,[54] and the Jewish Republican Party in 1928.[55] The latter two emerged from the efforts of ultra-Orthodox leaders in Subcarpathian Rus' to secure the autonomous status of the Orthodox communities in the region and their hold on them; they opposed both the prospect of a central Jewish Orthodox bureau in Bratislava controlled by rabbis in Slovakia and the attempts of Zionist activists to gain control of the Jewish communities. Led by the militant Rabbi Chaim Elazar Shapira of Mukačevo, the ultra-Orthodox camp allied with the Agrarian Party, which dominated the Interior Ministry and was thus in a position to decide the status of religious communities. Hence, Rabbi Shapira called on Jews to vote for the Agrarian Party, and he persisted in this stance even when, during the 1930s, right-wing and anti-Jewish elements on its agenda became more pronounced.[56]

In the first regional elections to the National Assembly, in March of 1924, the Communist Party proved its strength in Subcarpathian Rus', winning almost 40 percent of the votes.[57] In some districts it achieved an absolute majority: in Ťačová (Tyachiv) almost 52 percent, and in Svalava (Svalyava) 63 percent.[58] It remained a major force in the region throughout the interwar period, twice (1925 and 1935) gaining significant electoral victories.[59] Aryeh Ofir, a Zionist emissary from Palestine, documented this success in a diary he kept during a trip in the region. He lamented (20 October 1936) that ten members of the Zionist Hechalutz Hatzair in Mukačevo had left the movement to join the Communist Party, and he described (23 October) a similar trend in Užhorod—in both places owing to the appeal of the Soviet project of Jewish colonization in Birobidzhan. He also noted (21 October) that in Selo Slatina (Solotvyno) "all the communists [are] Jews."[60] The Communist Party did not await recruits; it also tried to infiltrate the ranks of Zionist groups to disrupt their activities.[61]

Like the Communist Party, the Agrarian Party, which dominated the country's political scene from 1922, employed aggressive methods. In the village Kaliny (Kalyny), for instance, a Jew forged ballots of both the Agrarian Party and the Jewish Party in the 1935 general elections. He then felt confident enough to boast that "the ruling party [i.e., the Agrarian Party] will make sure to ratify the election [results]," as it had done in previous elections.[62]

Elections in Czechoslovakia's eastern province offer more than just an example of political mud. They also elucidate how modern processes were shaped by, and had an impact on, ingrained social behavior. Jews in Subcarpathian Rus' viewed modern politics through traditional lenses and language, as reflected in election posters.[63] The "Jewishness" of a party turned into a yardstick for political legitimacy. Thus, in the general elections of 1925 Rabbi Shapira called on his community to "engage in a holy war" against the state's Jewish Party, described as "a sect of heresy."⁶⁴ The Jewish Party, for its part, responded by labeling its detractors "soul dealers" and stressed that not voting for the Jewish Party amounted to "a horrible desecration of the name of God" and "a sin, which shall haunt us forever."⁶⁵ Accordingly, the Jewish Party's platform for the 1925 campaign carried the title "The Ten Commandments of the Jewish Party."⁶⁶

Jewish Party propaganda went so far as to appropriate a favorite accusation that Rabbi Shapira used to fling at his rivals, claiming that its Jewish opponents were not really Jews. In the local elections of 1923, for example, a Jewish Party poster attacked the people of the Rights Party, representing Jews identified with Hungarian culture, as "half-Christianized, and their children are rags or Christianized. They are worse than non-Jews!" The poster called on "real Jews" to vote for the Jewish Party.⁶⁷ And in the general elections of 1925 the Jewish Party equated the Jewish Economic Party with the biblical figure of Esau.⁶⁸ Such tactics probably resonated with the Jewish public, as non-Jewish parties tried their hands, as well, at crafting such imagery: the Agrarian Party, for example, referred to the Zionists of the Jewish Party as "atheists who know nothing about Judaism and who live with non-Jewish wives."⁶⁹

Religious Wars

If tradition continued to play a significant role among Subcarpathian Rus' Jews, it emerged as a primary factor also among Carpatho-Ruthenians. The revival of Orthodox Christianity in interwar Subcarpathian Rus' set the stage for intense religious strife. The reemergence of Orthodox Christianity flowed from the exploitation of parishioners by many Greek Catholic priests in the form of the *koblina* and *rokovina*, traditional feudal taxes—both in cash and in labor—still in force at the turn of the twentieth century. The political interests of local Russophiles and Russian émigrés exacerbated this religious clash. Thus, a mere 577 followers of Orthodoxy in 1910 increased to more than 60,000 in 1921 and, assisted by Prague, to more than 110,000 in 1930.⁷⁰ This mass conversion involved violence, so that, in effect, "a religious war (not wholly metaphorical or bloodless) went on for some years," as historian Carlile A. Macartney observed.⁷¹

The Magyar sympathies of many Greek Catholic priests, at least in the eyes of Prague, commingled with anti-Catholic positions in the Czechoslovak government. Divisiveness also promoted Prague's interests insofar as it diverted attention from state policies and weakened opposition to them. But once the situation in Subcarpathian Rus' seemed to slide into anarchy, local and central officials stepped in. They abolished the *koblina* and *rokovina* (1920), ensured income as well as state pensions for priests (1926), and eventually institutionalized Orthodoxy by creating the Orthodox Mukačevo-Prešov Eparchy (1931). By the time the new Eparchy had come into existence, however, antagonism within the Orthodox camp, combined with the elimination of the feudal duties, facilitated the return of many who had left the Greek Catholic Church.[72]

Equally heated struggles raged among Jewish religious leaders in the region. One of the most vehement of these took place at the initiative of Rabbi Shapira against Agudath Yisrael, the Jewish Orthodox Party founded in Poland in 1912.[73] Partly driven by Agudath Yisrael's endorsement of agricultural settlement in Palestine, which resembled Zionist goals, Rabbi Shapira initiated a truly international Jewish war that pitted the mostly German and Polish supporters of Agudath Yisrael against the ultra-Orthodox camp of rabbis in Hungary, Romania, and Czechoslovakia. A meeting of ultra-Orthodox rabbis that Rabbi Shapira organized in Čop (Chop) in 1922 resulted in an open split and a ban on contact with members of Agudath Yisrael.[74] The move produced the desired results in Subcarpathian Rus': Agudath Yisrael remained a weak group throughout the interwar period, enhancing Rabbi Shapira's control.[75]

Rabbi Shapira's thirst for power among the Jewish communities of Subcarpathian Rus' equaled his religious fundamentalism.[76] And he thus responded to the political threat he saw in Zionism with violent diatribes: "all considered, they [Zionists] are neither Jews nor gentiles."[77] Such extreme statements placed Rabbi Shapira within a tradition of fierce rejection of the Haskalah (Jewish Enlightenment) and Reform movements by Orthodox authorities in Hungarian Jewry, beginning with Rabbi Moses Sofer, the rabbi of Pressburg (1806–1839), through such students of his as Rabbi Haim Sofer (no relation), the rabbi of Munkács (1867–1879),[78] and Rabbi Moses Schick, the rabbi of Huszt (1861–1879). Indeed, Rabbi Schick, a relatively moderate Orthodox authority, commented in 1845 on German reformers that "they are not Jews, but like complete gentiles and even worse."[79] Rabbi Shapira, however, "broke new grounds in the art of intolerance," as Alan Nadler has observed.[80] And for good reason: in the summer of 1934, for example, when a cholera epidemic in Mukačevo claimed many lives, Rabbi Shapira explained to the Jews who gathered at his synagogue that the

Zionists and their "house of heresy" (referring to the Hebrew Gymnasium) were to blame. He further warned parents not to send their children to the Hebrew Gymnasium, for God would "destroy and kill" them.[81]

But, as we have seen, he unleashed his tongue against other, far more "Jewish" opponents, including other Hasidic courts such as the Belzer Hasidic followers in Mukačevo. Rabbi Issachar Dov Rokach, the Belzer rebbe, came to town as a refugee from Galicia during World War I. After a few years of bitter personal feud between the Hasidic leaders, which involved mutual informing to the Czech authorities, Rabbi Rokach left in 1922. His followers in town thereupon split from the official Jewish community to form a separate communal body.[82] Invectives filled the language that Rabbi Shapira aimed at his rivals: from "Belz pigs" to "evil people . . . damned without redemption."[83] This power struggle—both courts adhered to an ultra-Orthodox ideology[84]—came to an end only after a decade. In 1934 the Belz group acknowledged Rabbi Shapira's authority and ended the formal division;[85] the enmity, however, persisted. These divides overlapped with another layer of social scission, as collective national aspirations claimed a place in the Subcarpathian Rus' market of ideas and promised salvations.

Fractured Society

Zionist dreams and aspirations in Subcarpathian Rus' appeared only after World War I, brought to the region by Jews from Poland and Slovakia or by local Jews who had been in Russian captivity during the war and were exposed to national as well as social discourses.[86] Zionists of all shades operated in Subcarpathian Rus', especially through youth groups. None of the movements functioned in a meaningful way before the early 1930s, however, and then only with the help of activists from beyond the region. Emissaries from Poland and Slovakia, for instance, established the left-wing and secular Hashomer Hatzair in 1929.[87] Bnei Akiva, connected to the religious Zionist Mizrachi, and the right-wing Revisionist Betar took their first steps in Subcarpathian Rus' that same year.[88] Hechalutz Hatzair, a left-wing movement with Marxist leanings, came into existence only in 1933, again with guidance from Polish Zionists.[89] The founder of the Hebrew Gymnasium in Mukačevo—the most important Zionist endeavor in the region—also began as an outsider: Haim Kugel was born in Minsk and studied in Palestine, Moscow, and Prague before reaching the town in 1924.[90]

Endless enmities and conflicts hampered the work of Zionists in the region. A state of "intra-Zionist hatred" remained fresh decades later in the memory of Sarah Udi, née Weisberg, who was born in Munkács in 1913.[91] And according to Shlomo Lipski, a Zionist emissary from Palestine, it led to mutual denunciations to the authorities on a daily basis.[92] Once the right-wing Revisionist Zionist Party emerged, it allied with the Traders Party, an affiliate of the Agrarian Party, thus adding further tension within the Zionist camp.[93] External adversaries also worked against Zionist goals and, as we have seen, no one more than Rabbi Shapira. The fierce struggles over ideology and communal power created an acute crisis of belonging— to one's family, to Judaism, and to the Jewish community, as well as to one's village or town. Breaching these boundaries proved taxing.[94] Zvia Weiser (Tomer), who participated in activities of Hechalutz Hatzair in Mukačevo, described this conflict:

> Hechalutz Hatzair . . . functioned as a meeting place for youth from poor and very religious families, in which the parents considered the word "Zionism" a curse. [They viewed] membership in the movement as a sin without forgiveness. We [thus] went to the movement secretly. . . . Hechalutz Hatzair was a contradiction to everything we had known. The conflict we faced, practically as children, was immense. The influence of the home was strong, coercive. [But] there was magic in Hechalutz Hatzair . . . [and] we drew strength from the atmosphere in the movement. With this strength we came home—to parents who refused to understand this new way.[95]

Others tried to combine their "new way" with the familiar world they sought to change. Hence, some pursued Zionist activity on *Shabbat* because of the free time it allowed, but not before attending synagogue with their parents, who voiced their opposition to Zionism clearly and loudly.[96]

In their battle against Zionism and the Hebrew schools, ultra-Orthodox leaders went so far as to agree to possible contravention of the biblical precept of observing *Shabbat*, as demonstrated by Avraham Perri's experience. Ultra-Orthodox authorities asked his father to enroll him in a non-Jewish high school rather than in the Hebrew Gymnasium in Mukačevo, although that meant he would need to write on Saturdays.[97] The father refused, and Avraham attended the Hebrew Gymnasium. In general, however, the efforts of ultra-Orthodox leaders proved successful. Zvi Neuman grew up in Mukačevo, a center of Zionist activity. Yet he explained that "relatively few went [to the Zionist youth movements], because most Jews were religious and under the influence of the rabbis."[98] Indeed, Zionist movements enjoyed very limited support among Subcarpathian Rus' Jews[99] and thus constantly experienced financial difficulties.[100] Then, too, some joined Zionist organizations simply as a means to escape their daily hardships and felt no connection to national worldviews.[101] Similarly, when the Arab Uprising unsettled Palestine between 1936 and 1939 and emigration to the Soviet project of Birobidzhan seemed safer and more lucrative, many of those who agreed to try that option showed no real commitment to communist ideology.[102]

Carpatho-Ruthenian nationalists also faced a fissured arena. Four different national narratives and political orientations had competed among Carpatho-Ruthenians since the middle of the nineteenth century. Some saw Carpatho-Ruthenians as Ukrainians; others propagated a regional Carpatho-Ruthenian identity; still others adhered to the Hungarian interpretation of Carpatho-Ruthenian history; and one faction looked toward Moscow.[103] The interwar period intensified these differing perspectives.

As in the case of Jews, foreigners labored to instill national identification among Carpatho-Ruthenians. Many immigrants from Russia and Galicia taught in schools throughout the region, propagating Russian and Ukrainian national ideas,[104] and some even assumed senior posts: the adviser on issues of language to the regional school administration, Ivan Pan'kevych, who also worked as a teacher at the Carpatho-Ruthenian Gymnasium in Užhorod (1920–38), immigrated to the region from Galicia and propagated a clear Ukrainophile approach.[105] Other Ukrainophiles and Russophiles—both locals and people from beyond the Carpathian Mountains—turned to cultural production. Andrei Vasil'evich Karabelesh, a popular Russian-language poet born in Subcarpathian Rus', taught in the 1930s in elementary schools in the region and at the Carpatho-Ruthenian Gymnasium in Mukačevo.[106]

But Ukrainophiles won the upper hand and steadily grew stronger. Significantly, many of the leaders of the Ukrainian national movement in the region worked as teachers, and during the interwar years they fostered a new generation of Carpatho-Ruthenians from all walks of life who grew up with identifications that transcended the limited time and place of village or town. The Ukrainophile Iuliian Revai, for instance, taught in elementary schools in the eastern part of the region after World War I. He later served (1923–1935) as department head in the Czechoslovak Ministry of Education in Užhorod, before becoming a minister in the short-lived Carpatho-Ukrainian cabinet (1938–1939).[107] Avhustyn Shtefan, Carpatho-Ukraine's minister of education in March 1939, likewise "served as the founding director (1922–1938) of the Commercial Academy . . . in Mukachevo [Mukačevo], which under his leadership became an important center for propagating a Ukrainian national spirit among Subcarpathian youth."[108] Shtefan was also instrumental in founding the Ukrainophile Populist Teacher's Society, later renamed the Teacher's Assembly, which attracted a large membership and by 1934 encompassed 1,211 of the 1,874 Carpatho-Ruthenian teachers in the region.[109]

While Russophile leaders such as Iosyf Kamins'kyi became intensely involved with the Russophile political effort in the region, Ukrainophiles made sure to dominate among teachers and students. Hence, as use of the Ukrainian language spread in regular newspapers, Russian appeared mostly in literary and academic publications. Czech observers in the 1930s could thus maintain that "compared with Russian, Ukrainian is today more dynamic in Subcarpathian Rus'."[110]

The population of interwar Subcarpathian Rus' experienced an intense and continuous state of fragmentation, as Jews and Carpatho-Ruthenians faced conflicting religious, national, ethnic, and political leaders and movements that vied for influence and power within each group. Most Jews remained attached to their traditional way of life and their Orthodox and ultra-Orthodox rabbis, leaving Zionists of all colors in a clear minority. Among Carpatho-Ruthenians, by contrast, new national and ethnic horizons gained more traction. While Ukrainophiles, Russophiles, and those seeking to advance a regional Slavic identity all failed to achieve preponderance, the first made the greatest progress. At the same time, Prague's increasingly aggressive policies aimed against Ukrainophile movements for fear of irredentism, especially after the Communist Party turn in 1926 to Ukrainianism concerning the Carpatho-Ruthenian nationality question, ensured that Ukrainophiles and their organizations adopted more forceful positions against the government.[111] As the social setting in Subcarpathian Rus' fractured, another conflict became apparent: between Jews and Carpatho-Ruthenians.

The Making of Conflict: Carpatho-Ruthenians, Jews, and the Rise of Political Resentment

Many Holocaust survivors from Subcarpathian Rus' commented in their testimonies on the positive nature of the relations between Jews and Carpatho-Ruthenians in the interwar years. Zvi Shafir, originally from the village of Svalava, explained that "the Carpatho-Ruthenians, more than 50 percent of the population, were much friendlier to Jews than the Magyars and the Swabians [i.e., local Germans] who lived in the area."[112] Ari Halpert, born in Mukačevo in 1923, described "very good relations" between the ethnic groups in the town, reflected in the ways neighbors treated each other and spoke the different languages, as well as in positive interactions between Jewish children and their non-Jewish peers.[113] Shmu'el Vyzer from Vyšný Bystrý (Verkhniy Bystryy) remembered that "relations with the [Carpatho-]Ruthenians were good."[114] Avraham Fuchs recalled his hometown, Sandrovo (Aleksandrovka), where Jews and Carpatho-Ruthenians "lived together with much understanding and peace, lives of farmers who work the land and share the daily hardships."[115] Rachel Amit from Apsha noted how Carpatho-Ruthenians took care not to disturb Jews around the synagogue on Saturdays.[116] And Aranka Siegal repeated her grandmother's description of her Carpatho-Ruthenian neighbors in the small village of Velké Komjaty (Velikiye Komyaty): "They [Carpatho-Ruthenians] concern themselves more with the land than with borders. They are busy with growing their food, and when their crops fail they blame the lack of rain, not the Jews. Also, we live modestly here. They have nothing to envy us for."[117]

Anti-Jewish events sometimes occurred. Most notably, a Magyar teacher in a Carpatho-Ruthenian school in Velký Berezný (Velikiy Berëznyy) accused two Jews from Užhorod of trying to draw blood from two Carpatho-Ruthenian children in 1930. The ensuing blood libel ended only in 1932, when lack of evidence, the protests of Jewish Party members, and President Masaryk's personal intervention brought the case to a close.[118] A few years later, German agents tried to spread Nazi ideas in the region.[119] Significantly, the initiative in these cases came from a Magyar and foreigners, not Carpatho-Ruthenians, and a report by members of a JDC committee who visited the area as late as 1938 corroborates the postwar testimonies of Jews.[120]

Political cooperation in the region reflected feelings related to joint experiences. In the local elections of 1923 in Subcarpathian Rus' a group of Jews founded the Party of Autonomy (Autochtonpartei), which aimed "to live with other people since [Carpatho-]Ruthenians, Slovaks, [and] Jews coexist in peace and quiet." They called on Jews in Mukačevo to eschew parties espousing Jewish separatism. Seeing Jews as part of a multiethnic society, Jewish Autochtonpartei activists declared, "Jews have no interests of their own."[121] Such political activity in Subcarpathian Rus' during the interwar period suggests the extent to which many Jews were integrated in the region.

No cooperation of this sort formed between Jews and Magyars. While Magyars had lost the dominant status they enjoyed before World War I to become a group that the new state treated with suspicion, even Jews who mourned Hungary's loss of Subcarpathian Rus' showed little interest in joint political ventures with local Magyar irredentists in the 1920s and 1930s, mostly because of the increasingly stronger anti-Jewish winds from across the border in Hungary.[122] Relations with local Germans also became strained, in this case under the impact of German nationalistic discourses in both Nazi Germany and Czechoslovakia.[123]

Yet the interwar years saw the rise of anti-Jewish sentiments among Carpatho-Ruthenians as well, and their relations with Jews slowly began to deteriorate. This gradual process of change calls for an analysis of the term *antisemitism*, challenging its straightforward and self-explanatory use. This approach, as David Engel has suggested, illuminates the crucial importance of place and time.[124] The general and all-encompassing usages of the term *antisemitism* have rendered it a rather blunt concept in need of much clarification of the distinctions that emerge in concrete contexts.[125] Since no substantial and widespread anti-Jewish tradition existed among Carpatho-Ruthenians, "eschewing 'antisemitism' as a ready-made category"[126] stems from an empirical imperative in this case. Relations between Jews and Carpatho-Ruthenians were embedded in the political and social dynamics of interwar Czechoslovakia, as well as in the collective emotional tones that accompanied them. Scrutinizing the unfolding situation, we see a process rather than a presumed condition commonly called antisemitism.[127]

As we have seen, while Zionism began to make some inroads among Subcarpathian Rus' Jews, Carpatho-Ruthenians also turned to national paths, encouraged by postwar settlements that afforded Subcarpathian Rus' an autonomous status within Czechoslovakia. Even though the various national movements could not win the support of the majority among Jews and Carpatho-Ruthenians, they provided the necessary frame for the disintegration of coexistence between Jews and Carpatho-Ruthenians.

This detrimental process consisted of three layers. First, while Jews welcomed Czechoslovak rule in the region—because of the promise it seemed to hold for Jewish life free of discrimination—Prague constantly refused to adhere to postwar agreements regarding autonomy. The Czech authorities also viewed Jews askance, suspecting them of Hungarian sympathies.[128] Jews' openness to the new state not only left Czech hostility unchanged but also aroused the anger of both Magyars and Carpatho-Ruthenians. As Jews moved to ally themselves with a regime that, like its Hungarian predecessor, viewed the region through a colonial lens—one Jewish commentator described Czechoslovak rule as "occupation"[129]—a rift grew between them and Carpatho-Ruthenians who were unwilling to continue assuming the status of a marginalized people in their homeland.

Jews' enthusiastic embrace of Czech schools in Subcarpathian Rus' especially infuriated Carpatho-Ruthenian leaders, who interpreted such choices of Jews in matters of education and language as treason against their Carpatho-Ruthenian neighbors.[130] Jews rejected Carpatho-Ruthenian schools as inferior, echoing the attitudes of Czech officials, and some also expressed uneasiness with the employment of Carpatho-Ruthenian priests as teachers.[131] Jewish leaders recognized the danger inherent in this situation early on. As Dr. Alexander Spiegel, president of the Union of Jewish Schools for Subcarpathian Rus', noted in 1923, "we would not want to be considered as a czechoslovakising [sic] element, thereby coming into sharp opposition with the entire autochthonous [Carpatho-Ruthenian] population."[132]

Finally, as these intergroup dynamics altered long decades of relations between Carpatho-Ruthenians and Jews, intragroup clashes came to characterize both collectives and further exacerbated ethnic tensions in Subcarpathian Rus'. Both Carpatho-Ruthenian and Jewish leaders showed incredible talent in devising competing accounts and movements claiming to represent each group's collective quality and destiny, thus promoting grave factionalism in the region and diminishing the sense of a common society.

Indeed, many Carpatho-Ruthenians came to see "the Jews" as obstacles to their emerging national sentiments and rights. Jews thus found themselves stuck in the midst of opposing national aspirations and claims, mainly between Carpatho-Ruthenians, Magyars, and the Czechoslovak state. As Carpatho-Ruthenians struggled among themselves—between conflicting national narratives—and against the Czechoslovak government in order to gain recognition of their regional collective rights, they began to move away from their Jewish neighbors. As Dr. Spiegel had feared, by the late 1930s many Carpatho-Ruthenians regarded Jews as agents of "Czechization."[133]

The rise of national strife in Subcarpathian Rus' after World War I thus added new facets of difference between Carpatho-Ruthenians and Jews—two groups of people who had previously adhered to local identities that cut across religious affiliations. The spread of national ideas, which promised Carpatho-Ruthenians several versions of justice and prosperity, sparked a loyalty crisis among Jews and discontent among Carpatho-Ruthenians, triggering interethnic tensions.[134] The social segmentation that prevailed at the time no doubt heightened the problems associated with choosing allies and maintaining or breaking loyalties. But what characterized these tensions? Looking beyond and around the term *antisemitism*, how should we probe the essence of the emerging conflict between Jews and Carpatho-Ruthenians in the interwar period? The use of research on emotions offers a way forward: as sociologist Abram de Swaan has suggested, "the social transformation . . . forms the context for a transformation of emotional concerns."[135] Anthropologists Catherine Lutz and Geoffrey M. White have also underlined the advantage of looking at emotions: "Incorporating emotion into ethnography will entail presenting a fuller view of what is at stake for people in everyday life."[136] The same holds true for research in history.

Sara Ahmed has addressed the study of emotions as a path to understand how people become invested in collective norms, focusing on social interactions and contacts that initiate "othering" through emotions.[137] And "emotional climate . . . refers to the collective emotions experienced as a result of a society's response to its sociopolitical conditions," according to social psychologists Daniel Bar-Tal, Eran Halperin, and Joseph de Rivera.[138]

Since a growing number of Carpatho-Ruthenians understood the deterioration in their sociopolitical status as related to the choices and positions of "the Jews," anti-Jewish resentments of a political nature spread in Subcarpathian Rus'. Referring to resentment works here, first, to focus the discussion: instead of the catchall *antisemitism*, we deal here with a specific phenomenon, one related closely to the way Prague administrated the region. Importantly, the usage of resentment highlights relational aspects, a key in the narrative presented above, and it also challenges the direct connection commonly made between antisemitism and hatred. This points to the merit of scholarship on emotions in this case: it pushes us to clarify what we actually mean when we use the word *hatred* to define an anti-Jewish stance or process. The position of Isaiah Trunk, an important historian of Jews in Poland and a pioneer in Holocaust research—that "the age-old, almost atavistic hatred of the Jews wherever they have lived unprotected— modern anti-Zionism can also be seen mostly as an inverse variation of this hatred—is such a familiar phenomenon that it needs no elaboration here"[139]—still enjoys wide currency, even if not in so crude a formulation. Besides the obvious questions that such statements beg—why did the Holocaust happen in the middle of the twentieth century, then, and not, say, at the end of the nineteenth century, and why at the heart of Europe and not in the Ottoman Empire?—they intentionally leave their arguments unexplained and brush aside cases where hatred played no role at all.[140]

At any rate, as "hatred may be defined as a secondary, extreme, and continuous emotion that is directed at a particular individual or group and denounces that individual or group fundamentally and all-inclusively,"[141] we clearly need to look elsewhere in the case of relations between Jews and Carpatho-Ruthenians. The concept of resentment fits well, as its component parts—a sense of deservingness followed by anger due to feelings of deprivation and injustice[142]—framed the political experience of Carpatho-Ruthenians from the hope of autonomy in the immediate post–World War I period to its frustration in the following two decades. The real and perceived role of Jews in this process bred more and more resentment. This situation deteriorated rapidly during the little-known Carpatho-Ukrainian autonomous phase, when it became closely associated with the ascending Ukrainian identification among Carpatho-Ruthenians.

3

A Little World War
Carpatho-Ukraine

IVAN OLBRACHT, the famous Czech writer who spent much of his time during the 1930s in Subcarpathian Rus', described the relations between Jews and Carpatho-Ruthenians in his novel *Nikola the Outlaw*: "Through centuries of association the Jews and [Carpatho-]Ruthenians have become used to each other's peculiarities, and religious hatred is foreign to them. . . . They see into each other's ritualistic mysteries and religious sorcery just as they see into each other's kitchens and rooms. . . . But beware of casting a new idea in their midst, for then at once two types of mind and nervous system will reveal themselves."[1] Olbracht thus captured the situation that obtained, as well as why and how it could change. As we have seen, new ideas in Subcarpathian Rus' had already begun to alter the interethnic dynamics between Jews and their neighbors while Olbracht was writing this piece. This chapter probes the building blocks of these ideas, which informed an emerging collective identity among Carpatho-Ruthenians after World War I. This "type of mind and nervous system," to use Olbracht's words, assumed intense political significance during the Carpatho-Ukrainian phase in the late 1930s, when two external forces, Ukrainian nationalists and Hungarian occupiers, introduced ethnic violence into the area and shattered its social fabric.

The tension that had emerged between Jews and Carpatho-Ruthenians in the interwar years reached a peak during the tumultuous months at the end of 1938 and the beginning of 1939, as Czechoslovakia crumbled under the pressure that would soon engulf most of Europe. The process of social disengagement in Subcarpathian Rus' and the subsequent social disintegration during World War II involved a set of local and external factors and agents. The Carpatho-Ukraine episode opens a window onto this multi-layered picture and the powers that decided the fate of Subcarpathian Rus'.

The political entity of Carpatho-Ukraine existed from October 1938 to March 1939, part of the Second Czecho-Slovak Republic, the last phase in the slow and painful demise of interwar Czechoslovakia.[2] As historian Mary Heimann has observed, the second Czecho-Slovak Republic "is usually skipped over in history books in a sentence or two."[3] While she has posited that "the Second Republic shows us what Slovak, [Carpatho-]Ruthenian and Czech variations on the contemporary European themes of anti-Semitism and Fascism looked like at the time and hints at how they might have developed had Germany and the Second World War not intervened,"[4] her focus lies with the Czech and Slovak cases.[5] Indeed, the limited literature on Carpatho-Ukraine provides details of the general events that framed its existence. However, the paucity of in-depth analytical attention and the abundance of ideological assertions have overshadowed several key issues investigated in this chapter. Significantly, no narrative at present explores the intricate web of relations and interactions between the groups that inhabited Carpatho-Ukraine, specifically between Jews and Carpatho-Ruthenians. Focusing on these social dynamics continues the previous chapter's inquiry into the meanings of the terms *nationalism* and *antisemitism* in the history of Subcarpathian Rus', with important implications for understanding the period of World War II in the region.

The End of Czechoslovakia: Carpatho-Ukraine

Carpatho-Ukraine grew out of the infamous Munich Pact of 30 September 1938: the recognition of an autonomous Slovakia on 7 October led quickly to an autonomous Subcarpathian Rus' four days later; Czechoslovakia had become the federated Czecho-Slovakia.

The first government of autonomous Subcarpathian Rus' lasted only sixteen days. On 26 October Czech authorities summoned its premier, Andrei Brodii, to Prague and arrested him for working toward the annexation of the area to Hungary, while minister Shtefan Fentsyk—suspected of serving as a Polish agent—found refuge in the Polish embassy. The Ukrainophile Avhustyn Voloshyn then took over the second cabinet. This signaled the rise of Carpatho-Ukraine (map 3); that is, the lands that remained after the First Vienna Accord (2 November) deprived the autonomous region of a southwestern strip of territory transferred to Hungary and left it with a population of 550,000 people. The vast majority (75 percent) were Carpatho-Ruthenians.⁶ The 2 November Accord also meant that the autonomous government moved from its previous capital in Uzhhorod, now controlled by Hungary, to Khust.

Internal strife and a bankrupt economy rendered Carpatho-Ukraine a failed autonomy at birth.⁷ Political violence and international intrigues allowed it only a fleeting existence that lasted barely five months. A bitter struggle between Russophiles and Ukrainophiles, as well as internal feuds in the latter camp, coupled with political inexperience and incompetence, rendered Carpatho-Ukraine an autonomy that could function only with continuous and firm direction from Prague.⁸ As we will see, external interference in the affairs of Carpatho-Ukraine quickly became the norm, which eventually brought about its downfall.

MAP 3. Carpatho-Ukraine, 1938–1939. Based on Paul Robert Magocsi, *A History of Ukraine*, 2nd rev. and exp. ed. (Toronto: University of Toronto Press, 2010), 659.

Indeed, seeking to provoke a situation that would trigger a Hungarian invasion, the Hungarian government sent into Carpatho-Ukraine special forces, the Rongyos Gárda, totaling hundreds of men, to carry out attacks. Polish incursions into the region from the north have received much less mention, but they, too, added to the atmosphere of violence and instability.[9] The paramilitary organization of Carpatho-Ukraine, the Carpathian Sich, in most cases failed to provide security in the face of this situation. On the contrary, several hundred armed Carpathian Sich men exacerbated it by terrorizing certain segments of the population.

Carpatho-Ukraine could not withstand these internal and external pressures. The end came quickly. In mid-January, following clashes between the Hungarian army and Carpathian Sich soldiers in the immediate vicinity of Mukachevo,[10] the Czecho-Slovak government appointed the Czech general Lev Prchala to the cabinet in Khust, the protests of Voloshyn and his associates notwithstanding.[11] In early March Czecho-Slovak president Emil Hácha dismissed the Carpatho-Ukrainian government in an atmosphere of impending doom, and fighting between the Czecho-Slovak army in Khust and the Carpathian Sich broke out on 13–14 March.[12] The next day, a desperate government sought to turn a troubled autonomy into an improbable state, creating what some contemporary commentators called a "republic for a day."[13] The bloody battles between the Carpathian Sich and the invading Hungarian army—while Prague ordered its forces to pull out of the region—could not save Carpatho-Ukraine. It vanished within days.

Conspiracies from Abroad: The Making of Carpatho-Ruthenian Experience

Subcarpathian Rus' took shape through constant interactions between foreign regimes imposed on it and local cultural and political orientations.[14] The short-lived Carpatho-Ukraine was the most pronounced example of this history. Caught in the midst of international struggles between visions of expansion and greatness held by Hungarian, Ukrainian, and German nationalists, the region became the object of fantastic dreams and conspiracies of politicians and ideologues from beyond and below the Carpathians. Most of those living there, however, knew nothing about the passions now attached to their homeland. And the dreamers, for their part, paid very little attention to those inhabiting that chunk of their designs.

Nazi Germany cared little about Carpatho-Ukraine nor about its potential to spur an independent Ukraine as a part of a German-dominated eastern Europe.[15] German Foreign Office documents indicate clearly that German policy makers took for granted the eventual demise of this political entity and searched for ways to maximize the advantages it could bring to German plans in the meantime.[16] In other words they sought ways to pit central and eastern Europeans against each other in order to set the stage for German expansion eastward. In this scheme Carpatho-Ukraine could not play any serious role.

While Nazi Germany geared toward war, Hungarian and Ukrainian nationalists planned grand futures. For both, Carpatho-Ukraine held importance, for the former as lost lands of a thousand-year Hungarian state, and for the latter as the springboard of a future Ukraine that would unite all those perceived as Ukrainians in eastern Europe. Not surprisingly, most Carpatho-Ruthenians harbored different notions and feelings about their hometowns and villages. Yet coming on the heels of the growing antagonism between activists and adherents of different Carpatho-Ruthenian national movements in the interwar period, the tumultuous months of Carpatho-Ukraine propelled many Carpatho-Ruthenians toward one particular group consciousness. Rogers Brubaker's interpretation of "nationness as event" captures the essence of this swift development.[17] During the period of Carpatho-Ukraine a *specific* kind of Carpatho-Ruthenian identification with Ukrainian nationalism "suddenly crystallized"; a collective self-understanding emerged from those months rather than caused them.[18]

Resistance to foreign domination and concerns about the continued marginalization of Carpatho-Ruthenians in their homeland constituted the core experience of the "event," the hasty rise and fall of Carpatho-Ukraine. This experience drew on a shift in Carpatho-Ruthenians' perceptions of place and time during the interwar era. As their world extended beyond the mountainous villages where most of them lived, an underprivileged existence dictated by the rule of strangers turned into a political problem in need of redress. This change, whereby daily material distress assumed political content, defined the new ways in which Carpatho-Ruthenians began to view other groups in the region at the time, mostly Jews and Magyars, no longer as neighbors who shared strong attachments to specific localities but as agents of powers that threatened their deserved freedom. This process transformed relations between many Carpatho-Ruthenians and their Jewish neighbors.

Local Conflicts, Imported Violence

As we have seen, no substantial anti-Jewish discourse emerged in Carpatho-Ruthenian society prior to the interwar period. In Máramaros County, which constituted nearly half of Carpatho-Ukraine, "very friendly" encounters obtained between Jews and non-Jews, as Rabbi Yekutiel Yehuda Greenwald, son of Rabbi Moshe Greenwald of Khust, wrote in 1945. "They lived as neighbors for generations; their grandparents and great-grandparents were good friends; the relations between priests and rabbis were very good; everyone respected the belief of the other."[19] Malkah Baldor, born in 1929, spoke of "very good" relations with non-Jews in Velyky Bychkiv, a predominantly Carpatho-Ruthenian locality, noting the absence of antisemitism there.[20] Clara Ilales remembered that in Belki relationships between Carpatho-Ruthenians and Jews were "good, good, better than between Jews here [in Israel]."[21] And Benjamin Kaufman recounted that in interwar Drahovo "life with the Carpatho-Ruthenians was . . . very good, very friendly."[22]

We have seen how Czechoslovak rule slowly altered this state of affairs. As ethnic, national, religious, and political divisions tore the social fabric of Subcarpathian Rus', a collective emotional discourse of resentment distanced Carpatho-Ruthenians from Jews. The crisis of the interwar years left a ruptured society, in which interethnic tensions had begun to spread. By the second half of 1938 this emerging tension gained threatening momentum with the arrival of "imported Ukrainians," as one observer called the Ukrainian nationalists who crossed into the region, mainly from neighboring Galicia.[23] Still, the anti-Jewish violence that erupted in Carpatho-Ukraine was not the exclusive domain of outsiders. Eva Slomovits, born in 1928 in Zarichchya, who attended a Carpatho-Ruthenian school and remembered "very close" relations with Carpatho-Ruthenian neighbors, said of the Carpathian Sich men, some of whom lashed out against Jews: "These were boys from the town. . . . They went with my sisters to school."[24] Ukrainian nationalists from bordering lands, however, predominated among the attackers and made sure to stir emotions. Although conflict had already fractured relations between Jews and Carpatho-Ruthenians, violence was a new expression of this rift and, indeed, was imported from places with a history of anti-Jewish aggression.[25]

Thus Jews' lives in Carpatho-Ukraine became fraught with danger. Rabbi Yehoshua Greenwald of Khust recounted "daily anti-Jewish measures,"[26] and some survivors described intermittent spasms of murder.[27] Many recalled "black lists" of Jews, whom the Carpathian Sich presumably planned to kill in the last days of Carpatho-Ukraine, in mid-March 1939. Few were murdered, but terror prevailed in the region.[28]

The violence included deportations of Jews from the autonomous territory to no-man's-land on the borders of autonomous Slovakia, Carpatho-Ukraine, and Hungary.[29] Esther Offer's father was born in Mukachevo, but he lived with his family in Khust. After Mukachevo had become part of Hungary in early November 1938, Carpatho-Ukrainian authorities expelled the family across the new border; they then made their way to Mukachevo, whence they returned after March 1939.[30] Other families experienced such enforced journeys as well.

Oral and written testimonies suggest that most Jews decided to retreat into their homes, families, and communities to weather the storm. Not everyone did so, however. Márton Szimkovics of Velykyi Bereznyi, for instance, joined with Magyars in the region, who also faced persecution,[31] against the rioting bands of the Carpathian Sich. He supplied them with rifles, while also conducting "reconnaissance work" in the service of Tivadar Kováts, director of the Hungarian National State Security Committee (Országos Nemzetvédelmi Bizottság).[32] While uncommon, such cooperation further distanced Jews from Carpatho-Ruthenians in an increasingly flammable atmosphere of interethnic tension.

The conflict between Jews and Carpatho-Ruthenians was real and related to regional contexts, but the violence of both locals and outsiders in the 1938–1939 winter months stemmed from beyond the Carpathian Mountains and was rooted in different political and social contexts. Hungarian occupying troops added another layer of imported violence, in this case against Carpatho-Ruthenians, and cemented a new degree of animosity that framed subsequent relations between Carpatho-Ruthenians and Jews.

March 1939: Hungarian Flags, Carpatho-Ruthenian Corpses

Internal friction characterized the leadership cadre of Carpatho-Ukraine. Contrasting political plans abounded, although none materialized, as much more powerful forces decided the fate of this Carpathian revolution. Bloodshed began in a fierce skirmish in Khust on 13–14 March, when the Czecho-Slovak army quickly subdued Carpathian Sich forces.[33]

This minor defeat foretold the debacle that would soon befall Carpatho-Ukraine, as the Czecho-Slovak army, on orders from Prague, retreated from the region, and the Hungarian army joined Hitler in crushing what remained of Czecho-Slovakia.

Jews saw Hungarian soldiers killing Carpatho-Ruthenians.[34] Rabbi Yehoshua Greenwald wrote shortly after the war that "Hungarian soldiers killed numerous Ukrainians."[35] In her memoir, written forty years later, Aranka Siegal described bodies of Carpathian Sich soldiers that she saw floating in the river that ran through her small town.[36] Eva Slomovits remembered that "these Sichoveks were rounded up . . . and they killed them, the Hungarians killed these young boys, a lot of them."[37] And Aharon Rat from Velyky Bychkiv related the incarceration of Carpathian Sich men in a school in the town, whence "every night [for several days] they would take some of them out and kill them in the forest."[38] The number of Carpatho-Ruthenian victims remains unclear. We know of around seventy-five battle causalities among Carpathian Sich soldiers, but no data exist to determine the number of combatants and civilians killed after the hostilities, in some places, such as Velyky Bychkiv and Solotvyno, in organized executions.[39]

Jews' accounts suggest that the Hungarian army entered Carpatho-Ukraine not only with the goal of a speedy occupation but also to terrorize opponents of Hungarian domination, chiefly Ukrainophile forces and their supporters. The volume of reports and correspondence about Carpatho-Ruthenians in the papers of Miklós Kozma, who was in charge of the Rongyos Gárda and the governor of the region from September 1940 until his death in December 1941, attest to those intentions. Especially telling are reports with titles such as "the Ruthenian question," "the Ruthenian problem," or "the Ukrainian question in Subcarpathian Rus'."[40] The common thread in these documents concerns the threat of Ukrainian influence in Subcarpathian Rus', related to anxieties about Bolshevism and the "danger" of Pan-Slavism.[41] The language, replete with references to "Ukrainian terrorists,"[42] leaves no doubt that the Hungarian authorities took these matters seriously. And it illuminates their actions as they crossed into Carpatho-Ukraine. Many Carpatho-Ruthenians sensed the peril: by the end of 1939, thousands of Carpatho-Ruthenians had fled to east Galicia, then under Soviet occupation.[43]

The suffering that Jews had endured for four months, culminating in the lawlessness of Carpatho-Ukraine's last days, prompted many to welcome Hungarian forces as liberators, and some hurried to brandish Hungarian flags.[44] As advancing Hungarian units made sure that their national colors dominated the landscape,[45] Jews' activities in this regard could only anger their Carpatho-Ruthenian neighbors. Carpatho-Ruthenians had already come to view "the Jews" as agents of Czech foreign rule, which they increasingly perceived as hostile during the interwar years. They now saw Jews' sympathies to local Magyars and to the Hungarian occupation as another traitorous move against Carpatho-Ruthenian society.

The anger over the killings of Carpatho-Ruthenians by Hungarian forces spread throughout Subcarpathian Rus' during the war, strengthening Ukrainophiles. In a report of the Royal Hungarian Border Area Police Captaincy of Ungvár (Uzhhorod), covering the period from June to September 1942, the author discussed the "secret Ukrainian organization," which had "spread to almost the whole Subcarpathian area.... Especially in the areas of the Huszt, Aknaszlatina, and Szolyva border police branch offices, where there are a significant number of supporters of Ukrainianism."[46] The author's claim, that the Hungarian authorities would soon "put an end to the dangerous movement," seems to have remained empty. A report of 2 February 1944 by the investigation department of the Royal Hungarian Gendarmerie (8th district) mentioned "the Huszt [Khust] movement" as decisive in fomenting unrest among Carpatho-Ruthenians in the area of Munkács (Mukachevo).[47]

The Hungarian authorities probably exaggerated the danger of "Ukrainianism." When, for example, thirty-three Carpatho-Ruthenians stood trial in a military court in Munkács in July 1942, accused of disloyalty to the state because of their alleged activity in a Ukrainian national organization, the court concluded, without any evidence, that the latter had "gained a special impetus among the secondary-school youth of [Carpatho-]Ruthenian ethnicity, who joined the organization en masse."[48] Yet these sources nevertheless reflect the spread and increasing strength of "Ukrainianism" among Carpatho-Ruthenians. Hungarian violence in this case provides an example of the way that, as political scientist Charles King has asserted, "violence does not always make identity, of course, but it can certainly push a particular identity to the top of one's repertoire."[49] This process shaped relations between Jews and Carpatho-Ruthenians under Hungarian and German occupations: the schism that had begun to separate the groups in the interwar years and widened under the Khust regime now turned into full-fledged enmity. In both periods foreign interventions in the region created a loyalty crisis that drove a wedge between the groups.

As we have seen, loyalty became a decisive element parallel to the expansion of Ukrainophile identification among Carpatho-Ruthenians. The colonial nature of the Czech regional administration between the world wars accelerated the spread of "Ukrainianism" and heated the simmering discontent in Carpatho-Ruthenian society with any stripe of foreign domination. This process peaked in Carpatho-Ukraine.[50] As historian Orest Subtelny has observed, the episode of Carpatho-Ukraine "helped to turn much of the region's population, especially the youth, into nationally conscious Ukrainians."[51] But this assertion actually clarifies little, for it begs the question: what were the ingredients of Ukrainian self-understanding that crystallized—to use Brubaker's terminology—in the public discourse in Carpatho-Ukraine during those five months?

What characterized this "Ukrainianism"? What marked it in the eyes of local leaders? And what did it come to mean in Carpatho-Ruthenian society? An earlier attempt at local self-rule during a time of political upheaval, the Hutsul Republic in 1919, offers clues. In the immediate aftermath of World War I, in February 1919, a number of demobilized Carpatho-Ruthenian soldiers, inspired by the short-lived Western Ukrainian Republic, founded a tiny state around the town of Iasynia, in the far eastern tip of Subcarpathian Rus'. Governing more than twenty thousand inhabitants, a government of four with an elected council of forty-two people survived for a bit more than four months until Romanian units occupied the area.[52] This brief episode has received very little attention, but the story of the Hutsul Republic contains several factors that merit discussion.

First, personal continuities stretched between the Hutsul Republic and Carpatho-Ukraine. Dmytro Klympush from Iasynia, the supreme commander of the Carpathian Sich, had played a central role in the Hutsul Republic. Stepan Klochurak, also from Iasynia, who had led the army and national council of the miniature state in 1919, served as Voloshyn's secretary and in various ministerial positions in March 1939. And the brothers Iulii and Mykhalio Brashchaiko, who had favored a path that would include Subcarpathian Rus' within the Western Ukrainian Republic in 1919, both served in various leadership positions in Carpatho-Ukraine.[53] These men came from different backgrounds, but they saw a common cause in resistance to outside interference in their homeland. Another proclivity united these people: they shifted between political loyalties. This highlights their main concern.[54] If considered from the standpoint of creating alliances and identifying threats in the service of overthrowing specific forces understood as hostile and oppressive—and these changed with time—the political fluctuations and maneuvers of Carpatho-Ruthenian leaders seem quite reasonable.[55]

The link between the Hutsul Republic and Carpatho-Ukraine also helps us to understand relations between Carpatho-Ruthenians and Jews. The anti-Jewish enmity among Carpatho-Ruthenians in Carpatho-Ukraine came after twenty years of evolving anti-Jewish resentment, and it was intertwined with the widespread impatience shared by many Carpatho-Ruthenians with Prague's policies in the region. No such processes preceded the Hutsul Republic; indeed, no interethnic tensions between Jews and Carpatho-Ruthenians marked its existence. Also, unlike Carpatho-Ukraine, the Hutsul Republic failed to attract serious interest of Ukrainian nationalists from the other side of the Carpathians, which ensured that anti-Jewish violence barely occurred around Iasynia at the time. Finally, the Hutsul Republic collapsed with no serious bloodshed and soon thereafter became part of Czechoslovakia. This new state seemed at first to hold some promise for Carpatho-Ruthenian life owing to postwar settlements in which Czech leaders initially agreed to grant autonomy to Subcarpathian Rus'. Hungarian rule, by contrast, brought with it several days of violence against Carpatho-Ruthenians, hardly a hopeful beginning.

This brief comparison points to the meanings of "Ukrainianism" among Carpatho-Ruthenians and to its impact on their relations with Jews. Ideas about freedom and oppression assumed political importance in Carpatho-Ruthenian society in reaction to Czech, Ukrainian, and Hungarian efforts to impose new political orders with little consideration for the local sensibilities in Subcarpathian Rus'. In the 1920s and 1930s "the Jews" became identified with "Czechization." Then in 1939 many Jews publicly welcomed Hungarian soldiers in the false hope that the latter would save them from the hands of the Carpathian Sich. Thus Carpatho-Ruthenian disappointment with Czech rule turned in November 1938 into excited anticipation when political freedom for Carpatho-Ruthenians seemed at hand. Hungarian occupation crushed these hopes. Jews, therefore, became unwilling onlookers in a process that peaked when Ukrainophile identification seemed to hold the most promise for Carpatho-Ruthenians while, at the same time, constituting a serious threat to much stronger powers preparing for unprecedented conflagration.

Conclusion: A Brief Critique of the Concept of Nationalism

An issue of contention in the study of nationalism concerns the divides of west and east and, concomitantly, (western) European and non-European (including eastern Europe). As historian Maria Todorova has pointed out, the level, if any, of outside influences on national movements in a particular place constitutes one facet of this debate.[56] Examining nationalism in Carpatho-Ukraine reveals the interplay between local and external trends of feeling, thinking, and acting nationalism. As we have seen, threads of thought and sentiment grew out of the specific contexts of Subcarpathian Rus'; violence, by contrast, came with Ukrainian nationalists from the other side of the Carpathian Mountains. In other words local contents of collective identification grew out of the historical soil of the region, which then found expression in a pattern of behavior imported and planted on that terrain.

This interpretation challenges the common assertion by scholars that most Carpatho-Ruthenians lacked interest in the politics of the region. Moreover, the image of Carpatho-Ruthenians as backward peasants unaware of the world around them draws on the colonial discourses and practices that many in fact tried to challenge.[57] Here we encounter one merit of saying what we want to say instead of using the word *nationalism*: we learn that concerns such as freedom, which have colored the struggles of many groups in human history, came to the fore in the case of Carpatho-Ruthenians as well. The use of the term *nationalism* masks this issue, and the added adjective *Ukrainian* elides the regional characteristics of the human interactions examined here. The invented divide between western and eastern Europe,[58] it seems, operates in similar fashion in the internal sphere of eastern Europe by creating a scale on which superiority and backwardness depend on national organizations that emerged earlier or later, respectively.

The correct question is, therefore, not whether Ukrainian nationalism caught the minds and hearts of many Carpatho-Ruthenians in the interwar years. The question rather concerns the meanings that Carpatho-Ruthenians attached to "Ukrainianism."[59] This chapter shifts the perspective to allow for consideration of both internal and external factors in the history of Carpatho-Ukraine. It thus shows that posing this question lays bare the connection between central issues and events (foreign domination, interethnic relations, the emergence of anti-Jewish attitudes among Carpatho-Ruthenians, and ethnic violence) that heretofore have eluded integrated examination.

Indeed, the analysis offered here links this critique of the concept of *nationalism* to the proposition in the previous chapter to view relations between Jews and Carpatho-Ruthenians beyond the conceptual limitations of *antisemitism*. The "Ukrainianism" that had attracted many Carpatho-Ruthenians during the period of Carpatho-Ukraine no doubt included an anti-Jewish component, but the reason for this aspect and the way it manifested itself in most cases between Carpatho-Ruthenians and Jews without violence calls for investigation of specific processes and contexts. As we will see in the next two chapters, the hostility that now characterized the stance of many Carpatho-Ruthenians to Jews rarely turned violent. The lack of a substantial history of long-term animosities between Jews and Carpatho-Ruthenians and the particular political and military conditions of Subcarpathian Rus' during World War II clarify this intergroup interaction. The general concept of *antisemitism*, at any rate, hardly sheds light on these regional particularities and the behavior patterns to which they gave rise. The next two chapters will expound further on the emotion-based framework introduced in the previous chapter, which deciphers the elements of the anti-Jewish mentality among Carpatho-Ruthenians under the oppression of the Hungarian occupation regime.

The story of Carpatho-Ukraine, at a national, ethnic, and religious crossroads in eastern Europe and during a time of political unrest, sheds light on a turning point in three related historical narratives: Czech, Hungarian, and Ukrainian. Analysis of Carpatho-Ukraine reveals how German war plans, the eventual helplessness of Czech authorities to hold on to the region, Hungarian irredentism and colonialism, and unfulfilled dreams of Ukrainophiles brought about the first instances of ethnic violence in Subcarpathian Rus', first on a small scale by Carpatho-Ruthenians against Jews and then, more lethal, by Hungarian occupiers against Carpatho-Ruthenians.

Mass violence continued to mark the increasingly difficult lives of the region's residents, as Hungary moved to establish its control in Subcarpathian Rus' and, whenever possible, carry out plans in service of a new colonial vision that would target Jews, Roma, and Carpatho-Ruthenians. The emerging antagonism between Jews and Carpatho-Ruthenians, at its height in Carpatho-Ukraine, left a broken society to face this violent onslaught that would change Subcarpathian Rus' society forever.

4

A Big World War
"Greater Hungary" and Genocide in the Carpathians

THE FORMERLY AUTONOMOUS area of Carpatho-Ukraine—now renamed Kárpátalja—remained under military rule until June 1939, when the Hungarian Regent, Miklós Horthy, appointed Baron Zsigmond Perényi as head of a civil administration to govern the area.[1] Perényi, a landlord with an estate in Nagyszőllős (Vynohradovo), had spent the interwar years in Budapest and now returned to the region. He was a committed Hungarian nationalist and a trusted member of the conservative class that had ruled Hungary since 1920.[2] But his political vision of Hungary remained rooted in bygone days, and turning Subcarpathian Rus' into a part of a "Greater Hungary" in line with the political language of ethnonational singularity and the international atmosphere of conflict and ethnic violence required more forceful figures in leading positions. Accordingly, in September 1940 Miklós Kozma, another leading conservative who had stood at the head of the Rongyos Gárda in 1938 and 1939 after serving (1935–1937) as minister of interior in the far right-wing government of Gyula Gömbös, became the appointed governor (*kormányzói biztos*) of the region. Kozma not only embraced discriminatory actions against Jews and other groups in the region, which had begun immediately after the Hungarian occupation; he sought to alter completely the social makeup of Subcarpathian Rus' through harsh discrimination, daily violence, arrests and torture, political persecution, and, whenever possible, mass deportations—targeting Jews, Roma, and Carpatho-Ruthenians. These policies spelled great suffering and disaster for almost all the inhabitants of the region. As non-Magyars, they constituted "problems" to a Magyar-dominated "Greater Hungary."

Imagining "Greater Hungary"

Historian Alon Confino has argued that we should turn our attention to central cultural elements in German history, particularly the study of memory in the Nazi period, in order to understand why and how the elimination of Jews became an imaginable possibility in modern German society. Confino highlights the very real implications of a collective imagination as it infused the society and politics of Nazi Germany with meaning.[3] Confino's approach may serve to explore the act of collective imagining as a basic political process in other cases, such as the obsession in Hungarian society after World War I with "Greater Hungary."[4]

As we have seen, Hungary's ruling elite before World War I chose aggressive policies that advanced assimilation of the kingdom's non-Magyar groups into the Magyar population—"magyarization"—with a view to consolidate a Magyar majority in a "Greater Hungary." Hungary's defeat and humiliation in World War I and its aftermath triggered radical change: the country had lost two-thirds of its pre–World War I territory and three-fifths of its population, mostly in the borderlands.[5] During the chaotic period of 1918–1920, one goal united the Hungarian Left and Right and provided all political camps with legitimacy, from Mihály Károlyi's socialist and democratic experiments and Béla Kun's communist regime to the conservative forces of Miklós Horthy and the extreme rightists around Gyula Gömbös: the preservation of pre–World War I Hungarian territories and the fight against the invading Czech and Romanian armies in the north and east. All joined the struggle, and all believed in it as a just cause. And when Horthy, who had become regent of the kingdom on 1 March 1920, and the Hungarian government accepted the Trianon Treaty on 4 June, all felt the weight of the disaster.[6]

A new mood took hold of Hungary's ruling cadres during the interwar years, permeated with the xenophobia and drive for ethnonational "homogenization" and expansion that had become a staple of European politics at the time.[7] The guiding political principle in imagining "Greater Hungary" now shifted from "magyarization" to exclusion. In 1934 Horthy set the tone by suggesting that the post–World War I Turkish-Greek "population exchanges" should inspire similar policies vis-à-vis the minorities in Hungary.[8] Horthy's concern focused particularly on the large German minority, about whom Hungarian nationalists had been anxious since the middle of the nineteenth century.[9] Bálint Hóman, Hungary's minister of culture and education for almost a decade between 1932 and 1942, viewed the deportations of Carpatho-Ruthenians, Romanians, and Serbs from Hungary as no less necessary. Wartime conditions sharpened this position. Henrik Werth, Chief of the General Staff of the Hungarian army in 1941, urged the expulsion of Hungary's Slav, Romanian, and Roma populations together with the Jews, making an explicit connection between the two latter groups.[10] Others joined the state's leaders in expressing such visions: in 1942 a Hungarian official could imagine the expulsion of three million Romanians from Transylvania after the war, provided Hungary found itself in the winning camp.[11]

"Greater Hungary" thus stood at the heart of the political consensus in Hungary and fostered the rise of increasingly exclusionist and violent ideas as legitimate political futures.[12] Such visions took immediate physical form in Subcarpathian Rus', as the Hungarian occupiers changed street names and used new postage stamps that declared that Munkács (Mukachevo) and Beregszász (Berehovo) had "returned" to Hungary.[13] But turning the region's society into a part of an imagined "Greater Hungary" spurred mainly destructive impulses that left almost no one untouched.

Anti-Jewish Policies: Framing the Magyar Nation

As we have seen, Hungarian soldiers committed small-scale massacres of Carpatho-Ruthenians as they marched into towns and villages in Carpatho-Ukraine. Some also lashed out at Jews. Shmu'el Vyzer, for example, who was fifteen years old in 1939, remembered that an old Jew waited for the arrival of Hungarian soldiers on the main road of Felsőbisztra (Verkhniy Bystryy), exclaiming, "Long live the Hungarian army." Still a soldier beat him and tore his beard.[14] And a number of Jews from Beregszász provided information in their testimonies about the pillaging and looting of Hungarian troops.[15]

The new Hungarian authorities quickly moved from sporadic violence to institutional persecution. The plight of forty-nine-year-old Sámuel Hollender from Nagybereg (Beregi) illuminates the underlining rationale of the new rulers. On 13 February 1939 the subprefect (*alispán*) of Bereg County and Ugocsa County suggested incarcerating Hollender because of anti-Hungarian remarks he had allegedly made the preceding October, before the Hungarian occupation. The two gendarmes who had arrested Hollender on 23 November 1938 acted "according to information" from one Béla Fábián, a local Magyar whose motives remain unknown, though his actions reflect how relations between Jews and Magyars in the region had soured in the previous two decades. The gendarmes, however, stressed that such "anti-Hungarian activity" stemmed from support for the Czech Agrarian Party and "will induce anti-Hungarian feelings among the population." The Royal Hungarian Gendarmerie's company commander in town promptly notified the Hungarian military command in nearby Beregszász, emphasizing that Hollender's internment was "very much, almost absolutely necessary."[16] The correspondence about the case mentions seven other individuals from Nagybereg whose "anti-Hungarian activity" as "Czech sympathizers" or simply their identification as "Communists, Social-Democrats and Agrarian Party leaders" rendered their internment "necessary . . . as soon as possible."[17]

This case illustrates how the stormy waters of warfare and international conflict that redrew the borders of Subcarpathian Rus' a number of times after World War I left Jews to face multiple and conflicting allegations from both the state and their neighbors of having retained their loyalties to a past regime or transferred them to a new one. Similar to the way Czech authorities in the 1920s viewed Jews as loyal Hungarians, now Hungarian authorities, like many Carpatho-Ruthenians, perceived Jews as loyal Czechs. Hollender's case also demonstrates an imagined necessity in the eyes of state authorities that already held the possibility of far more sweeping policies to ensure a "Greater Hungary" purged of people perceived as subversive.

The emphasis on disloyalty used by the gendarmes in Nagybereg resonated with central decision makers. Shortly thereafter, in June 1939, the Ministry of the Interior applied it to all Jews in the region as "suspicious elements . . . who are problematic from a political and economic perspective."[18] Jews in Subcarpathian Rus', however, hardly possessed the kind of economic power that such language suggested. In fact, the Hungarian occupation and the beginning of war in September 1939 fueled a decline in the economic condition of an already impoverished population. Decree 1939/1100 of the prime minister (4 February 1939) had singled out Jews for economic persecution, which deprived thousands of families in the territories occupied in November 1938 of their business licenses. Decree 1940/3380 in May 1940 targeted Jews in the area occupied in March 1939.[19] Some Jews managed to transfer their businesses to Christian employees, acquaintances, or friends. The latter, operating as straw men, enabled the original owners to continue to receive at least some of the profits.[20] Still, a JDC report of November 1939 described the region's Jewish population as "the poorest of the poor."[21]

The language of these decrees follows the same logic as that of the gendarmes who dealt with Sámuel Hollender's case: those deemed disloyal to the Hungarian state because of their alleged hostility to Hungarian interests in the interwar years could not enjoy the privileges of Hungarian citizens. Economic interests and the influence of Nazi Germany no doubt pushed this discriminatory process forward, but these decrees, as well as the anti-Jewish legislation in Hungary, aimed first and foremost to define and delineate the ethnonational political body.[22]

Indeed, the Hungarian authorities used the Second Anti-Jewish Law (4 May 1939) to define *Jew*,[23] and many non-Jews hurried to submit the necessary documents to prove their non-Jewish origins. The mayor's office in Ungvár, for example, dealt with requests to verify non-Jewish ancestry, based on documentation showing that applicants, their parents, and their grandparents were born as Christians and had since remained members of Christian denominations.[24]

The so-called Race Protection Law (Fajvédelmi törvény) of 8 August 1941 sought to cement the separation between Jews and non-Jews by prohibiting "mixed" marriages. It had no effect on relations between Jews and Carpatho-Ruthenians, however, as it aimed "to protect the purity of the blood and the spirit of those who belong to the community of the Magyar race."[25] Instructions concerning this law in Subcarpathian Rus' elaborated the legal implications of a possible offense: a letter from the head of the prosecutor's office in Huszt (Khust) to the municipality of Nagyszőllős (27 November 1941) clarified that the main criminal liability could apply only to Jews, whereas the authorities should view their non-Jewish spouses or partners in extramarital relations merely as accomplices.[26] Ethnic Hungarians, then, were also "protected" from culpability in such cases.[27]

The legal attack against the Jews in Hungary culminated in September 1942 with a law that prohibited Jews from acquiring agricultural land and enabled the government to confiscate land owned by Jews.[28] Local authorities in Subcarpathian Rus' tried to push for more encompassing legislation. Officials in Bereg County had already requested (March 1941) the prime minister to modify existing laws in order to prevent Jews from buying real estate; they stressed that this would save Munkács, Beregszász, and other county towns from "Judaization."[29] No such modification took place, and the 1942 law probably affected most Jews in the region in a rather minor way.[30] The significance of this anti-Jewish legislation, however, lay in the political, not the economic, realm: like the change of street names, it attempted to realign space according to ethnonational criteria.[31]

These anti-Jewish measures proved effective in framing the Magyar collective and separating it from a central "other," but the image of "Greater Hungary" left little room in the future state for the presence of Jews. As we have seen, it portrayed a new political geography of most of the Danube Basin, in which a large Magyar majority would control a territory unwelcoming toward non-Magyar populations. This vision translated into destructive impulses and initiatives whenever an opportunity presented itself, and it prompted a multilayered attack against most of the region's inhabitants.

Mass Deportations, Multilayered Violence: Jews, Roma, Carpatho-Ruthenians, 1938–1941

The Hungarian authorities began to expel Jews from Subcarpathian Rus' immediately after the Hungarian occupation of the southwestern part of the region in November 1938. These somewhat unorganized instances quickly became routine. Once Hungarian forces conquered the rest of the region in March 1939, they applied this practice there as well. By December 1939 several thousand Jews had been forcefully removed, first, until March 1939, to no-man's-lands between Czech, Slovak, and Hungarian territories, and later to Poland.[32]

The National Central Alien Control Office (Külföldieket Ellenőrző Országos Központi Hatóság—KEOKH), a body within the Public Security Department in the Ministry of the Interior, planned and oversaw many of these deportations.[33] The head of the KEOKH branch office in Sátoraljaújhely instructed (6 March 1940) the chief constable (*főszolgabiró*) of Ungvár to prepare a list of expelled Jews in his area of jurisdiction.[34] The correspondence and lists concerning the town of Radvánc (Radvanka) exemplify the extent of the deportations. At least seventy-one heads of families, almost all of whom, according to the Public Notary Office in Radvánc, were Jewish men born outside of Hungary, had already been deported or were "under the effect of an expulsion decision." The documents provide no clear indication about whether the deportation orders pertained to family members as well, but a request—that if they "have their own income and live in a separate household, they should be enlisted as independent persons and should be included on the list with the data required for heads of households"—implies as much. If so, the total number of targeted Jews in Radvánc amounted to around three hundred, nearly half of the town's Jewish population.[35]

It seemed at first that evidence of Hungarian citizenship would protect Jews from deportation, and obtaining it thus consumed the time and energies of many Jews, both those who had arrived in the region in World War I as refugees and those whose families had settled there in the nineteenth century but never felt the need to take care of their legal status. The set of required documents included birth certificate, parents' marriage certificate, residence permits, official employment and tax information, and proof of real estate ownership, if relevant.[36] Jenő Krausz from Bustyaháza (Bushtyno) wrote to his son on 17 April 1941, explaining that he had been to visit the border police in Aknaszlatina (Solotvyno) "because of the *citizenship* documents I have been ordered to submit. It cost me a lot of money and pains: the fifty pengős that you sent, and I sold my pocket watch to be able to send [the documents] to Pest to the Ministry."[37] Yet, as we will see, the essence of citizenship in Hungary had changed and no longer relied on formal status. Such efforts would therefore often prove futile during the extensive deportations that began three months later.

The brief military control of the Hungarian army in east Galicia in July 1941, as Hungary joined Nazi Germany in its attack on the Soviet Union (22 June 1941), served as a pretext for the first major attempt to implement large-scale deportations from Subcarpathian Rus'. Writing to Hungarian prime minister László Bárdossy, the Hungarian governor of the region, Miklós Kozma, declared on 10 July 1941: "At the beginning of next week, I will push all the non-Hungarian Galicians who escaped here, the uncovered Ukrainian agitators, and Gypsies across the border."[38] While Roma appear explicitly in the letter, the two other groups point to a more inclusive operation than the text suggests, illuminating two related rationales for exclusion and persecution. The first group referred to Jews as quintessential foreigners, the second to Carpatho-Ruthenians as a security threat, an idea that undoubtedly emerged from the brief confrontation of the Hungarian army with the Carpathian Sich in mid-March 1939.[39] The deportations of Jews and Roma in summer 1941 did not eventually include Carpatho-Ruthenians, yet the latter occupied a central place in the worldview and designs of the Hungarian authorities.

The correspondence of Bárdossy and Kozma reveals the extent to which Carpatho-Ruthenians attracted their attention. They discussed German agents in charge of "Ukrainian propaganda" in the region; vague plans about the deportation of family members of Carpatho-Ruthenians who had "just escaped from here [to the Soviet Union]"; the annulment of Hungarian citizenship of those escapees; anti-Hungarian Ukrainian leaflets; and the departure of "six [Basilian] Fathers" from the region, who "will never return."[40] Furthermore, the day after Kozma had written to Bárdossy, he boasted in his diary: "Pest has started to move, and is following me in the new situation. 1) Foreign citizens; 2) Military zone;[41] 3) Ukrainian agitators; 4) Gypsies."[42] Kozma again explicitly tied Hungarian designs regarding three non-Magyar groups in the region in a way that could facilitate sweeping deportations. Others shared his agenda. A few days after his letter, Árpád Siménfalvy, the lord lieutenant (*főispán*) of Ung County and the town of Ungvár, wrote approvingly (16 July): "It is a matter of common knowledge that His Excellency Kozma is removing Jews of non-Hungarian citizenship from Subcarpathia to the north and is using this occasion to cleanse Subcarpathia from wandering Gypsies, too."[43]

The regional authorities were not the only ones to concern themselves with broad projects of violent deportations. The head of the KEOKH, Sándor Siménfalvy, issued (12 July) the central decree for the deportations of summer 1941, relating to all of Hungary and targeting no one group in particular, speaking instead of "foreign citizens."[44] Most of the central and local decrees featured similar language, such as "aliens" and "non-Hungarian citizens,"[45] for while Jews stood at the top of the list of victims—and, with Roma, were the most defenseless—the Hungarian authorities targeted other groups as well.

The brothers Sándor and Árpád Siménfalvy grew up in Subcarpathian Rus', in Nagyszőllős.[46] Their roles in the deportations of summer 1941 throw into sharp relief the central place of Magyar officials who hailed from the territories that Hungary had lost after World War I in translating "Greater Hungary" from public imagination to political reality.[47] Many more took part in the task. The fact that both the KEOKH and the Subcarpathian Rus' governor's office devised and carried out plans for these forced population transfers proves that all concerned agreed, drawing on the broad ideological consensus that had crystallized in the interwar period.[48] Several state authorities thus furnished more than enough perpetrators on the ground: gendarmes and policemen in the border police branches, who gathered the victims, beat and robbed them, and transported them to the border; and soldiers who literally dumped the deportees on the other side of the Carpathian Mountains. Shmuel Yung was born in 1920 in Taracújfalu (Novoselytsya). The village notary refused to provide his family with Hungarian citizenship certificates, even though all were born there. When the gendarmes came to deport the family, "they asked no questions—whether any person was born there or not." The gendarmes took Shmuel, his parents, his brother, and two sisters by truck to Huszt, where they waited for three days before a train transported them to Kőrösmező (Iasynia), the site of a transit and registration camp established by the KEOKH for the mass deportation campaign. They stayed there for three or four days, with barely any food and sleeping on the floor, after which "the Hungarians brought us to Horodenka, in east Galicia, and left us in a large open area."[49]

Hungary's leaders decided to put an official end to large-scale deportations on 15 August 1941[50] not because of any difference of opinion with their regional representatives, nor due to any concern for the fate of their victims, and also not in response to the pleas of Jewish leaders in Budapest,[51] but first and foremost because the German occupying forces in east Galicia made it clear that they would not allow their continuation.[52] The Germans on the other side of the Carpathian Mountains evidently grasped the numerical significance of words such as *foreigners* and *non-Hungarian citizens*, and they stopped the flow of deportees.

The Hungarian orders targeted people without Hungarian citizenship—that is, those bereft of the protection a state extends to its citizens. But the term *citizenship* in this case had already lost its conventional legal meaning and had become a corollary of ethnic identification as defined by the state. This constituted a clear example of the kind of biopolitics that, according to philosopher Giorgio Agamben, marks the modern era *par excellence*.[53] In fact, clause 7 of Decree 3850/1941 ME (in effect since 23 May 1941) by the prime minister, which amended previous laws concerning the citizenship of the inhabitants of Subcarpathian Rus', explicitly excluded Jews from the possibility of regaining Hungarian citizenship status based on citizenship before the Trianon Treaty.[54] So it mattered not at all whether Jews held the required papers to show their formal belonging to the Hungarian state; the latter had already labeled them unwanted strangers and, if needed, collected or simply destroyed identification papers, which virtually turned the people who had held them into "non-Hungarian citizens."[55]

These deportations therefore threatened many more than solely Jews without Hungarian citizenship. The goal was to deport as many Subcarpathian Rus' Jews as possible. In some localities the authorities accomplished this objective with terrible success. In Lipcse (Lypcha) in Máramaros County, for instance, only 80 of the 542 Jews who had lived there remained after the deportations of 1941.[56] In Csicser,[57] in Ung County, only nine of the original fifty-four Jews survived in 1941.[58] And in Szinevér (Synevyr) the entire Jewish community was erased.[59]

While the drive for total uprooting of the region's Jews has been well established in recent scholarship, nowhere has the key question—why?—emerged. Was this simply a manifestation of an extreme position aimed exclusively against Jews? Or, rather, was it part of a far-reaching vision regarding the future of Subcarpathian Rus'? Here a simplified notion of anti-semitism blurs a complex reality, where anti-Jewish positions intermingled with other interests of the state and evolved into actions in concrete contexts that afforded a chance to pursue multiple goals. Multilayered mass violence also occurred in the other borderlands that fell into Hungarian hands during World War II: Romanians in Transylvania and "Serbs, Bosnians, Montenegrins, gypsies, or Jews who did not (themselves or their parents) have citizenship within the territory of Greater Hungary before October 31, 1918" in the Délvidék[60] faced the violence of the state.[61] Arrests, torture, and mass deportations began immediately with the Hungarian occupation of the Délvidék in April 1941, culminating in January 1942 in the massacres of thousands of Serbs and hundreds of Jews in the Šajkaš region and in Novi Sad. Serbs—another group without real power at the time but still feared as a "security threat" even before the rise of organized partisan activities among Serbs in the Balkans—suffered the most: the Hungarian authorities expelled thirty thousand to German-controlled Serbia, despite strong protests by the German authorities. The requirements regarding citizenship and date of settlement remained dead letters in this case as well.[62]

These forced movements of people exemplify the potential of violence inherent in colonial projects that aim to reshape subjugated groups (in whole or in part) to resemble the masters, what Homi Bhabha has described as mimicry. He has explained that colonial discourses that seek to transform colonial subjects in the image of the occupier contain an inherent ambivalence: the "reformed other" turns out as almost the same as his or her conqueror, *"but not quite."* This imitational slippage—for, by essence, all imitations remain incomplete—already points to potential processes, whereby *"mimicry*—a difference that is almost nothing but not quite—[turns to] *menace*—a difference that is almost total but not quite."[63] In an age that left no space for differences, and certainly not such menacing ones, these discourses led to murderous results.

Indeed, "magyarization" had produced, at best, mimicry in Subcarpathian Rus' and elsewhere. As we saw in Chapter 1, most Carpatho-Ruthenians, living in small towns and villages, would not turn into Hungarian-speakers, and while a minority of Jews in the region commanded the Hungarian language, they were precisely a mimic: Hungarians, *but not quite*, and in this case not quite at all. Literature Nobel Prize laureate Imre Kertész, originally from Budapest, described an encounter in a German concentration camp with Jews from Munkács: "Among one another and with the Latvians they use Yiddish, but they also speak German, Slovakian, and a smattering of who knows what, *only not Hungarian*."[64] Such characterization applied all the more to Jews from the small towns and villages of Subcarpathian Rus'. Naftali Deutsch, for example, remembered that in his village, Magyarkomját (Velikiye Komyaty), "most of the Jews and non-Jews could not speak Hungarian and only a few could read and write Hungarian."[65] Moreover, the period of Czechoslovak rule in the region heightened the failure of Hungarian mimicry and thus the menace presented by an area and inhabitants that refused "reform." Whether or not they held in their hands pieces of paper with formal designations could not change the essential gaze through which the Hungarian authorities now saw Jews as a collective. The history of colonial domination in the region therefore conditioned the mass violence that came with changing ideological and political winds.

The number of Jews violently deported from Subcarpathian Rus' in the summer of 1941 remains unknown. We know that from 15 July until 9 August more than fifteen thousand Jews were deported—this figure includes a few thousand people from other parts of Hungary—and two thousand more, imprisoned in Kőrösmező, would soon face expulsion.[66] Yet deportations commenced in some places even before the official government decree of 12 July; in Huszt, for example, the Hungarian authorities had deported about six hundred Jews in three days, beginning 10 July.[67] Also, the operation lasted almost another week after 9 August, and the Hungarian authorities probably could not register every victim, especially owing to the participation of different forces and the destruction of entire communities in some cases. It is thus reasonable to posit that as many as twenty thousand Subcarpathian Rus' Jews—about one-fifth of the region's Jewish population—were deported in the summer of 1941. Most of them found a cruel death at the hands of Ukrainians and mainly in the Kamenets-Podolsk mass killing by German units and their accomplices at the end of August 1941.[68]

As we have seen, it was "a matter of common knowledge" that the Hungarian authorities also deported Roma, but the available sources provide no hint about the number of victims. What came of the plans regarding Carpatho-Ruthenians? Mainly because of the stand of the German authorities beyond the Carpathians, who would not accept more deportees from Hungary after 15 August, the Hungarian government could not even begin to organize and carry out deportations of Carpatho-Ruthenians. But the summer of 1941 signaled a new level of commitment to the idea of "Greater Hungary" and of mass violence in its service. This multilayered assault continued in 1942.

Making Life Unbearable: Carpatho-Ruthenians and Roma, 1939–1943

The massacres of Carpatho-Ruthenians in March 1939 set the tone for the political persecution that would descend on Subcarpathian Rus' society under Hungarian control. Tens of thousands of Carpatho-Ruthenians, not only those suspected of being "Ukrainian agitators," suffered arrest, torture, internment, expulsion, and death during the Hungarian occupation.[69] Vincent Shandor, for example, a leading Ukrainophile who served as the representative of Carpatho-Ukraine in Prague, reported on the arrest and torture of his sister and brother.[70] The exaggerated threat of a "secret Ukrainian organization" in 1942, and reports that it had "spread to almost the whole Subcarpathian area," made life very hard for many Carpatho-Ruthenians.[71] And as Budapest reversed the Czechoslovak land reform,[72] the regional authorities transferred thousands of Carpatho-Ruthenians from rich to poor lands.[73] Since many Carpatho-Ruthenians eked out a subsistence living at the time, these measures exacerbated their daily struggle.

The drive against Carpatho-Ruthenians targeted their culture as well. For example, the Hungarian authorities strove to purge the Ungvár city library of books in Hebrew and Yiddish, as well as books from "the [Carpatho-]Ruthenian book list."[74] Ukrainophile cultural activities came under particular attack, and Ukrainian-language publications ceased to appear.[75] Russophiles fared no better: Kozma reportedly threatened "to crush into powder and send to the grave anyone who dare call himself a Russian."[76] The persecutory justification here centered mainly on loyalty, which explains why Kozma permitted an Uhro-Rusyn orientation, that is, a limited regional identity tied to Hungary.[77] It remains unclear how many Carpatho-Ruthenians saw themselves as "Uhro-Rusyns," but the relative success of "Ukrainianism" during the interwar period and in Carpatho-Ukraine, coupled with Hungarian oppression and violence, must have seriously limited the appeal of the Uhro-Rusyn idea. In any case, according to the Hungarian future advocated by Bálint Hóman, Henrik Werth, and other Hungarian nationalists, a victorious Hungary would need not resort to such enforced loyalty. If Hungarian leaders and officials could imagine the mass deportation of Romanians from Transylvania after the war, they could easily envision an identical fate for the stateless and largely defenseless Carpatho-Ruthenians.

The Roma population in the region suffered worse, as they represented the ultimate outsiders and were described in anxiety-ridden language. The commander of the gendarmerie unit at Csap (Chop), for example, referred to Roma as "the home of dirt and infectious disease."[78] Contrary to received wisdom,[79] the Hungarian authorities treated Roma as a "question to be fundamentally solved" from the outset of their occupation of the region.[80] At times the Hungarian authorities viewed Jews and Roma as interrelated "problems": the chief constable of the town of Nagykapos,[81] for instance, requested "regulation" of "wandering Gypsies," adding that a "similar regulation is needed with regard to wandering Jews."[82] The logic of the persecution of Jews in this document follows simultaneously anti-Jewish and anti-Roma anxieties, which echo the general drive of the Hungarian state against those perceived as "foreigners" and "wandering"—again, without much consideration for their formal status. Indeed, "wandering" could easily expand to include, as in Nyitra-Pozsony County, not only nomadic Roma but also settled Roma "without sufficient income." In fact, the legal committee of that county suggested dealing with the "Gypsy question in general" as a struggle against "undesirable elements."[83] The rationale for persecution of Roma thus emanated from an acute impulse, beyond the threat of disloyalty: the urge to remove a group perceived as foreign, unreliable, and inherently diseased and dirty.

This harsh anti-Roma position entailed policies that included raids, enforced curfew, internment, and withholding of food-ration coupons. Raids against Roma became common in all of Hungary during World War II,[84] and regional and local authorities carried them out in Subcarpathian Rus' on a regular basis. The subprefect of Bereg County and Ugocsa County ordered the chief constables under his authority to conduct raids in June 1939, and gendarmerie units in Nagybereg, Mezőkászony (Koson), Bátyu (Bat'ovo), Beregszász, Bene, and Nagybégány (Velyka Bigan) complied.[85] Gendarmes in Ung County received similar orders in May and again in October and November 1940.[86] The documents describe, for example, that an "individual was denounced for road trespassing and four individuals were ID-checked,"[87] or that "the patrols of the [gendarmerie] unit checked the identities of thirty-seven individuals during the raid."[88]

The accounts of victims depict the suffering such language disguises. Kalman Sabo, a Rom from Beregszász, recalled his humiliation at the hands of Hungarian gendarmes, describing in detail how one had beaten him severely in 1943, when he was only nine years old.[89] Morris Muller, a Jew from Huszt, confirmed that Roma in town "had a hard time,"[90] and Yaakov Halpert, a Jew from Nagyszőllős, commented that Roma suffered even more than Jews under the Hungarian occupation.[91]

Such an atmosphere no doubt helped Hungarian officials imagine the deportations of Roma in the summer of 1941 as "common knowledge," as Árpád Siménfalvy, the lord lieutenant of Ung County and the town of Ungvár, wrote on 16 July.[92] Many public officials furthermore called for the internment of Roma in labor camps that year.[93] The raids now tightened. Whereas in 1939 and 1940 many Roma managed to move between counties to avoid raids, the subprefect of Ugocsa County issued strict orders to his chief constables to track down Roma who might escape from raids in the neighboring Szatmár County in May 1942.[94] In the summer and fall of that year Roma faced further discrimination, hardship, and violence, as authorities forbade them to leave their residences between sunset and sunrise and provided food-ration coupons only to Roma (and their families) employed as musicians or in field, wood, or mud work.[95] Life had become unbearable in such conditions, but the region's Roma would soon experience even harsher tribulations.

"Jews Have No Place": 1942–1943

The Hungarian authorities in Subcarpathian Rus' put the Jews at the top of the list of groups targeted for persecution. The status of statelessness and foreignness, attached to the region's Jews collectively, combined with the exclusionary anti-Jewish religious and political discourse that spread in the 1920s and 1930s in Hungary.[96] Jews were also almost completely powerless, and the Nazi-led genocidal assault in German-dominated Europe set a supportive international tone, even though violent deportations—not mass killings—guided Hungarian policies in realizing "Greater Hungary" in Subcarpathian Rus'.

As we have seen, the wave of mass deportations in summer 1941, the first large-scale episode of mass violence in Hungary during World War II aimed at Jews en masse, came to a stop mainly as a result of the refusal of German authorities in east Galicia to allow its continuation,[97] which left Hungarian occupation authorities unsatisfied. The German occupiers on the other side of the border, who had just begun to murder entire Jewish communities,[98] would not accept more Jews into the territories under their control, and Kozma's efforts to persuade them failed.[99] Various figures in the Hungarian extreme Right, including senior officers in the army,[100] turned to Berlin in their efforts to deport all the Jews in the region in 1942.[101] But extremists held no monopoly on such ideas, certainly not in Subcarpathian Rus'.[102] The deportation of *all* Jews had appeared on Kozma's agenda since he became governor,[103] well before leading Nazis began to pressure the Hungarian government to include the country's Jews in the "final solution"—indeed, a year before any decision about a European-wide "final solution."[104] After Kozma died in December 1941, others in the region kept his vision alive. In April 1942 Árpád Siménfalvy sent a long report to the Ministry of the Interior with parts of the minutes of the annual meeting of the Ungvár municipal committee. He suggested establishing a national authority to plan and carry out "the relocation of the Jews":

The year 1942 will be the year of great efforts and decisions. . . . Thousands of tanks, airplanes, and armies of millions are fighting for the final victory, cultures crumble and nations sink from one day to the other in the trapdoor of history. This incredible struggle with its horrible devices and consequences stands unparalleled in world history; and behind it the contours of a new European order, a world based on a Christian national worldview, a new millennium, a new European life are forming. . . . Jews have no place in the ongoing world struggle and in the new Europe that will emerge from it. . . . We Hungarians have to literally liquidate this [Jewish] question based on our own strength and resolution . . . because it would mean a terrible threat to our homeland if we postpone this question or wait for external forces to solve it.[105]

The envisioned order of Hitler's Europe created a sense of heightened urgency, but it remained in the hands of Hungarians to prove their "European legal standing that is worthy of our Hungarian national mission."

Local authorities, enthusiastic to partake in the task, abounded with ideas that, following Árpád Siménfalvy's prescription, would restrict Jews' place. The chief notary of Huszt, József Bíró, proposed, for example, to address the housing problem in town by simply confiscating apartments of Jews.[106] Others refused to allow the stop in mass deportations in summer 1941 to deter them and pressed forward with small-scale deportations whenever possible. The Aknaszlatina Border Area Police Office, for instance, informed the Financial Directorate at Máramarossziget in June 1942 of the expulsion of nine Jews from Aknaszlatina. The officials of the Financial Directorate made "arrangements . . . so that all the public debt of the expelled individuals should be insured and recovered."[107] In December 1942 the same office requested the district notary office to "inform us in due time about the discharge date from military service [labor battalions]" of five additional Jews from the same town who were slated for expulsion.[108]

Jews in neighboring northern Transylvania also faced a concerted drive to push them out of the country. Like Árpád Siménfalvy, retired army general and member of the Bihar County Committee (in the western part of the region) Sándor Báthory-Szűts, who counted among the local Hungarian conservative elite, suggested in March 1942 that the government "should immediately set up an agency with the appropriate powers, whose task is the practical preparation of the resettlement of Jews and its implementation."[109] Others in the region agreed with Báthory-Szűts but preferred to act rather than wait for directives from Budapest. In Csíkszereda (in the eastern part of the region), whence the Hungarian authorities had already deported Jews in 1940, deportation orders rained down on Jews in 1942.[110] Károly Herskovits, the wife of the head of the Jewish community, turned for help to Margit Slachta, the founder of the Sisters of Social Service (1923) and a well-known opponent of anti-Jewish measures in Hungary. Herskovits wrote to her (16 June 1942) that since the return of Hungarian rule in August 1940, "Jews have been almost constantly deported from the town."[111] Slachta thereupon sought the assistance of Countess Móric Esterházy (18 June 1942), a member of the Hungarian Red Cross, mentioning that similar events had plagued the lives of Jews in Borszék and warning that "the general situation is rapidly deteriorating; it seems that the Hungarian state would like to follow the example of Slovakia."[112] Emma Strobl, a member of Slachta's Sisters of Social Service, confirmed the widespread agreement about Árpád Simménfalvy's "national mission" when she informed Slachta (10 July 1942) of her conversation with the town's police chief: "we should not think that this [the deportations] is the will of only one man. . . . A lot of people are backing it."[113]

The Experiences of Jews: Crisis, Disintegration

Jews responded in several ways to the persecution and mass violence of the state. Some managed to hide in order to escape deportations. Fifteen-year-old Sam Moskowitz fled with his family from Dombó (Dubove) during the deportations of summer 1941. They spent two or three weeks deep in the Carpathian Mountains, as he "knew every little mountain in the area."[114] Others made their way to Budapest, where the big city afforded better opportunities to avoid the authorities and find jobs.[115] But many of the Jews in the towns and villages throughout the region could not leave, primarily because they were very young or very old, or would not leave because they preferred to remain with their families, who needed their support. Most of these families now consisted of women, children, and the elderly; the Hungarian army had inducted Jewish men into forced labor battalions.[116]

Many of the men in these battalions suffered atrocious journeys during the war and its aftermath, especially those in units that the army sent outside of Hungary, to the war zones against the Soviet army or as slave laborers in copper mines and railroad construction for the German occupiers in Serbia. One survivor related the misery he endured in a testimony right after the war.[117] He shared a cattle car with around forty other forced laborers on their way to the Eastern Front. After eleven days, in temperatures that dropped as low as minus 45 degrees Celsius, "teeming with lice . . . we set off on foot to Stary Oskol. We marched in blizzards. . . . A certain Major Morva hit us with a whip to move [us] faster. . . . There were many victims by the time we reached the next village." They made it to Stary Oskol just in time to get caught in the havoc of Axis retreat.

The German defeat in Stalingrad and the destruction of the Second Hungarian Army in Voronezh (January 1943) signaled the beginning of the westward movement of the Soviet army and the looming defeat of Nazi

Germany and its Axis partners.[118] But for the men in the Hungarian labor battalions it meant a new phase of murderous violence. "It was terrible. On the way Hungarian soldiers plundered us and beat us up . . . and took our clothes and left us there naked. . . . A lieutenant from Kisvárda beat up an attorney from Kisvárda so bad, claiming that the attorney killed his mother and father, that he was taken away half-dead. After half a day he died.[119] After being completely robbed, we were set free. . . . We had to retreat without guards and a commander, exposed to all kinds of dangers." Retreating Germans posed an especially deadly threat.[120] "One evening Todt men attacked us [in Rosovka]: they beat us and plundered us. . . . One of them stabbed me with his bayonet." Yet this individual survived and, with much luck, remained with his ever-shrinking unit as it withdrew through Kiev and Brest-Litovsk, eventually returning to Hungary in October 1944.[121]

In Subcarpathian Rus', in the meantime, the wives, parents, children, and friends of these men struggled with the difficulties and distress of daily life. Shmu'el Vyzer experienced economic deprivation and material want as "hard, very hard"; the authorities had taken the license of his father's sawmill in Felsőbisztra.[122] Miki Herbstman, whose family lost its shop in Mezőkászony and its vineyards, recalled that "it was a very difficult time for Jewish people."[123] These acts of official robbery exacerbated the food shortages, which from 1941 onward meant hunger and malnutrition for many non-Jews as well as Jews.[124]

Sam Moskowitz referred to the violence of Hungarian policemen and "Hungarian hooligans" and said that "life [in Dombó] became very very miserable."[125] Most of the time, however, the Hungarian police tried to prevent large-scale public disorder on the streets, which created conflict with Hungarian soldiers, who sometimes engaged in organized attacks against Jews. An infantry company commander in Munkács, for instance, thought that Jews' homes would serve nicely as sites for a "partisan exercise" in May 1942, just before his unit left for the front. The rationale stemmed from the state's policies and security anxieties prevalent in the Hungarian army, which had just played a central role in planning and perpetrating mass killings of Serbs and Jews in Hungarian-occupied Délvidék. Jews, a group collectively deemed foreign and slated for removal, now also became, like many Carpatho-Ruthenians and Serbs, "the enemy." The "exercise" quickly turned into real-life "looting and assaulting of Jews."[126]

Whereas soldiers only passed through Subcarpathian Rus', the daily presence of the dreaded Hungarian gendarmes ensured that many could not forget their violence. Morris Muller described how they mistreated Jews on the streets of Huszt.[127] Sometimes the gendarmes beat their victims severely.[128] In particular, the torture of the victims in the gendarmerie's investigation headquarters in the region, the Kohner Castle above Munkács, served as a reminder to all the region's inhabitants of the occupation authorities' power over their lives.[129] Two letters from a mother and father in Beregszász to their son, Shimon, probably written in January 1944, convey a sense of the atmosphere in those days. "We cannot relax for even a minute," wrote the mother. And the father added that "we have had enough, too much. . . . I wanted to write a lot of things but I am not capable of gathering my thoughts."[130]

Most Jews in the region felt equally incapable of dealing with information about the ongoing genocide against Jews in German-dominated Europe. And when, nevertheless, firsthand accounts conveyed the dreadful news, repression and denial became the order of the day. Katherine Bodek's uncle managed to survive the summer deportations of 1941 and returned to the region. He told his family about mass murder on the other side of the Carpathian Mountains, but "we didn't believe him"; they thought that he had lost his mind.[131] Jean Greenstein heard local Germans, who had joined the SS and were on leave at home in Nagyszőllős, talk about the murder of Jews. "Of course, nobody believed it."[132]

Refugee Jews from Poland and Slovakia also brought terrifying details with them of the unfolding mass murder. Eva Slomovits remembered the "horror stories" of a Polish Jewish woman. "We thought she was crazy. We couldn't believe it."[133] According to Sarah Holender, "We didn't want to believe it."[134] If the refugee Jews met rejection and disbelief, they also received much-needed help from Jews in Subcarpathian Rus'.[135] But the local Jews' disintegrating lives and communities seemed horrible enough and consumed their physical and mental capabilities, rendering the reported details of the genocide unimaginable.[136] Unable and unwilling to grasp the political imagination of a "Greater Hungary" that demanded their utter exclusion, most Jews in Subcarpathian Rus' refused to contemplate the Nazi fantasy aptly described by Alon Confino as "a world without Jews."[137] They thus pushed knowledge of the mass killing of Jews out of the public sphere and buried it under a "social sound of silence," to borrow sociologist Eviatar Zerubavel's term.[138]

Jews and Carpatho-Ruthenians: Facing Persecution Apart

This "sound of silence" echoed the helplessness of most Jews in Subcarpathian Rus' at the time. Active resistance to the oppression of the Hungarian occupying authorities rarely occurred, and when it happened, it showed a level of interethnic cooperation that hardly existed in other spheres of life.

In May of 1939 a group of Jews formed a communist underground cell in Nagybocskó. Local Magyar and Carpatho-Ruthenian communists also joined it. The leading figures among the Jews in the group met often and discussed the events of the war; the flight of local communists to the Soviet Union[139] and financial support for their families; the need to raise money to fund the cell's operations; and the formation of partisan units to prepare for Soviet occupation of the region. The most substantial activities dealt with the preparations for and assistance to a group of Soviet paratroopers, who were dropped in the vicinity of the town on 4 January 1942. At the head of the Soviet soldiers stood Oleksa Borkaniuk, a Ukrainophile Carpatho-Ruthenian who had served as the secretary of the influential Communist Party in Subcarpathian Rus' in 1935; his team included Samu Sámuel Hábermann, a Jewish tailor who joined the cell in 1939 and shortly thereafter crossed the border to the Soviet Union. The Hungarian authorities had uncovered the cell well before 1942, however, and during January and February arrested its members along with the Soviet soldiers. The cruel interrogations included torture and some cases of murder. The trials that followed resulted in six death sentences and long prison terms.[140] One other small-scale resistance attempt in the region met a similar fate.[141]

For the most part, however, the onslaught of the Hungarian occupation, which could have only exacerbated the divide between Jews and Magyars, failed to unite Jews and Carpatho-Ruthenians. Fircha Hermal, for example, explained that the relations between Jews and Carpatho-Ruthenians in Alsóverecke (Nyzhni Vorota) deteriorated quickly during the Hungarian occupation.[142] In Nagybocskó, where Hungarian troops had massacred Carpatho-Ruthenians in March 1939, some Carpatho-Ruthenians joined Jews in the communist underground, but others reportedly assisted the Hungarian authorities in anti-Jewish actions.[143] A similar hostility drove some Carpatho-Ruthenians in Técső (Tyachiv) to cooperate with the Hungarian authorities against their Jewish neighbors, notwithstanding the exhortations of the local Greek Catholic priest.[144] Yet most Carpatho-Ruthenians throughout Subcarpathian Rus' shunned contact with the authorities. The anti-Jewish resentments among them, which climaxed as Hungary invaded the region, persuaded many that Jews deserved no aid. The persecution that descended on Carpatho-Ruthenians cemented their choice to turn away from their Jewish neighbors.

The hostile distance between Jews and Carpatho-Ruthenians and between Jews and Magyars rendered the "social sound of silence" all the more essential. As Helen Fein has argued, one's anticipation of coping with a given threat determines her or his acknowledgment of warning signs. The less Jews could depend on support from non-Jews, the more powerless they were, and therefore the less ready to face the possibility of destruction.[145] When persecution and mass violence again intensified in the spring and summer of 1944, it would leave no doubt for Jews that their past lives with their Carpatho-Ruthenian neighbors lay in ruin.

Conclusion: Hungary Before March 1944: Shifting the Focus, Changing the Narrative

This chapter has reexamined the history of Hungary during World War II by shifting the focus regarding both time and place. First, it has centered the period between November 1938 and March 1944 as worthy of analysis without viewing it as merely preliminary to a predetermined German occupation. Scholarship with titles such as "Prelude to the Holocaust in Hungary" or "The Last Chapter" clearly imparts that meaning.[146] This chapter, by contrast, strives to capture at least a bit of the often forgotten quality of every history: it might have taken a different course or it might not have happened at all, and we should therefore think about it as a forward-moving process pregnant with possibilities.[147]

This chapter has also sought to understand wartime Hungary in its borderlands rather than the still prevalent tendency to look at Budapest and areas within the Trianon boundaries.[148] As the occupied border territories stood at the heart of the widely shared political imagination of Hungarian society after World War I, it is crucial to direct our analytical lens on them. The multiethnic, multilingual, and multireligious societies of those regions posed burning "problems" for the Hungarian authorities, and the ways they chose to write about them and the policies they put forward and implemented to address them tell us much about wartime Hungary.

We learn that anti-Jewish policies evolved, first and foremost, according to vital Hungarian interests, and not primarily as a result of pressure from Berlin. As Kinga Frojimovics has rightly argued, the KEOKH functioned, at least partly, as a "'dejewification commando' operating in Hungary before the Germans occupied the country."[149] Indeed, for the Jews in Szinevér, as we have seen, *total* destruction occurred in the summer of 1941—before the German leadership sent its diplomats to pressure the Hungarian government to deliver the country's Jews for annihilation in Nazi death camps and well before the German occupation of Hungary. As the war dragged on, the government of Miklós Kállay (March 1942–March 1944), fearing German defeat and responding to the destruction of the Second Hungarian Army in Voronezh in January 1943, sought contact with the western Allies and consistently refused to deport Jews as part of the Nazi "final solution."[150] Still, the mass deportations in the summer of 1941 and subsequent persecutions in Subcarpathian Rus' were very much part of a genocidal process, insofar as we understand genocide not as a synonym for mass murder but as a thorough effort to eradicate a society and culture, which is precisely how Raphael Lemkin, who coined the term *genocide*, explained it.[151] Yet even those who seek to change the narrative about Hungary before March 1944 focus almost exclusively on anti-Jewish policies, thus missing the significant connections that typified the multilayered mass violence designed and carried out by the state.

The goal of a Magyar-dominated "Greater Hungary" prompted policies that targeted Roma and Carpatho-Ruthenians in Subcarpathian Rus' in addition to Jews. Legislators in Budapest, county subprefects, and local gendarmes made sure that harassment, discrimination, violence, and sometimes death pervaded daily lives. But some moments between 1938 and 1944, particularly during the summer of 1941, opened windows of opportunity for violence to escalate in order to realize the ultimate desire of the authorities: to remove as many of the region's non-Magyar inhabitants as possible. This goal of breaking the social fabric of Subcarpathian Rus' continued to serve as a compass also after those windows closed, forcing de-escalation of violence to the more routine persecutions and depredations of state authorities that still tore families and communities apart. "Dejewification" certainly figured as a central aspect of this process, but what meanings flashed in the minds of many people as they imagined it?

The integrated exploration in this chapter uncovers how images of disloyalty and foreignness fed animosities against Jews, Roma, and

Carpatho-Ruthenians, picturing them as threats to the ethnonational Magyar state. Attitudes and emotions against the three groups found anchors in the distant or near past: Carpatho-Ruthenians as Russophiles reminded Hungarians of Russian forces that helped the Habsburgs crush the Hungarian revolution in 1849,[152] and memories of Ukrainophiles in the autonomous Carpatho-Ukraine were all too fresh. Also, the association of both Russophiles and Ukrainophiles with the Soviet Union further heightened concerns about disloyalty and foreignness. Roma aroused more intense anxieties, which stemmed from their seemingly inherent predilection to a wandering and filthy existence, and all these justifications commingled with Christian anti-Jewish positions and sentiments to place the Jews as the most dangerous threat in the struggle for "Greater Hungary." Earlier chapters herein pointed to the benefits of deconstructing the term *antisemitism* when discussing the relations between Jews and Carpatho-Ruthenians. Here we see that the components of antisemitism shed light on policies of mass violence that aimed at more than solely the Jewish communities of Subcarpathian Rus'. Digging into the meanings of antisemitism thus lays bare not only the links between the layers of this assault but also the particular drive for a "dejewified" "Greater Hungary." In other words elucidating this multidimensional picture clarifies the specific victimization that descended on Jews.

The next chapter explores the impact of the German occupation of Hungary in March 1944 on the project of "Greater Hungary," tackling a common dichotomy in the study of history and one with loaded implications in this story: break versus continuity.

5

Site of Hatreds
Destruction in Subcarpathian Rus'

THE GERMAN ARMY rolled into Hungary without firing a single shot on 19 March 1944. Attempts by Budapest in 1943 to establish contact with the Allies and propose peace in advance of a dreaded occupation of the country by the Soviet army had failed. The German invasion, Operation Margarethe I, aimed primarily to prevent Hungary from opting out of the Axis, while also securing Hungary's economy and resources for the German war effort. Hitler and the German authorities blamed the Jews of Hungary for the tension between the two countries, and they also saw them as a grave military danger at a time when the Eastern Front moved steadily westward toward the Carpathian crest and in view of a possible invasion of the Allies in the Balkans. Including the Jews of Hungary in the German "final solution" program thus figured as a crucial strategic objective—both militarily and ideologically—of the German leadership in March 1944.[1]

Adolf Eichmann, who had overseen the deportations of millions of Jews across Europe to Nazi death camps, now gathered his Sondereinsatzkommando with one goal: the deportations to Auschwitz of Hungary's Jews.[2] These committed Nazis followed the German army into Hungary solely to apply their expertise in genocide against a population perceived as the ultimate threat to Nazi Germany. They carried out policies in the service of a total worldview, according to which the continued existence of large Jewish concentrations in Nazi-dominated Europe—mostly in Hungary and Romania—accounted for the major economic, political, and military problems in the Axis and signified a colossal failure of the Nazi revolutionary effort. The later stages of the war therefore brought the anti-Jewish hatred that stood at the heart of the Nazi movement to a peak and the commitment to kill Jews to new heights of intensity.

As we have seen, Hungary's leaders saw the world differently. Rather than a global utopia, they imagined a "Greater Hungary." Jews figured as the first enemies on their list, as on the Nazis', but they wanted them out of the country, not necessarily dead. Moreover, some Hungarian nationalists conceded the role of at least some of the Jews of Budapest, particularly the financial elite, in the future of "Greater Hungary," while excluding completely from this vision all the Jews in the multiethnic and multireligious borderlands. Their policies spelled suffering, dislocation, and death on a massive scale, but they never thought to realize their vision through systematic mass murder. Many of them hated Jews, certainly the Jews who lived in the territories occupied by Hungary since 1938, but without the apocalyptic anxiety that radiated from Berlin.

By 1944 the German and Hungarian states had attacked Jews as a group "with similar justification over a lengthy time period," to borrow from political scientist Roger Petersen's explanation of hatred.[3] When Germany invaded Hungary in 1944, the Hungarian authorities in Budapest, Subcarpathian Rus', and elsewhere in the country quickly grasped the potential of the encounter between these two different anti-Jewish hatreds. If, as Sara Ahmed has maintained, "hate is a negative attachment to an other that one wishes to expel . . . from bodily and social proximity,"[4] and since Hungarian leaders took advantage of opportunities before March 1944 to further their vision of "Greater Hungary," they now saw new hope in the German invasion.

The Hungarian Authorities: Change and Continuity

The new situation brought changes in the Hungarian leadership. Pro-German rightists assumed the top positions in the government. Döme Sztójay, who had served as the Hungarian ambassador in Berlin (1935–1944), became prime minister, and Andor Jaross of the far-right Party of Hungarian Renewal (Magyar Megújulás Pártja) became minister of the interior. Under Jaross two extreme rightists who hated Jews passionately, László Baky and László Endre, filled powerful posts regarding anti-Jewish policies and actions: secretary of state in the Political Department and secretary of state in the Administrative Department, respectively.[5] A positive working relationship quickly developed between these central figures in Budapest and Eichmann's entourage of mass murderers.

László Ferenczy, lieutenant colonel of the Royal Hungarian Gendarmerie, functioned as liaison between the gendarmerie and the German Security Police (Sicherheitspolizei) and stood at the head of the effort to ghettoize and deport the state's Jews in 1944. Apart from exceptional commitment, he brought to this position more than two years (March 1940–July 1942) of experience as the commander of the gendarmerie's investigation unit in Kassa, which played a role in the violent oppression in Subcarpathian Rus' under Hungarian occupation.[6] In 1944 Ferenczy situated his headquarters in Munkács (Mukachevo), and Dieter Wisliceny worked next to him as Eichmann's representative.[7]

The German invasion induced changes in the Hungarian administration in Subcarpathian Rus' as well. The mayor of Munkács, Aladár Vozáry, lost his job, and Árpád Siménfalvy lost his place as the lord lieutenant (*főispán*) of Ungvár (Uzhhorod) and of Ung County and Ugocsa County, in both cases probably because of the presence of Jews in their lives. Vozáry's wife was Jewish,[8] and Árpád Siménfalvy had maintained contact with Jewish leaders in his hometown, Nagyszőllős (Vynohradovo), especially during the 1920s and 1930s.[9]

Yet many regional and local Hungarian officials kept their posts. The region's governor since 1942, Vilmos Pál Tomcsányi, took an active role in the ghettoization process until its conclusion at the end of April, when he resigned. No less important, the mayors of Ungvár and Beregszász (Berehovo) and the chief notary of Huszt (Khust) stayed in place and personally oversaw the ghettoization and deportations of large numbers of Jews from the ghettos and concentration places in their towns. And Colonel Győző Tölgyessy, head of Gendarmerie District VIII (Kassa), including Subcarpathian Rus', who had commanded the gendarmes in his district since 1942, willingly led them also after March 1944 as they harassed, beat, expelled, plundered, and killed.

Both change and continuity facilitated the deadly attack against the Jews of Subcarpathian Rus' and thus the realization of "Greater Hungary." Those Germans who pursued the murder of Jews wherever they encountered them could not have carried out their plan in Hungary if it had not matched a highly influential national longing that had framed Hungary's troubled alliance with Hitler since 1938. The overlapping interests of Hungarian authorities and German genocide specialists in the spring and summer of 1944 brought about the speedy ghettoization and mass deportations of some 440,000 Jews. It began in the mountains, on the slopes of the Carpathians.

Everyday Destruction: The End of Jewish Life in Subcarpathian Rus', March–June 1944

As we saw in Chapter 4, a wide consensus among the Hungarian authorities perceived the Jews of Subcarpathian Rus' as an inherently disloyal group and thus particularly dangerous in a borderland area. The early attack on the region's Jewish communities in the spring of 1944 thus derived from entrenched Hungarian priorities. These concerns now corresponded with the perceptions of the German occupiers.

Expulsions and Ghettoization

The representatives of the SS in Hungary tackled the task of destroying the Jewish communities in Subcarpathian Rus' immediately, determined to accomplish their goal at lightning speed. They first called for a ghettoization process in Subcarpathian Rus' that would last no more than several days and end by 6 April. But rather than facilitate the process, military considerations actually interfered: the commander of the First Hungarian Army rejected the Germans' request, explaining that it would disrupt the army's deployment in the region.[10] The German occupiers nevertheless pushed forward and established Jewish councils throughout Subcarpathian Rus' in the first days of April, acting before central, regional, or local Hungarian authorities made any decisions about such bodies. In Ungvár, for example, the Jewish Council (Zsidó tanács), consisting of six departments, was well in place by 7 April, following "the orders of the German command."[11] The Jewish councils in Munkács, Beregszász, and Nagyszőllős likewise began to function in early April.[12]

Budapest, in the meantime, provided the legal framework for the anti-Jewish policies. On 4 April the Ministry of the Interior initiated the registration of the state's Jewish population, instructing (Decree 6136/1944. VII. res.) local authorities to request Jewish communal organizations to submit lists of all Jews.[13] In the following two weeks this vital information landed on all the relevant desks. The public notary of Királyháza (Korolevo), for example, submitted the required list to the chief constable (*főszolgabiró*) of Nagyszőllős on 8 April, mentioning in addition "five baptized Jews, who are Jews according to the racial law."[14] And the mayor of Ungvár, László Megay, sent the list of Jews in his town to the Ministry of the Interior on 18 April with copies to the local police headquarters and the local gendarmerie unit.[15]

As the names of the victims accumulated on paper, László Baky set in motion other necessary processes. The day of 7 April was particularly busy. He first sent out his detailed ghettoization order (Decree 6163/1944. res.),[16] after which he held a meeting about the deportation of Jews from Gendarmerie District VIII (Kassa).[17] The Hungarian government then decided (12 April) to formally turn Subcarpathian Rus' and northern Transylvania into "military operational zones," retroactive since 1 April, and appointed Vilmos Pál Tomcsányi, the governor of Subcarpathian Rus', as government commissioner for the military area.[18] László Endre chaired a meeting in Munkács that day to discuss the details of ghettoization in Subcarpathian Rus',[19] and Tomcsányi issued his own Decree 162/1944 for ghettoization in the region, largely based on Baky's instructions.[20] Local authorities followed suit and published their own orders, such as the one by the mayor of Ungvár, which announced the beginning of the "relocation of Jews" on 20 April.[21] Ghettoization in Subcarpathian Rus', in fact, began on 16 April and ended within several days.[22] Tomcsányi resigned at the end of April for reasons that remain unclear, and András Vincze, a retired lieutenant general of the Hungarian army, assumed his position.[23]

Laws and decrees pouring from the capital lent legal legitimacy to ethnic discrimination and forcible mass displacement, as the Hungarian authorities in Subcarpathian Rus' devised and carried out anti-Jewish steps of their own accord. Local authorities in Munkács, for example, showed initiative in late March by deciding that all the town's Jews must wear a yellow patch on their clothes, even though Decree 1.240/1944 M.E. on the marking with a yellow Star of David of all the Jews in Hungary (defined by law) above the age of six went into effect only on 5 April.[24] Significantly, the government Decree 1.610/1944 M.E. on ghettoization was promulgated on 26 April,[25] by which time the mayor of Ungvár and the town's police chief could report on the ghettoization of almost seventeen thousand Jews of Ung County and Ungvár.[26] The urgency expressed in these steps reveals the broad consensus at work and the way that local and regional officials in effect understood them as continuous with the anti-Jewish campaign in the period before March 1944.

Ghettoization completely altered the physical settings of towns and villages across the region, and it transformed the ways many residents—both Jews and non-Jews—felt about the places they called home.[27] In Huszt, for instance, the Hungarian authorities crammed more than five thousand Jews into three separate streets, changing the town's landscape significantly.[28] Many Jews from villages and towns in Bereg County were driven into the Kont and Vály brick factory and the Weiss farm in Beregszász. Most of the town's Jews were forced into the barrel factory of Reismann and Neufeld; the elderly and the sick were concentrated in one street.[29] Aladár Vozáry, the mayor of Munkács until the German occupation, described ghettoization there as "an earthquake, an avalanche has shaken the town and its inhabitants. . . . Whoever has a heart, it aches."[30] A few days after the conclusion of ghettoization in town, the authorities reduced the area of the ghetto: "They make the Jews empty two streets within an hour. The crazy running and hurrying begin again."[31]

In Nagyszőllős the Hungarian authorities turned the central synagogue into a prison, later conducting in its courtyard the registration of the town's Jews just before deportation.[32] Thirty wealthy Jews in Huszt suffered arrest and abuse in the town's central synagogue throughout the ghetto period in order to drain them and the community of financial resources and use them as hostages to prevent resistance. Eitan Porat recalled that every evening "we heard their screams."[33] The perpetrators thus transformed that space, which Jews associated with protection, solace, and belief, into the embodiment of suffering, despair, and destruction. As literary scholar Elaine Scarry has explained, torture often involves the objectification and externalization of the prisoner's pain, which enhance it as "world destroying."[34] In Munkács the German occupiers, together with very willing Hungarian gendarmes, added to the torment by coercing their victims to partake in it. They gathered many Jews on the first Saturday after ghettoization and ordered them to destroy the interior of synagogues and Jewish study houses in what became known by the victims as "the black shabbat."[35] In almost every town across the region, synagogues became tools of mass atrocities.

The Hungarian authorities quickly realized that the large number of Jews in the ghettos and concentration sites throughout the region posed problems owing to food shortages, overcrowding, and poor sanitation conditions. On 14 April, before the start of ghettoization, the local authorities in Huszt informed superiors in Ungvár that, contrary to the oral orders conveyed at the meeting in Munkács on 12 April, they could not receive the Jews of the Ilosva (Irshava) district. The following day, the gendarmerie captain in Beregszász rejected the attempt to place these Jews in his town.[36] Ten days later, the new mayor of Munkács, István Engelbrecht, requested higher authorities to help him provide food for the Jews relocated to his town.[37] Whatever the response was, the Jews of Ilosva and the surrounding area were nevertheless sent to the brick factories in Munkács.[38] Naftali Deutsch remembered that the Jews of his town, Magyarkomját (Velikiye Komyaty), obeyed the authorities' order to gather at the synagogue on 16 April and marched eight kilometers to neighboring Ilosva. After spending the night in a large yard used to store building materials, gendarmes led them to the nearby train station in pouring rain, "feeling miserable, and fearing an unknown future." Freight wagons transported them to Munkács.[39] The difficulties caused by moving Jews into ghettos and concentration sites required no more than such ad hoc solutions. As we will see, those in charge of ghettoization in Subcarpathian Rus', in any case, perceived it as a temporary measure; most of them knew nothing about further plans in mid-April (or later), but they assumed that the region's Jews would not stay there for long.

Jews sometimes tried to hinder expulsions and ghettoization. Sam Moskowitz recounted that the local authorities in Dombó (Dubove) received bribes in order to announce a typhoid epidemic, which called for quarantine and rendered the immediate expulsion of the town's Jews impossible.[40] But the scheme could not save them. In May the Hungarian authorities expelled the 1,006 Jews in the town to the ghetto in Técső (Tyachiv).[41] Moskowitz could not forget the beatings, humiliation, and robbery as gendarmes gathered them in the synagogue in Dombó.[42] A similar attempt in Dolha (Dovhe) likewise failed, and the village Jews were relocated at the beginning of May to the Weiss farm in Beregszász and deported to Auschwitz at the end of the month.[43]

Many ensured the efficiency of the deportations. Survivors from Huszt mentioned the chief notary, József Bíró, who took part in humiliating Jews in the town's ghetto.[44] Survivors from Beregszász stressed the central role of the mayor, Kálmán Hubay, in the anti-Jewish persecution.[45] Other kinds of authority figures also took part. In Nagyszőllős, for example, a Magyar schoolteacher, Victor Ortutay, worked as one of the stenographers who wrote down the details of family members right before they entered the freight wagons.[46] The careers of these three officials stretched before and after March 1944, which, again, points to important continuities. In addition to lists of names, ages, professions, and deportation dates, people such as Ortutay, Hubay, and Bíró also drew up lists of property and money.

Mass Robbery

The official registration of the possessions, currency, and valuables of Jews robbed by Hungarian authorities in the process of ghettoization and deportations followed the procedure laid out in appendix E to Baky's Decree 6163/1944. res. It stipulated that the seized objects and currency of each apartment should be recorded on a list with two copies.[47] The people engaged in this work in Subcarpathian Rus' left an extremely detailed paper trail. In Beregrákos (Rakoshyno), for example, the authorities expropriated twenty-six cows, noting the exact weight of each.[48] In the ghetto in Szeklencze (Sokirnitsa), to which gendarmes expelled the Jews of Felsőkalocsa (Nehrovets') on 16 April, an unnamed midwife, who participated in the search for hidden valuables, found silver and gold necklaces, earrings, watches, rings, medallions, and one pair of gold earrings with a diamond—all concealed by sixteen Jewish women.[49]

The Hungarian gendarmerie took the lead in the mass robbery of the Jewish population, in which brutal interrogations put the wealthiest at great risk. Ellen Hersh, who grew up in an affluent family in a suburb of Ungvár, referred to the harsh beatings that her father suffered to force him to reveal information about valuables that the gendarmes believed he had hidden. "There was a lot of torture going on in the ghetto. . . . This was done daily to people, to many people."[50] A survivor from Gánya (Hanychi) relayed that in the ghetto in Técső, to which gendarmes had expelled him, "during the search for valuables the gendarmes undressed us completely and checked if we had hidden something. Meanwhile they were constantly beating us."[51] In the larger ghettos the gendarmes set up special cells to imprison and torture affluent Jews together with those suspected as communists. According to one survivor, Jews held in the so-called barrack 7 in the Felszabadulás street brick factory in Ungvár, the main ghetto in town, "were treated very badly, beaten all the time."[52]

The regional authorities sometimes used mass robbery as a tool of social change. Following Decree 50.500/1944 K.K.M. (21 April) and anticipating Decree 58.000/1944 K.K.M. (21 May) of the Minister of Trade and Transportation, the authorities in Ungvár finalized (10 May) a list of 168 shops and industrial businesses owned by Jews and ready for distribution with priority to Magyars who had suffered loss or injury as a result of aerial bombing.[53] In the village of Veléte (Velyatyn), almost every one of the seventy-nine expropriated estates was carved up between different Magyar caretakers.[54] Other cases, however, exhibited straightforward favoritism: only two people took control of the seventy estates of Jews in Gyertyánliget (Kobyletska Polyana).[55] And in Lipcse (Lypcha) the Hungarian authorities first (12 April) plundered the meager amounts of money in the hands of the town's Jews, before expelling them (18 April) to the ghetto in Iza (Iza); six days later these Jews were moved to the larger ghetto in Huszt.[56] Finally, after the deportation of the Jews to Auschwitz in mid-May, Magyar caretakers received more than seventy-seven thousand cadastral hold (around 110,000 acres) of the victims' fields and meadows. One Béla Gribószky, however, managed to put his hands on more than a third of the plunder.[57]

The German occupiers also engaged in mass robbery in Subcarpathian Rus'. Upon arrival in a town, they arrested several Jews and informed the community leaders of the sum they demanded for their release.[58] Theft of property and valuables was also common. In Munkács, for instance, they seized the large house of Péter Zoltán, a wealthy Jew, to use as headquarters, confiscating all the contents and valuables in it.[59] Here, "Greater Hungary" and "Greater Germany" clashed. In addition to the prevalent inclination of people to enrich themselves in such situations, Hungarian leaders strove to utilize the wealth and possessions of the Jewish victims as building blocks in their ethnonational project. The German invaders, however, reached into the same pile of plunder with the view to add to the power of Nazi Germany and attempt to offset the costs of mass killing.[60] The widespread poverty of the Jews in Subcarpathian Rus' usually left all perpetrators disappointed.

Yet the atmosphere of competition pushed the Hungarian authorities to strip Jews of all their assets and belongings right to the very end of the deportation process. The gendarmes in Huszt beat and sometimes killed anyone found in possession of money or valuables just before they pushed their victims into the deportation trains.[61] Katherine Bodek summarized that episode in Ungvár in two words: "just awful."[62] And in Kassa, before the Hungarian guards handed the trains over to their German counterparts, they harassed and threatened the victims in the hope of squeezing from them whatever possessions they had managed to salvage. One survivor from Huszt stated that "my sister was even pulled off the train [in Kassa] and was undressed by a Hungarian gendarme, who threatened to shoot me if he found something on us, but he found nothing. He even took the underwear off my older sister before he let her get back on the train."[63] Such wanton violence cut deep into the minds and souls of the victims, whose bodies and worlds fell apart with every blow and act of humiliation.

"I Lost My Mind": Victims

Contemporary accounts reveal the misery that came to dominate the daily existence of Jews in Subcarpathian Rus' as they faced genocide. In May, Hermina Klein managed to smuggle a letter to her daughter in Vác, describing the experience of ghettoization in Nagyszőllős:

> We have been in this miserable place for three weeks now. . . . In my most horrible nightmare I could not imagine that one could live in these conditions. Ten thousand people are terribly crowded here. In our house [4 rooms, a storeroom, and an attic] now dwell 230 people. There is nothing more dreadful than to roll around on the concrete floor here, sick and blind, awful. They expelled us from our home and robbed all our belongings and property for which we had labored for thirty-six years. All of it was taken from us in ten minutes. . . . My only hope is that I will not be able to bear this wretched life much longer.[64]

Other Jews in the region indeed found themselves unable to continue living in such conditions and committed suicide.[65] And some sensed that their situation defied imagination as well. In a few letters sent surreptitiously from the Munkács ghetto to Budapest, a mother stressed to her daughter that "you could not imagine our plight here."[66] Eugen Schoenfeld wrote sixty years later about the same ghetto: "We entered a period of anomie, of social disorganization. This disorganization was evident in the breakdown of all normal life. My mother, for instance, who was very Orthodox and all her life adhered stringently to [the] law[s] of Kashruth, the ritual pre and proscription pertaining to edible food, was now forced to violate these religious laws."[67]

These testimonies underscore historian Amos Goldberg's assertion that persecution and mass violence for the most part overwhelmed Jews and that, rather than induce various forms of resistance, the genocidal attack invaded and crushed their inner selves, leaving many to experience their mental and spiritual worlds fading away into a terrifying nothingness.[68] Samuel Moskowitz from Kálnik (Kalnik) conveyed just this sense of absence when describing his decision to flee and avoid expulsion to the ghetto in Munkács. At that point in the interview the interviewer asked, "What was going on in your mind when you say goodbye to your mother and your sister?" Moskowitz replied, "I have no mind, I have no mind, I lost my mind."[69]

Sexual violence, while not widespread, added another dimension of horror to the process of annihilation.[70] Aranka Siegal recounted that two German soldiers broke into a house in Beregszász one evening and raped a woman and her daughter; Dr. Feher, the husband and father, "could no longer bear to live, he wrote in a note, and then shot himself with a hunting rifle."[71] In Munkács, drunken Germans raped a Jewish woman.[72] These accounts confirm recent research that argues that Germans in Nazi-dominated Europe did not shy away from sexually assaulting Jewish women and other people considered inferior according to Nazi racism.[73] Women also joined this kind of abuse, as midwives—sometimes neighbors—assisted the authorities in searching for money and valuables on the bodies of Jewish women and girls, while gendarmes undressed their victims, hit them, and gazed at the public violation of personal integrity. In Huszt a local midwife named Sárosi (first name unknown) gained notoriety by beating pregnant women.[74] One survivor, who mentioned Sárosi, added in the next sentence: "The gendarmes behaved in an awful way as well. I am ashamed to recall what happened even now, after so many things."[75]

Emissaries of Zionist movements from Budapest, some of them natives of Subcarpathian Rus', tried to organize efforts to hide or escape to Budapest or even to Romania and Slovakia, places that posed much less danger to Jews at the time.[76] Zvi Prizant from Huszt, a member of the Dror-Hechalutz Hatzair movement, moved to Budapest in 1941. In April 1944 he was sent with false ID papers to his hometown to build hiding bunkers, an effort that failed almost everywhere in the region as it required more than just a few weeks before ghettoization.[77] He thus returned for a short time to Budapest, only to appear again in Huszt with another member of his movement, Menachem Baumgarten. This time, he tried to persuade as many Jews as possible to risk the road to Budapest rather than enter the ghetto.

Most of the Jews in Huszt and elsewhere in Subcarpathian Rus' proved unwilling to listen to Zvi Prizant and other emissaries like him. Jean Greenstein, who had already encountered disbelief in Nagyszőllős when he reported the killing of Jews in Nazi-dominated Europe before March 1944, now tried again. He told friends and acquaintances that a German officer, an ethnic German from his town who had returned with the German occupiers, had warned him of the deportations to "annihilation camps," but "nobody believed it."[78] Most Jews preferred to cling to hopes about Soviet forces that would soon occupy the region or to rumors about the transfer of Jews to labor camps elsewhere in Hungary. Sheindy Levi from Beregszász explained that "we did not believe [information about mass murder of Jews], we did not want to believe . . . which human being could accept such information[?] . . . We did not want and we refused to think about it."[79]

Still, Zvi Prizant noted after the war, "With great effort we managed to send eleven people from Huszt and they all arrived safely to Budapest."[80] Two factors may have helped some Jews in Huszt to escape: the assistance of Jewish youth in the ghetto police, as noted by Zvi Prizant,[81] and the position of the town's rabbi, Yehoshua Greenwald, who supported this course of action.[82] Helena Rosenfeld, for instance, explained in 1946 how she managed to obtain Christian identification papers and flee to Budapest from the town, together with her husband, her daughter, and her three sons. She and her family made it out of the region right before deportations commenced.[83]

Deportations

Eichmann arrived in Budapest with the clear intent to deport all the Jews of Hungary to Auschwitz, but he knew that he required the Hungarian authorities on all levels to achieve his goal. Historian Christian Gerlach has thus suggested avoiding the "Eichmannization" of the Holocaust in Hungary,[84] but scholars have yet to reach agreement with regard to the timing and nature of the joint German-Hungarian decision-making process in the spring and summer of 1944.[85] Concrete plans for mass deportations appear for the first time in a telegram from Edmund Veesenmayer, the German Plenipotentiary in Hungary, to the German Foreign Office on 23 April. The language suggests a focused decision to deport the Jews of the borderlands: Subcarpathian Rus', northeastern Hungary, northern Transylvania, and the Délvidék.[86] Furthermore, the Vienna transportation conference, which gathered between 4 and 6 May, discussed *only* the deportation of Jews from Subcarpathian Rus', northeastern Hungary, and northern Transylvania;[87] indeed, the ghettoization of the Jews in Trianon Hungary would not begin until 5 June.[88]

Vital Hungarian and German interests converged in the deportations of the Jews of Subcarpathian Rus' and the other borderlands. Hungary's leaders saw this as an opportunity to further their vision of "Greater Hungary" and strengthen their hold on the borderlands by removing Jewish populations seen as disloyal right from the very beginning of the Hungarian occupation of these regions between November 1938 and March 1941. They also needed to abide by Horthy's promise to Hitler to provide one hundred thousand laborers (probably more), which the German army, mostly the Luftwaffe, needed badly.[89] And the German army would get border territories without a group believed to pose a military threat, while Eichmann could begin to fulfill his mission in Budapest. It was the first time in his career that he personally commanded his whole team and directed a genocidal scheme of unprecedented proportions.[90]

Perhaps the timing of the Ungvár mayor's request on 24 April, a day after Veesenmayer's telegram, that the minister of the interior and the region's governor make sure to deport the ghettoized Jews, as they posed a health hazard to the town's residents, was not mere coincidence.[91] In fact, in a meeting in Ungvár on 15 April, a day before the beginning of ghettoization, the mayor was informed that the soon to be incarcerated Jews would remain in his town no longer than the end of May.[92] As we have seen, about a week would pass before all the relevant people reached a decision about mass deportations, but the participation of Wisliceny in that meeting in Ungvár strongly indicates that all involved understood in mid-April that ghettoization in Subcarpathian Rus' would soon lead to forced removal of the Jews from the area.

The details of the deportation process in Subcarpathian Rus' were finalized in a series of meetings held by László Ferenczy in Munkács between 8 and 12 May.[93] Between 11 May and 6 June[94] the Hungarian authorities deported around ninety thousand Jews from Subcarpathian Rus' on approximately thirty trains.[95] The last train departed from Huszt on 6 June and brought to completion the destruction of more than a century of Jewish communal life in Subcarpathian Rus'. It also marked a major victory for those treading on the murderous path toward "Greater Hungary." Similar to other such terrible triumphs, this moment came just as Stalin's army pushed toward the Carpathian Mountains, ready to consume in its fire any last illusion about the future of Hungary.

Fantasizing "Greater Hungary" on the Brink of Disaster, June–October 1944

Almost five months passed between June and the Soviet occupation of Subcarpathian Rus'. During that period, even as Axis defeat grew imminent, many on all levels of the Hungarian authorities kept their gazes fixed on the horizon of "Greater Hungary." In addition to the deportation of Jews this vision required the obliteration of their memory. Thus, the local press reported in May that authorities in Munkács planned to demolish the former ghetto area and rebuild a neighborhood for Magyar residents who would arrive from other parts of the country.[96] A decree (24 May) by László Megay, the mayor of Ungvár, asked the town residents to "remove all the signs and address-signs that call Jews to mind from all the houses, shops, and workshops" within three days, adding that "everyone should consider following this order to be a patriotic duty."[97] Finally, the Ministry of the Interior instructed (June) the public administration offices across the region to demolish synagogues, which would yield construction material for the state as well as make land available.[98]

The drive to erase all traces of Jews mirrored the relentless effort to find Jews hiding in the region. At the end of June gendarmes discovered five Jews who had received shelter from three gentiles in Szernye (Serne) with the help of the town's notary and a local merchant.[99] Eleven Jews were found hiding in the area of the former ghetto in Munkács in late July.[100] And a month later a Hungarian soldier caught Jean Greenstein and three other people leaving their bunker in the area of the former ghetto in Nagyszőllős, in which they had lived for three months until they ran out of food and water.[101]

Meanwhile, stealing had become a social norm in "Greater Hungary." The police chief of Ungvár noted as late as 9 October that "most crimes in town are theft," attributing the phenomenon to decreased public morale associated with the looting of apartments previously owned by Jews.[102] "Public morale fell awfully" at the time, observed Aladár Vozáry right after the war.[103] While László Ferenczy wished to imagine the deportations of Jews as facilitating law and order,[104] reality proved the opposite.

As before March 1944, imagining "Greater Hungary" spurred hatred and translated into mass violence that aimed at populations other than Jews alone. Roma were next in line. We have seen that drawing up lists of Jews prefigured the process of ghettoization and deportation. Lists of

Roma, such as the "Gypsy census" conducted by the public notary office in Nagyrákóc (Velikiy Rakovets) in July 1944, pointed to similar intentions.[105] Such acts of registration in other parts of Hungary served subsequent deportations of Roma, mostly after the Arrow Cross takeover of the country on 15 October.[106]

As testimonies of Roma from the region show, violence against them in 1944 grew particularly acute after the conclusion of the anti-Jewish deportations. According to Kalman Sabo from Beregszász:

> As soon as the Jews were sent away in the train carriages, our turn came. . . . One morning the gendarmes, around 30 of them, came on horses [to our tabor] and gave two minutes for all of us to line up on the street. We all came outside. The gendarmes held two- or three-meter-long sticks in their hands; they beat anyone who came out late. . . . They ordered us to stand in two lines. . . . They told us that we have two minutes to run home. There were pregnant women and mothers with small children who could not run. They beat them. . . . In the evening, people were already running to the nearby forest.[107]

Like Jewish women, Roma women fell victim to sexual assault. El'sbeta Gabor from Beregszász reported, "Hungarians and Germans . . . came to our tabor every evening, picked young girls and took them away. Well, it is a shame to talk about that. They brought them back after some time. Everyone cried."[108] And Iolana Tokar from Ungvár remembered the degradation she felt when Hungarians gathered all the Roma in town in a bathhouse, and "they shaved everyone, including the girls. It was humiliating, as Hungarian soldiers stood on the other side of a barbed wire fence."[109] This public display of (male) power flowed from well-established notions among Hungarian authorities about Roma as filthy and dangerous.

The anti-Roma violence and the efforts to capture Jews in hiding proceeded even as the authorities prepared to evacuate the region and flee the advancing Soviet army. July, August, and September saw a flare of decrees and correspondence dealing with various aspects of the withdrawal.[110] The pace of warfare, however, soon rendered their detailed procedures irrelevant: Soviet aircraft bombed the region frequently in September and October,[111] and heavy Soviet artillery preceded the entry of troops in towns like Munkács.[112] "Greater Hungary," a nightmare for its victims, had now become a crumbling fantasy. The disastrous war, which had initially promised to transform the vision to reality, now crushed it under the weight of boots, wheels, chains, and bombs.

Carpatho-Ruthenians: Bystanders

During the hectic months from spring to early fall of 1944 Hungarian officials—preoccupied with mass deportations of Jews, anti-Roma violence, and large-scale expropriation—had little time to turn their attention to the Carpatho-Ruthenian population and its place in their vision of "Greater Hungary." Yet how did Carpatho-Ruthenians react to the German invasion? How did they perceive Hungarian intentions and policies in the new situation? And how did they respond to the persecution, ghettoization, and deportation of their Jewish neighbors?

The vast majority of Carpatho-Ruthenians refused to cooperate with Hungarian and German authorities, but they also lent little help to their Jewish neighbors. They thus seem to fit the misleading term *bystanders*—misleading, for it blurs the reality in which, literally, they were standing, and it implies a behavior characterized by indifference. Following the pathbreaking scholarship of historian Gordon Horwitz on Germans who lived around the concentration camp at Mauthausen,[113] historian Victoria Barnett and, more recently, political scientist Ernesto Verdeja have called for a critical look at descriptions of bystander behavior that rely on words such as *indifference* and *inaction*.[114] Focusing on Hungary during World War II, historian Tim Cole has added to this discussion by shedding light on Magyar bystanders as active people.[115] These analyses, however, focus on bystanders among the dominant group: Germans around Mauthausen and Magyars in Hungary. We still know little about bystanders in Hungary who themselves faced state violence and whose conditions and experiences differed from those of their Magyar neighbors.[116]

Many of the discussions on bystanders among subjugated groups in Nazi-dominated Europe usually identify patterns of collaboration along with the much less common cases of help and rescue. As Timothy Snyder has remarked concerning eastern Europe, these accounts rarely address crucial aspects of the histories of the places and societies of bystanders, producing shallow descriptions that portray bystanders only when they kill Jews or watch as others murder. Bystanders thus appear in many historical narratives as if from nowhere. And almost always we see these people through the lens of sources produced by Jews or the perpetrators.[117] Focusing on the gory dimensions of violence between neighbors in Buczacz during World War II, historian Omer Bartov has argued that "much of the gentile population in this region [east Galicia] both collaborated in and profited from the genocide of the Jews." He therefore asserts that "the category of bystanders in these areas was largely meaningless, since everyone took part in the events."[118] Events in Subcarpathian Rus' (and in other places), however, unfolded differently, and deciphering the meaning of *bystanding* actually constitutes the crux of the matter here.

Events in Subcarpathian Rus' also included horrendous scenes of violence in the process of ghettoization and deportation. In Alsóapsa (Nyzhnya Apsha), where mostly Jews and Carpatho-Ruthenians lived, "locals acted really shamefully; they were glad to see the Jews would be deported," according to the joint testimony of eight survivors. And in the ghetto in Aknaszlatina (Solotvyno), where the Jews of Alsóapsa were held, "when gendarmes took us to the freight cars, they beat us where they could, chased us and trod on the fallen people."[119] Hungarian gendarmes in Ilosva acted similarly and beat Jews "to a pulp" in the course of the expulsion.[120] Yitzhak Gershuni recounted such abuse in Técső, on the way from the ghetto to the train station, and he specifically mentioned that non-Jews witnessed the horror.[121] Esther Offer described an acquaintance in Huszt, who "was standing in a street corner [during the deportation] and she was clapping her hands."[122] The cruelty of perpetrators reached the highest levels in the larger towns, where the violence included murder on the streets in front of many non-Jewish observers. Two sisters from Munkács remembered the abuse and humiliation of their parents during the expulsion of Jews from the ghetto to the brick factories prior to deportation. "On the way the policemen beat the people with whips until they bled. When my elderly father collapsed and could not march any further, a policeman shouted at me not to be standing there, saying: the old guy can die alone just as well. They whipped our 85 year old mother . . . the whole way to the brickyard."[123]

Those who openly welcomed the misery of their Jewish neighbors were hardly indifferent. Expressions of Schadenfreude—pleasure and even gloating in view of the victimization of Jews—point to an active stance that stemmed from the political resentment that emerged against Jews in the interwar period.[124] But the majority who turned their gaze away also made a choice. While recent studies have traced the participation of collaborators in mass violence to "ethnic resentment,"[125] the widespread anti-Jewish resentment among Carpatho-Ruthenians gave no impetus for aggression, mostly because no deep-seated anti-Jewish discourse existed in Subcarpathian Rus'. Resentment, however, proved sufficient to propel a decision that, in effect, sanctioned anti-Jewish violence. Following historian Daniela Saxer's observation that "emotions in social interactions don't appear singly, but in clusters,"[126] it becomes clear that fear enhanced resentment in this case. Carpatho-Ruthenians had already suffered at the hands of the Hungarian authorities, and now, as the front approached, many feared for their future.[127] Thus, both emotions combined to push Carpatho-Ruthenians away from their neighbors rather than to join hands with them against the violent state.

The association of Jews with "Czechization" still fresh in their minds and hearts, many Carpatho-Ruthenians responded to mass violence against a group that they no longer perceived in 1944 as belonging within their social and cultural world, even as the state engaged in violently recasting that world *as a whole*. A considerably limited sense of agency in this case of bystanding brings to mind the position of Jews in the region five years earlier, when they saw and heard the violence of Hungarian soldiers against Carpatho-Ruthenians in mid-March 1939 (Chapter 3). Similar to Carpatho-Ruthenians in 1944, Jews in 1939 saw the violence against their neighbors, at least in some sense, through the recent history of interactions between the groups—in that case the anti-Jewish hostility and some violence in the brief period of Carpatho-Ukraine. Many Jews in 1939, like their neighbors five years later, could do very little, even if they had wanted, to help those Carpatho-Ruthenians targeted by the Hungarian army. As with the analysis of the visions, policies, and actions of state authorities, this discussion of social interactions and breakdown underscores the importance of considering the entire period of the war, before and after March 1944, in order to understand the perceptions and choices of *both* Jews and non-Jews.

Examining bystander behavior as a form of action—but not necessarily violence, let alone killing—suggests an important correction to a common cliché: genocide and other forms of mass atrocities happened, are taking place right now, and will most probably mar the future *not* because most people usually remain indifferent; mass violence has occurred and will occur because most people adhere to positions and emotional states that, explicitly or implicitly, approve of it. This approach also highlights the relational aspect: a certain kind of action results from a particular history of contact, in this case between Jews and Carpatho-Ruthenians. Unlike in east Galicia, anti-Jewish hatreds and communal violence figured neither in the history of Carpatho-Ruthenians nor in their individual memories and thus also not in their political worldviews. Anti-Jewish resentment in this case worked to ensure very little interference in mass violence driven by anti-Jewish hatreds brought by outsiders, Germans and Hungarians. Restoring agency, even if constrained, to those we usually call bystanders means we face not deterministic realities—indifference or violence—but patterns of behavior to study, comprehend, and therefore perhaps even alter.

Rescue

Not all Carpatho-Ruthenians succumbed to fears and resentments and abandoned their Jewish neighbors. Both individual and collective attempts to help and rescue Jews occurred. Most notably, a small Carpatho-Ruthenian underground network that formed in the vicinity of the small town of Dombó in Máramaros County engaged in, among other activities, hiding Jews in several bunkers in the forest. We know the names of two Carpatho-Ruthenians involved in the effort, Yuri Anofray and Nikola Nosa, and we know that the latter kept contact with a partisan group under Soviet command, which carried the name "Stalintsy."[128] Another partisan detachment of about ninety Carpatho-Ruthenians and ten Jews operated in the area, led by one Petro Kushnir. Martin Pearl, who escaped from his town of Gánya, around six kilometers south of Dombó, joined them. He recalled good relations between Jews and non-Jews in the unit.[129] Despite warning by the authorities,[130] other small partisan groups, also including Jews, maintained themselves in the region, though they saw very little combat, if at all.[131]

Some managed to survive without the help of local partisans. Gabriel Mermall and his son Thomas escaped from Poroskő (Poroshkovo), thirty kilometers north of Munkács, to the mountains and forests. Keeping a diary during part of the time, Gabriel continued to write after the war, thus creating a fascinating combination of diary and memoir. After Gabriel and Thomas slipped away from their town, they headed to a Carpatho-Ruthenian family, good friends of Gabriel's sister. The family suggested that Gabriel and Thomas hide with one of the sisters who lived alone in a separate house, but she eventually would not keep them. They then moved on to a local German friend of Gabriel's, who directed them to another family in the depth of the forest. That family, too, would not let them stay, and they tried another house down the road. This time, they were betrayed to the authorities, but, thanks to a woman from their previous attempt, they succeeded in escaping. Running deep into the forest, they encountered the son of the man who would save their lives. Ivan Gartner, a Carpatho-Ruthenian, not only took the father and son—people he had never before met—to a secluded and relatively safe place in the mountains; he also supplied them with food every week for thirteen weeks. Then, when he decided that remaining in the forest might be too dangerous, because of the battles raging in the area, he took Gabriel and Thomas to his home and put them in the roof of the stable, at enormous risk to his whole family.[132]

The arrival of Soviet units of the 4th Ukrainian Front in October 1944 saved people like Gabriel and Thomas, but it also introduced one last wave of multilayered mass violence into the region during World War II.

The Fall of Nazi Europe: Misery for All, October 1944–Summer 1945

The Soviet occupation regime in Subcarpathian Rus' worked to ensure the incorporation of the region as part of postwar Soviet Ukraine.[133] This vision branded local Germans and Magyars not only as people associated with enemies but also as obstacles to the political consolidation of the area as a Soviet stronghold south of the Carpathian Mountains.[134] Political persecution and mass deportations hit the region again. The Soviet authorities ordered all Magyar civilians of military age to report for three days of labor in mid-November. Those who complied and those caught in other ways—around forty thousand people—found themselves imprisoned in a new concentration camp established near the town of Svalyava, whence deportations headed toward labor camps in the Soviet Union.[135] Arrests and deportations of local Germans who had not fled before the arrival of Soviet forces followed in March 1945.[136] Among those arrested, some had just endangered their lives saving Jews. One Dr. Tóth, for instance, together with others, hid and fed several Jews on a farm near Ungvár and in a wine cellar in the town. Maurice Katz, one of the Jews in that group who himself assisted Tóth in the rescue activities, managed to get him out of Soviet custody and smuggle him with a group of around twenty people to Romania.[137]

József Strausz, a resident of Mukachevo (formerly Munkács) of German descent, escaped imprisonment in 1944 only after Amos Rubin, a Jewish boy he had just saved, testified on his behalf at the Soviet military command in town.[138] In the summer of 1945, Strausz again needed help, and this time Amos's father, Eliyahu Rubin, who had survived Auschwitz and returned in April, provided a positive statement on his behalf. Amos Rubin's mother also survived and made her way back in July, and the family soon departed for Palestine. Left without his protectors, József Strausz was eventually deported by the Soviet authorities to labor camps, where he died in 1947.[139] Soviet deportations also engulfed many Carpatho-Ruthenians. Ivan Gartner, the rescuer of Thomas and Gabriel Mermall, for example, spent six years with his son Vassiliy in Siberia.[140]

Around fifteen thousand Jews from Subcarpathian Rus' who survived Nazi concentration camps and death marches returned to the region in the months after the end of the war in Europe in May 1945, mostly searching for relatives.[141] We know, for example, that 2,384 survivors registered to receive some assistance and relief in Uzhhorod (formerly Ungvár) by the end of June 1945.[142] Many survivors across the region met with hostility from their former neighbors. The anti-Jewish resentments among Carpatho-Ruthenians, as well as the desire to hold on to property and possessions formerly owned by Jews,[143] proved sufficient to produce a general animus against the survivors.[144] In contrast to neighboring Poland, Hungary, and Romania, however, no anti-Jewish violence erupted in the region after World War II. As during the war years, since no deep-seated anti-Jewish tradition characterized the lives of Carpatho-Ruthenians in Subcarpathian Rus', they expressed their anti-Jewish enmity without recourse to violence.

The violence that Jews did encounter in Subcarpathian Rus' in 1945 emanated from Soviet occupation authorities. Some Jews who had returned from German concentration camps became victims of deportations to Soviet labor camps. George Zimmermann from Budapest, for example, survived harsh conditions in a forced labor battalion in the Hungarian army. Soviet forces freed him from his Hungarian tormentors near Munkács, which quickly became Mukachevo, where he stayed only to be arrested by Soviet authorities and sent to the camp in Svalyava. He recalled meeting there many other Jews who had made it through the war in Hungarian labor battalions, and he described the overcrowding and exhaustion that claimed victims on a daily basis among the camp inmates—Jews, Magyars, and Germans.[145] Esther Offer survived Auschwitz and returned to Khust. Soviet soldiers tried to break into the house where she and other Jewish female survivors spent their first night back in the town. They screamed for help, and an officer in a nearby house fired shots in the air that chased the soldiers away. Esther Offer and the other women left the next morning for the Romanian border.[146] Indeed, fear spread among survivors,[147] and the vast majority of Jews left the region either before or shortly after June 1945, when the Soviet Union officially annexed it.[148]

A period had ended: a region meant to form part of an imagined empire—"Greater Hungary"—now, war-torn and ravaged, came under the rule of another, very real, empire. The latter now completed the destruction of the region's native society and culture that the Hungarian authorities had begun and, in effect, incorporated it into the postwar system of nation-states that, as historian Mark Levene has shown, united long-term political visions of *both* Axis and Allied powers, West and East—all the significant differences notwithstanding.[149]

Conclusion: The Fall of "Greater Hungary" in Subcarpathian Rus'

The German invasion of Hungary gave the Hungarian authorities all over the country an opportunity to move rapidly in their quest to remake society in the frame of "Greater Hungary." In Subcarpathian Rus', local and regional officials—those who had served before March 1944, as well as the newcomers to their jobs—eagerly planned, initiated, and implemented anti-Jewish and anti-Roma policies according to the ethnonational design. They operated on familiar grounds. As we saw in Chapter 4, the persecution and deportations of Jews and Roma in order to transform Subcarpathian Rus' into a Magyar-dominated region had begun well before the spring of 1944. Clear continuities thus stretched from 1938 through 1941 and 1942 to 1944, as the Hungarian regional administration carried out violent deportations in line with a political goal that meant the world for the vast majority of Hungarians.

Not by chance, then, ghettoization began in Subcarpathian Rus', and besides the small-scale anti-Jewish operations in the Délvidék in late April and May,[150] it was the only region where ghettoization preceded the state's official decree. As in 1941 and early 1942, initiative and promptness underlay Hungarian anti-Jewish policies in Subcarpathian Rus' and the Délvidék. Wide agreement called for a speedy realization of "Greater Hungary" in the borderlands; without that, Eichmann would never have managed to include the Jews of Hungary—around 300,000 of the approximately 450,000 deported by July 1944 (more than two-thirds) had lived in the borderlands[151]—in the Nazi "final solution."

The history presented in the last two chapters thus challenges the still prevalent tendency to think about the Holocaust in Hungary as an event that stemmed primarily from German goals. Indeed, drilling down on the period of the German occupation in Subcarpathian Rus' in its entirety—both chronologically and thematically—shows the extent to which the destruction of the region's Jewish communities in 1944 figured as a central element in the broader vision of "Greater Hungary." In other words looking beyond June 1944, to consider Hungarian policies and the anti-Roma violence until October 1944, elucidates how the swift ghettoization and mass deportations of Jews from Subcarpathian Rus' was not an isolated event in the region's history, not even in 1944. If we view the history of Jews and the history of the places where they lived as closely intertwined, placing this case of mass violence in its proper historical context helps explain it.

As we have seen, an integrated approach also proves vital if we are to understand the relations between Jews and their Carpatho-Ruthenian neighbors. Tracing the rise of anti-Jewish resentment on political grounds in the 1930s offers a perspective to grasp the bystander behavior that characterized most Carpatho-Ruthenians as they witnessed the cruel termination of Jewish life in Subcarpathian Rus' during World War II. Unlike in the German-occupied Soviet territories, where many people attacked their Jewish neighbors and murdered them, Carpatho-Ruthenians rarely turned against Jews and, in general, preferred not to cooperate with the occupiers of their homeland. Not everyone in eastern Europe hated Jews and took advantage of every opportunity to kill them. The case of Subcarpathian Rus' demonstrates that mass violence requires no necessary assistance of local populations; their *active* acquiescence, even as they, too, face the state's violence, more than suffices. The response of Carpatho-Ruthenians to the suffering of people they knew quite well and, as we saw in Chapter 1, with whom they shared a lot in common, figured painfully in the disintegration of the worlds of tens of thousands of Jews as the places they felt at home, the buildings in which they had worshiped, everything they had labored to create, and all they had cherished now stood in ruin within a matter of days and weeks.

Ultimately, Hungary's leaders and the authorities in Subcarpathian Rus' managed to achieve the most in their striving for a "Greater Hungary" just as the rapid Soviet advance westward put any future for Hungary, let alone a great one, in danger. The Soviet occupation of Subcarpathian

Rus' in October 1944 not only put an end to Hungary's rule there but also brought fear, suffering, and misery for tens of thousands of people who seemed to the Soviet authorities to pose obstacles to Moscow's control. One last round of multilayered mass violence, mostly against Magyars and ethnic Germans, placed the region firmly within the Soviet empire. It would remain the most western outpost of the Soviet world for the next half century, reaching into the Danube Basin across the Carpathians. With the region's multiethnic and multireligious social fabric shattered and its economy and politics oriented to the east, a new era had begun, one in which "Greater Hungary" in Subcarpathian Rus' was a thing of the past.

Conclusions, Comparisons, Implications

THE CONCERTED ASSAULT on Subcarpathian Rus' society to transform it into an integral part of "Greater Hungary" ultimately failed. Yet it destroyed the region's Jews and wreaked havoc on Roma and Carpatho-Ruthenians. The military defeat of Hungary in the Carpathians initiated one last round of mass violence, as Soviet occupation authorities targeted Magyars and local Germans in order to consolidate their hold on the region and incorporate it into Soviet Ukraine. A substantial Magyar population still lives in and around Berehovo today, and one might encounter Hungarian on the streets in Mukachevo and Uzhhorod, but most of the people in the larger towns speak Russian—a legacy of Soviet times—and local dialects of Carpatho-Ruthenian still thread through the mountain villages.

No one hears Yiddish any longer—a silence echoed in the empty and altered spaces that tens of thousands of Jews once considered home. The former central synagogue in Beregszász, for example, functions as a cinema today, and its physical transformation has left no traces of its past as a prayer house. And after Hungarian and German occupiers murdered the living in Munkács, local authorities in postwar Mukachevo removed the dead in the old Jewish cemetery to make room for a garage. It closed down after several years, leaving only a large empty field (fig. 2).[1] This void epitomizes the destruction of Subcarpathian Rus' society as it faced the pressures and mass violence of global warfare, changing borders, and large-scale attempts to alter society according to visions of state and nation building.

FIGURE 2. The empty field in the place of the old Jewish cemetery in Mukachevo, Ukraine, 2012. Source: Author's collection.

This process sowed friction between Jews and Carpatho-Ruthenians for the first time when Prague controlled the region during the 1920s and 1930s. Available sources show no traces of any significant anti-Jewish sentiments among Carpatho-Ruthenians before World War I, and Jews' accounts and testimonies about the interwar period confirm this. The geographic seclusion of the region facilitated both groups' efforts to maintain traditional ways of life, which included a strong element of popular mysticism rooted in the thick forests that cover the Carpathian Mountains; Jews respected gentile sorcerers, Carpatho-Ruthenians believed in the powers of "miracle rabbis," and all accepted that supernatural forces dominate life. Anti-Jewish contempt of a religious nature and Christian theological views about the inferiority of Jews remained weak forces in this atmosphere, all the more so as the presence of Jews in the region in substantial numbers dated to the early nineteenth century, not hundreds of years as in most of Europe. Finally, the small minority of Carpatho-Ruthenian elites, both secular and religious, busied themselves much more with struggles that revolved around ethnic, national, and religious identities than with ideas about Jews; most Carpatho-Ruthenians remained aloof from these debates until well into the 1920s.

Relations between Jews and Carpatho-Ruthenians thus present a case of an eastern European society with no tradition of what we call anti-semitism. Applying this general term to explain the breakdown of that situation fails to provide analytical clarity and actually conceals the particular elements that account for the detrimental change. Constructs that defined Jews and Carpatho-Ruthenians as part of ethnonational collectives rather than in relation to a specific location or religious faith began to spread after World War I and *only then* bred conflict and brought an end to the shared lives of Jews and Carpatho-Ruthenians. But national activists and movements alone provide no explanation without the contexts that made them a dominant factor in intergroup dynamics. Indeed, the stance of the Czechoslovak government with regard to Subcarpathian Rus' determined the collective notions and emotions that characterized the new ways in which growing numbers of Carpatho-Ruthenians began to ponder their place in the world beyond their villages and small towns. That Prague refused to grant autonomy to the region, in contradiction to the Treaty of St. Germain-en-Laye (1919), and that Jews chose to support the new rulers, mostly by sending their children to Czech rather than Carpatho-Ruthenian schools, proved decisive.

Jews thus seemed to serve as agents of "Czechization" and obstructers of Carpatho-Ruthenian collective aspirations. This sense of betrayal and the belief that the behavior of Jews kept Carpatho-Ruthenians in a subordinated sociopolitical status facilitated the rise of anti-Jewish resentments. This political experience of Carpatho-Ruthenians in Czechoslovakia, which drew on common perceptions of deprivation and injustice, coincided with the growing Ukrainophile orientation among Carpatho-Ruthenians. Local Ukrainophile leaders, together with Ukrainian nationalists from Galicia, capitalized on the concentration of the region's Russophile activists in the political sphere and steadily gained influence in culture and education, spreading the Ukrainian language and winning the hearts of Carpatho-Ruthenian students to their cause. While outsiders from Prague created a situation that cast doubt on Jews' loyalties to their Carpatho-Ruthenian neighbors, Ukrainophiles stirred emotions and deepened the new divide between the groups.

The hectic period of autonomous Carpatho-Ukraine, as the region became known between October 1938 and March 1939, intensified the situation and saw the only instance in the history of Subcarpathian Rus' in which Carpatho-Ruthenians engaged in anti-Jewish violence; it remained sporadic, however, despite the prodding of the foreign Ukrainian nationalists who played dominant roles in the attacks. Another external force, the Hungarian army, put an end to this short-lived violence by destroying Carpatho-Ukraine and pursuing Ukrainophile activists and militiamen, in some cases targeting noncombatant Carpatho-Ruthenians and leaving thousands dead within several days.

Some Carpatho-Ruthenians in Carpatho-Ukraine thus acted first as perpetrators only to become victims within several months. Many Jews publicly welcomed Hungarian soldiers, who seemed to save them from peril, even as they witnessed the violence of these troops against their neighbors. As this occurred in a region with no substantial history of long-term interethnic animosities and since no Carpatho-Ruthenian anti-Jewish violence took place under Hungarian and subsequent Soviet occupations, concepts such as *antisemitism* that wrongly put groups on opposite sides of allegedly ongoing conflicts cloud analysis. Rather, the picture of multiple actors and processes—Czechoslovak rule in the region and its violent termination, Hungarian expansionist aims, and the frustrated political hopes of Ukrainophiles—and their convergence in specific contexts emerges as key to understanding the fate of Jews as an integral part of the history of Subcarpathian Rus'. Indeed, zooming in on the multilayered nature of mass violence in Subcarpathian Rus' under Hungarian domination clarifies the reasons for it, the dynamics of it, and how it led to the annihilation of Jewish life in the region.

Explaining Genocide in Subcarpathian Rus'

The small-scale killing operations of the Hungarian occupiers against Carpatho-Ruthenians in March 1939 foretold trying times and the violence to come. Indeed, Carpatho-Ruthenians, not only those suspected as Ukrainian sympathizers, continued to suffer persecution and violence under Hungarian rule. Roma also faced a barrage of humiliating restrictions and violence. The authorities perceived Roma as dirty and criminal, blamed them for spreading disease, and saw them as unreliable, which justified the imposition of curfews, withholding food-ration coupons, and the frequent raids meant to harass, intern, expel, and, in general, turn daily lives into an endless struggle for basic freedom and necessities. The drive of the Hungarian authorities to establish an ethnonational "Greater Hungary" under the cover of world war—a project that enjoyed wide consensus in Hungarian society and politics, from Right to Left—provided the rationale for mass violence against Carpatho-Ruthenians and Roma, but it imagined Jews as the most urgent danger.

The links between the layers of violence against different groups in Subcarpathian Rus' elucidate the persecution and mass deportations of Jews, as they allow us to identify specific meanings of anti-Jewish stances and how they translated into policies and violence that aimed at more than just uprooting Jews. Ideas and anxieties about disloyalty and foreignness played crucial roles in the exclusionary mind-set that rendered most of the region's inhabitants—hundreds of thousands of Jews and non-Jews—unwanted strangers in their homes, as Budapest moved to redefine the notion of home and the legal concept of citizenship in line with ethnonational criteria. Taking the whole historical picture of "Greater Hungary" as a subject of investigation throws the limited analytical potential of the term *antisemitism* into sharp relief. In contrast to its common use as the main or even sole reason to persecute and kill Jews during World War II (and in other periods) and its explicit or implicit association with hatred, here it serves to prompt research questions: what kind of positions and emotions constitute antisemitism in this case? What made them operational at *specific* junctures? And what kind of actions did they prescribe?

The Hungarian leadership in Budapest and the authorities in Subcarpathian Rus' took advantage of national and international opportunities to diminish the strength of minority groups through mass deportations. Nazi Germany's attack on the Soviet Union in the summer of 1941, which the Hungarian army joined, offered just such an occasion. The multilayered mass deportations in summer 1941 forcibly removed twenty thousand Jews from Subcarpathian Rus' to east Galicia, destroying several Jewish communities in Máramaros County completely. This amounted to one-fifth of the region's Jewish population. The Hungarian authorities planned and perpetrated this instance of mass violence without any pressure or involvement from Berlin; indeed, the deportations stopped because they *clashed* with German interests in east Galicia, where German occupiers, busy with mass murder of Jews, would not accept the influx of more Jews into their hands. Furthermore, the papers of the governor of Subcarpathian Rus' at the time, Miklós Kozma, and the documents and correspondence of other Hungarian authorities show clearly that Roma suffered arrest and expulsion as well. Finally, Hungarian designs that sought to target at least *some* Carpatho-Ruthenians in this instance remained unfulfilled owing to the termination of the deportations by the German authorities on the other side of the Carpathians. The number of Carpatho-Ruthenians—the *majority* population in the region—and the clear priorities of the Hungarian authorities with *all* Jews and Roma ensured that, throughout the war, most Carpatho-Ruthenians suffered heavily but managed to survive and remain in the region.

If German action in the summer of 1941 thwarted the full implementation of Hungarian intentions, the German invasion of Hungary in March 1944 allowed Hungarian authorities to resume their efforts. And the latter hurried to finish the task. The swift ghettoization and mass deportations of Jews from Subcarpathian Rus'—where the process began almost two weeks before the government issued the official decree on ghettoization—resulted, above all, from the sense of continuity with anti-Jewish measures and violence before March 1944. The small SS force (eight officers and forty enlisted men) stationed in the Kassa Gendarmerie District,[2] which included Subcarpathian Rus', had almost no impact on the course of the operation. The anti-Roma violence that came on the heels of the anti-Jewish campaign—completely unrelated to German plans—likewise drew on anti-Roma hatred and policies of Hungarian perpetrators in the region since 1938. Hence, instead of thinking about the annihilation of Jews in Subcarpathian Rus' mostly as a product of Nazi ideology and the German invasion of Hungary, we observe the decisive impact of Hungarian ethnonationalism, continuities from 1939 through 1944, and the ways in which the interaction between wartime German and Hungarian interests and designs, not only concerning Jews, at times intensified the process of mass violence against Jews and at other times de-escalated it, albeit with the aim, in any case, of driving all Jews out of the region.

Carpatho-Ruthenians witnessed the victimization of Jews in Subcarpathian Rus' without participating in the violence, either before or after March 1944. There was neither a Jedwabne in Subcarpathian Rus' nor cases of postwar anti-Jewish violence such as in Kielce or in other places in Poland, Romania, and Hungary. The anti-Jewish resentments among Carpatho-Ruthenians, which originated during the time of Czechoslovak rule, ensured that most of them preferred to remain behind closed doors while Hungarian gendarmes brutally deported their Jewish neighbors and left some to die on their doorsteps. The attack of the Hungarian state against Carpatho-Ruthenians no doubt cemented this choice. The changing relations between Jews and Carpatho-Ruthenians thus call for critical engagement with another common concept in the study of the Holocaust (and other mass atrocities): *bystanders*.

A broad time span, before as well as after March 1944, again proves essential, for it allows joint consideration of two instances of bystanding in the region: Jews who saw and heard the violence of Hungarian occupiers against some Carpatho-Ruthenians in mid-March 1939, and Carpatho-Ruthenians who saw and heard the violence against all Jews in spring 1944. Despite clear differences between these events, this frame challenges the general tag "indifference" that much scholarship employs to describe bystanders. Here, by contrast, the specific intergroup dynamics in Subcarpathian Rus' throughout World War II point to the active *yet not violent* behavior of *both* Jews and Carpatho-Ruthenians as they responded to the mass violence around them that shattered their society. The attack of the Hungarian state on the people of Subcarpathian Rus' thus stands as an example of how mass violence obliterates lives *and* social ties that, in this case, encapsulated a way of life of both Jews and non-Jews that today, from the vantage point of our world of nation-states, we find difficult even to imagine.

Rethinking the Holocaust in Hungary

The analysis offered here of mass violence in Subcarpathian Rus' suggests a need to rethink the established narrative about the Holocaust in Hungary. The German invasion of Hungary has so far stood at the center of research about these events, addressing antisemitism, the "collaborating" Hungarian state bureaucracy, and the plans and policies of Nazi Germany.[3] Looking primarily at the post-March 1944 period, limiting the discussion almost completely to the anti-Jewish measures, and employing the paradigm of collaboration has effectively pushed much of the history of Hungary aside. Specifically, the histories of the state's multiethnic and multireligious border areas during the war have received only limited attention, whether in relation to the period before the German invasion or after it. Examining these borderlands facilitates an understanding of the history of Hungary during World War II *as a whole*—without viewing March 1944 as a point of rupture, and involving non-Jews as well as Jews, Hungarian designs and policies in addition to those of Nazi Germany, and local, regional, and national initiatives rather than collaboration.

Scholarship has begun to show how the persecution and destruction of the Jewish communities in the Hungarian borderlands of northern Transylvania and the Délvidék[4] occurred within changing constellations of multilayered mass violence against Romanians, Serbs, and Roma.[5] At the end of the war, moreover, Hungarian officials, some of whom had just taken an active part in the ghettoization and mass deportations of Jews, again took advantage of foreign occupation—this time Soviet—to further Hungarian ethnonationalism: they engaged in the mass deportations of around two hundred thousand ethnic Germans from Hungary.[6] For one last time "Greater Germany" and "Greater Hungary" came into conflict.

Considering the political vision of "Greater Hungary" thus challenges the model of collaboration in the case of the Holocaust in Hungary. The attempt to use the war to enlarge the state's territory and ensure a Magyar majority within it functioned as a central motivation in the destruction of the Jewish communities in Hungary. It entailed much violence, at times murderous, but driving out those perceived as inherently disloyal and foreign to the imagined state, not systemic mass murder, constituted the primary intention. German mass killers wanted to murder the Jews they managed to seize, but in many cases, certainly in Axis states, they could accomplish that *only* when it intersected with national interests. Germans indeed murdered the vast majority of Jews from Hungary who lost their lives during World War II, primarily in Kamenets-Podolsk in the summer of 1941 and in Auschwitz in the spring and summer of 1944. But those sites of mass murder stood at the end of the genocidal process that the Hungarian state initiated and carried out through moments of both friction and cooperation with Berlin, *before* as well as after March 1944.

Applying the term *collaboration*, then, elides the perspective of the history of Hungary and obfuscates the designs and actions of local, regional, and national officials. Rethinking collaboration through the case of Hungary thus helps place the Holocaust more clearly in the context of World War II and in the course of modern European history, in which the project of "Greater Hungary" emerged and assumed violent dimensions.

Holocaust Scholarship: Shifting the Perspective

The historical picture that emerges from this reexamination of the genocide of Jews in Hungary resonates with recent studies on Romania and Croatia during World War II. This new research highlights multilayered mass violence and probes the modern histories of state and nation building to understand the meanings of this violence. It thus shifts the perspective of Holocaust scholarship from questions that center on Nazi Germany and its anti-Jewish genocidal campaign to incorporate local and regional patterns of violence during World War II and their complex roots and dynamics, including the intricate webs of collective and individual motivations they generated that account both for moments that escalated violence and for moments that reduced it in scale and intensity. New work on the history of Bulgaria in the twentieth century has not yet integrated Jews, though it, too, suggests the need to reconsider how we understand the fate of Jews during World War II, certainly in southeast Europe.

Historian Vladimir Solonari has written extensively on the efforts of the regime of Ion Antonescu, Romania's military dictator between September 1940 and August 1944, to build an ethnonational "Greater Romania" under the cover of war, targeting non-Jews as well as Jews and focusing on the state's borderland regions. These processes of mass violence stemmed from Romanian, not German, interests. As in Hungary, antisemitism and the violent removal of approximately two hundred thousand Jews from the border areas of Bukovina and Bessarabia to Romanian-occupied Transnistria—including systematic mass murder of Jews in all those territories from summer 1941 until well into the spring of 1942[7]—constituted a *central* element in a *broader* program of mass violence, which targeted other non-Romanian groups (mostly Roma, Bulgarians, Magyars, and Ukrainians) for exclusion and persecution and included a vision of "returning" supposedly ethnic Romanians "home." Jews figured as the first victims on the list, but Solonari asserts convincingly that we cannot understand their specific victimization properly without scrutinizing the whole historical picture.[8]

The wider history proves particularly significant in light of the deescalation of violence against Jews after October 1942, when Antonescu decided to *refuse* to deport Jews from the Regat (Romania's core provinces of Walachia and Moldavia) and southern Transylvania to German hands for murder in the Belzec death camp as part of the Nazi "final solution." Antonescu remained determined to follow this change of policy until King Michael's coup in August 1944 that, shortly before the Soviet invasion of the country, removed Antonescu from power. Approximately 375,000 Jews would thus survive the war in Romania.[9]

As in the case of Miklós Kállay's government in Hungary, Antonescu's decision stemmed from his assessment, from the summer of 1942 onward, that Germany would lose the war. Yet also as in Hungary, Antonescu sought to realize the vision of "Greater Romania" in other ways, such as the failed plans for large-scale emigration of Jews from Romania to Palestine in 1943.[10] Moreover, Antonescu approved a plan drafted in December of 1942 by the Under-Secretariat for Romanization, Colonization, and Inventory. According to Solonari, it "amounted to nothing less than an elaborate plan for the comprehensive ethnic cleansing of Romania," which would have destroyed the communities of more than one million non-Jews in Bessarabia and Bukovina and all Jews in Moldavia.[11] The course of the war, foreign policy considerations, and bureaucratic rivalries left this plan on paper,[12] though it demonstrates the importance of looking at anti-Jewish designs and violence during World War II within histories of states on the deadly paths of "ethnic homogenization."

The literature on Croatia during World War II has recently begun to view the mass murder of Jews through an integrated analysis as well. Historian Alexander Korb focuses his criticism on the tendency to see the Independent State of Croatia as merely a puppet of Nazi Germany. Rather, Korb turns our attention to perceptions and objectives of the Ustaša leaders and authorities as they sought to realize their utopian image of a "pure" Croat state. Korb argues that antisemitism in wartime Croatia intersected with other motivations in the broader frame of an ethnonational vision that targeted Jews mostly because of their alleged disloyalty and support for the main "enemy" group and the vast majority of the victims: Serbs. By the end of 1941 the state had murdered around twenty-five thousand Jews and almost two hundred thousand Serbs.[13]

German and Croat visions and agendas intersected in the destruction of Jews and Jewish communities in Croatia between 1941 and 1943.[14] But the mass killings of Serbs, which gave impetus to social unrest and armed resistance, interfered with the designs of the German occupiers in the Balkans to control the area and exploit its economic potential with minimal military presence. Consequently, German pressure on Zagreb slowed down the pace of murder from late 1941 onward and even pushed some changes in anti-Serb policies, though another 150,000 Serbs would die at the hands of the state by the end of the war.[15] Also, as in Hungary, German killers paid no attention to the persecution and mass killings of Roma by local Croat gendarmes and Ustaša perpetrators. These actions flowed solely from the vision of the desired Croat nation and state. The close association of Roma with the Balkans and their tendency to move between Serbia and Croatia rendered them both a security threat and a hindrance to the strict ethnonational view imagined in Zagreb and by authorities throughout the country.

A national worldview that rendered whole populations intrinsically treacherous also figured prominently in little-studied Bulgaria. As the state joined Nazi Germany's attack on Yugoslavia and Greece in April 1941, it took hold of the borderlands of western Thrace and eastern Macedonia. From the time that Bulgaria emerged as an autonomous entity in the Ottoman Empire after the Berlin Treaty (1878), its leaders pursued aggressive and violent policies meant to consolidate a territorially expanded ethnonational state.[16] They had all but failed to achieve this goal, despite the sacrifices and enormous violence of the struggle against the Ottoman Empire, Serbia, and especially Greece over Macedonia in the first decade of the twentieth century, the two Balkan Wars in 1912–1913, and World War I.[17] The frustrated collective dream had therefore now finally come true.

The work of historian Theodora Dragostinova on the relations between Bulgaria and its Greek minority brings to light the conflict between Bulgaria and Greece and between Bulgarian and Greek nationalists over Thrace, Macedonia, and especially over the shifting loyalties of their inhabitants.[18] With this history in the background the Bulgarian occupiers during World War II turned to implement their ethnonational design: they deported tens of thousands of Greeks from western Thrace and thousands of Serbs from eastern Macedonia, and they resettled tens of thousands of Bulgarians in their place.[19] The now celebrated pioneer of Genocide studies, Raphael Lemkin, explained that the Bulgarian occupation authorities in western Thrace initiated "measures aimed at changes in the composition of the population," which meant the closing of Greek churches and schools, centrally coordinated mass robbery, and the mass deportations of more than one hundred thousand Greeks from the region, especially following the ruthless suppression of the spontaneous revolt of Greeks against Bulgarian rule in and around the town of Drama in September 1941.[20] Since the Bulgarian authorities foresaw no future for Greeks in the region, Lemkin posited that these persecutions constituted "a *real* genocide policy," affirming his broad understanding of the term as denoting precisely such wholesale social and cultural destruction—not necessarily accompanied by outright mass murder.[21]

The intensity of the anti-Greek persecution and violence left a clear mark. Greeks who survived the oppression of Bulgarian occupation ensured that their children saw "the Bulgarians" as "bloodthirsty people," "barbarians," and "slaughterers," who harbored "hatred from time immemorial" against Greeks.[22] Jews in western Thrace and eastern Macedonia also faced the reality of an occupying power bent on realizing an ethnonational vision, certainly in border areas during a time of global war that heightened concerns over loyalty and security. Jews in these regions had lived as Greek or Yugoslav citizens after World War I, which implied political loyalty. That the authorities falsely identified the Jewish population in Macedonia with communist and partisan activities confirmed them as dangerous.[23]

Yet accounts of the persecution and mass deportations (March 1943) of Jews from these regions (almost twelve thousand people) have largely placed this case of mass violence in the context of German plans and the "final solution."[24] In fact, narratives about the rescue of Jews in Bulgaria within its pre-1941 borders (almost fifty thousand people) still overshadow the annihilation of the Jewish communities in the borderlands and the vested interests of the Bulgarian authorities who initiated, planned, and brutally carried out the arrests, concentration, mass robbery, and deportations.[25]

Unlike in Hungary, the history of Jews in Bulgaria in its pre-1941 borders and their level of social integration undoubtedly played an important role in the combined efforts of Jews and non-Jews—community and political leaders, members of professional associations, and prominent figures in the Bulgarian Orthodox Church—to protect Jews from deportations to German hands in March and again in May 1943.[26] Indeed, de-escalation of anti-Jewish violence in Bulgaria began well after Hungary and Romania, and only after the mass deportations of Jews from the borderlands, which aroused no comparable social outcry and took place despite the very clear signs already in March 1943 of German defeat. The Bulgarian authorities, in any case, remained committed to the ethnonational vision, and they pursued other courses of oppression against the Jews who managed to evade deportations: large-scale expulsions from the capital and other cities to the countryside, recruitment of men to forced labor projects, and mostly a systematic policy aimed to ruin Jews economically.[27] And it worked: the vast majority of Jews in Bulgaria after the war (forty-five thousand of fifty thousand), reduced to poverty and pushed to the margins of society, left, mostly to Palestine/Israel. Antisemitism played a role in this story only in as much as it gained *concrete* meaning from the broader ethnonational drive of the Bulgarian state, which, following the violent dismemberment of Yugoslavia in April 1941, doomed the Jews in western Thrace and eastern Macedonia.

We thus see clearly that what we call the Holocaust in southeast Europe actually unfolded as several cases of mass violence that assumed murderous proportions through diverse processes tied to national and often-times local contexts, especially in multiethnic and multireligious borderlands. The emerging historiography on states in southeast Europe during World War II points to the ways in which territorial ambitions, ethnonational visions, views about the purported loyalties of Jews and non-Jews in border zones, and the persecution and mass murder of several groups, affected the content of anti-Jewish positions and emotions and the course of anti-Jewish policies and violence. As we have seen, all these elements also figured in the history of Subcarpathian Rus'.

These Holocausts (plural), then, remind us that the histories of Jews in Europe intermingled inseparably with the histories of Europe. This point deserves emphasis, as precisely the Holocaust has made it difficult for scholars to see Jews as part and parcel of the societies in which they once lived.[28] The tendency to think about the history of Jews as a closed universe has framed two central concerns in the emergence of Holocaust studies as an independent field: insistence on the singular nature of the Holocaust in history and on antisemitism as a unique impetus for persecution and genocide. These elements constitute an emotional and ideological agenda that in effect places the Holocaust apart from history and thus sits uneasily with the new direction in Holocaust scholarship I have outlined above.[29] Indeed, the few intersections of Holocaust history with work on genocide and mass violence during World War II have caused much controversy. More broadly, the potential meeting points between the study of the Holocaust and scholarship on genocide have yet to overcome these emotional and ideological hurdles.[30]

A significant turn in the study of genocide has put aside the endless debates about the definition of the concept of *genocide* and broadened the agenda to include analyses of mass atrocities, whether or not they assumed genocidal proportions—whatever threshold is used. Adam Jones's recent collection of essays, *The Scourge of Genocide*, which includes chapters on subjects such as torture and structural violence, typifies this new approach.[31] Donald Bloxham and Dirk Moses, the editors of the authoritative *Oxford Handbook of Genocide Studies*, have endorsed this position explicitly: "This collection is committed to probing the limits and utility of the concept of genocide for historical understanding, and placing the crime back in its context(s) that may often include mass non-genocidal violence. We do this because the focus on upper case *Genocide* often entails a focus on outcomes rather than causes and processes that may or may not produce the mass killing which many think is the substance of genocide."[32] This passage highlights a fundamental point: the study of mass atrocities requires rigorous historicization and sensitivity to *unfolding* events. As with *genocide*, we may reconsider the usefulness of the term *Holocaust* in order to delve into the contexts of the events and processes subsumed by the word. As we have seen, multilayered mass violence—some, but not all, involving mass killing—characterized Hungary during World War II and practically all of eastern and southeast Europe. Grounding the Holocaust in the different regional and local modern histories—which require much further research—reveals underlining factors and linkages that drove mass violence and that have already begun to change the ways in which we think about the genocides during World War II that together we call the Holocaust.[33]

Genocide in the Carpathians has taken such a path, pointing to a future of Holocaust scholarship beyond the limits of Holocaust studies by reference to the histories of Czechoslovakia and mostly Hungary. Viewed through the prism of Holocaust studies, pieces of general—that is, not Jewish—histories serve as background in order for us to learn more about the Holocaust. This work looks in the opposite direction and turns to the Holocaust because study of it offers invaluable insights about key topics such as state formation, citizenship, relations between groups in multiethnic societies, and the choices people make in the midst of warfare and mass violence. It is precisely because of the view of the Holocaust as a focal point in human affairs, and particularly in the modern world, that it deserves attention that could transcend the ideological and emotional constraints of Holocaust studies. This study, I hope, moves us a little bit in this direction.

Reference Matter

Notes

Introduction

1. These terms and their mis/ab/uses have drawn many comments, much criticism, and often whole essays. The composite "east-central Europe" seems rather awkward; an effort to avoid the politicized Eastern Europe of communist times by a geographic reconciliation that would content all sides. The resulting geography, however, remains fluid and unclear (which states or regions are included and why—and who decides?) and invites questions about the absence of a "west-central Europe." "Central Europe," when applied to eastern Europe, raises even more geographical question marks with related political and ideological dimensions. My choice of "eastern Europe" here relies on the longer perspective of the construction of the West-East divide in modern European history, beginning with the Enlightenment and thus predating the geopolitical considerations of the second half of the twentieth century. See Larry Wolff, *Inventing Eastern Europe: The Map of Civilization on the Mind of the Enlightenment* (Stanford: Stanford University Press, 1994). Indeed, the state authorities that ruled the region during the first half of the twentieth century imagined it in the frame of this West-East divide, which translated into specific policies.

2. A major exception is the recent two-volume study of Mark Levene, *The Crisis of Genocide* (Oxford: Oxford University Press, 2013), vol. 1, *Devastation: The European Rimlands, 1912–1938*, and vol. 2, *Annihilation: The European Rimlands, 1938–1953*. See also Omer Bartov and Eric D. Weitz, eds., *Shatterzone of Empires: Coexistence and Violence in the German, Habsburg, Russian, and Ottoman Borderlands* (Bloomington: Indiana University Press, 2013).

Piotr Wandycz's important study, *The Price of Freedom*, demonstrates the contrast between the potential inherent in studying Subcarpathian Rus' and its neglect. In his introduction Wandycz used the example of Uzhhorod, the provincial center, to describe the effects of frequent border changes, but the region all but evaporates from the rest of the text. Piotr S. Wandycz, *The Price of Freedom: A History of East Central Europe from the Middle Ages to the Present* (London: Routledge, 2001), 8.

3. Tara Zahra, *Kidnapped Souls: National Indifference and the Battle for Children in the*

Bohemian Lands, 1900–1948 (Ithaca, NY: Cornell University Press, 2008), 8, refers to the illuminating case study of the post–World War II Julian March on the border between Italy and Yugoslavia by Pamela Ballinger, *History and Exile: Memory and Identity at the Borders of the Balkans* (Princeton, NJ: Princeton University Press, 2003), esp. 261–265.

4. For a critical view on this issue see Holly Case, *Between States: The Transylvanian Question and the European Idea During World War II* (Stanford: Stanford University Press, 2009). In a penetrating study of Last Judgment iconography throughout the Carpathian Mountains between the fifteenth and eighteenth centuries, historian John-Paul Himka addressed this methodological issue, admitting his "habit of working for years within the normal paradigms of my discipline, the national paradigm." This initial position led him to think he "would be able to trace the evolution of Ukrainian Last Judgment iconography," indeed, "that there was one single [Ukrainian] iconographic tradition, of which the Carpathian icons were just surviving examples." The evidence, however, uncovered "a local, sometimes even microregional, tradition," unrelated to the medieval traditions of Kyiv. As his research unfolded, he thus understood that "shedding assumptions . . . was about as important as discovering the facts" and that this procedure of writing history points to "possibilities that have not been fully realized by the historical profession." John-Paul Himka, *Last Judgment Iconography in the Carpathians* (Toronto: University of Toronto Press, 2009), 3–4, 6, 10, 94, 140–142, 194–200.

5. Celia Applegate, "A Europe of Regions: Reflections on the Historiography of Subnational Places in Modern Times," *American Historical Review* 104, no. 4 (1999): 1182.

6. Charles King, "The Micropolitics of Social Violence," in *Extreme Politics: Nationalism, Violence, and the End of Eastern Europe* (New York: Oxford University Press, 2010), 55–76, esp. 69–76.

7. Case, *Between States*. Two recent studies that provide challenging accounts of nation and state building from the local and regional perspectives are Uğur Ümit Üngör, *The Making of Modern Turkey: Nation and State in Eastern Anatolia, 1913–1950* (Oxford: Oxford University Press, 2011), which focuses on the Diyarbekir Province; and Ward Berenschot, *Riot Politics: Hindu-Muslim Violence and the Indian State* (New York: Columbia University Press, 2011), which deals with Ahmedabad, the largest city in the Indian state of Gujarat.

8. For an analysis that concentrates on "Greater Hungary" as a eugenic vision, see Marius Turda, "In Pursuit of Greater Hungary: Eugenic Ideas of Social and Biological Improvement, 1940–1941," *Journal of Modern History* 85, no. 3 (2013): 558–591.

9. Subcarpathian Rus' and northeastern Hungary together made up the Felvidék, the area that Hungary had occupied in November 1938 and March 1939 during the violent disintegration of Czechoslovakia by Nazi Germany. Hungary took northern Transylvania from Romania in August 1940, according to the Second Vienna Accord, and the Hungarian army entered the Délvidék—mostly the Bácska and Baranya regions in northern Yugoslavia—as it joined Nazi Germany's attack and dismemberment of Yugoslavia in April 1941.

10. For discussions of colonialism and genocide see A. Dirk Moses, ed., *Empire, Colony, Genocide: Conquest, Occupation, and Subaltern Resistance in World History* (Oxford: Berghahn, 2008). On Hungarian policies in the Hungarian-Slovak border territory of the Felvidék see Leslie M. Waters, "Learning and Unlearning Nationality: Hungarian National

Education in Reannexed Felvidék, 1938–1944," *Hungarian Historical Review* 2, no. 3 (2013): 538–568. On the Hungarian settler colonial project of transferring in 1941, following an agreement with the Romanian government, more than three thousand families (altogether around fourteen thousand people) of the Bukovina Székely—essentially an entire group of Magyars beyond the borders of Hungary—to Bácska, see Enikő A. Sajti, *Hungarians in the Voivodina, 1918–1947* (New York: Columbia University Press, 2003), 250–272.

11. This study focuses on relations between Jews and Carpatho-Ruthenians, as both groups lived throughout the region and many towns and villages were home only to Jews and Carpatho-Ruthenians. Magyars (ethnic Hungarians) lived almost exclusively in the areas in the southwest of the region, at the foot of the Carpathians, primarily in the larger towns (see map 2). Even there, however, they lost their numerical dominance in the 1920s and 1930s, owing in large part to emigration following the defeat of Hungary in World War I. In Mukačevo (present-day Mukachevo in Ukraine), for example, Magyars numbered a bit more than 12,500 in 1910 among some 7,500 Jews and less than 1,500 Carpatho-Ruthenians, but only 5,500 in 1930 alongside more than 11,300 Jews and almost 6,500 Carpatho-Ruthenians, the increase of the latter two groups a result mainly of high birthrates and movement from villages and smaller towns to larger towns in the region. See data in Paul Robert Magocsi, *The Shaping of a National Identity: Subcarpathian Rus', 1848–1948* (Cambridge, MA: Harvard University Press, 1978), 356.

12. This work follows Paul Robert Magocsi, the foremost specialist on the history of the region and its Carpatho-Ruthenian population, in the choice of the name Subcarpathian Rus'. See Magocsi, *Shaping of a National Identity*, 277–281. Names of places throughout this study correspond to the forms in use in the different periods of the region's history. When a location in Subcarpathian Rus' is mentioned for the first time, its present-day form in Ukrainian is provided in parentheses. Other spellings of place names remain as they appear in quotes and titles. See also Paul Robert Magocsi, "Mapping Stateless Peoples: The East Slavs of the Carpathians," *Canadian Slavonic Papers* 39, no. 3–4 (1997): 301–331.

13. Magocsi, *Shaping of a National Identity*, 105–129.

14. For an account centered on the Greek Catholic perspective see Athanasius B. Pekar, *The History of the Church in Carpathian Rus'* (New York: Columbia University Press, 1992).

15. *Kárpátalja Településeinek Vallási Adatai (1880–1941)* (Budapest: Központi Statisztikai Hivatal, 2000), 16–17.

16. Eduard Winter, ed., *Die Deutschen in der Slowakei und in Karpathorussland* (Munster: Aschendorffsche Verlagsbuchhandlung, 1926). Large numbers of Germans had settled in the region before the Ottoman occupation of Hungary (1526), but they fled the wars and tribulations of the sixteenth and seventeenth centuries. In the aftermath of World War I many Germans left the region for Germany and Austria.

17. Claude Cahn, *The Misery of Law: The Rights of Roma in the Transcarpathian Region of Ukraine*, European Roma Rights Center, Country Reports Series, no. 4 (1997), 8. On the Carpathian groups of Roma, which include those in Subcarpathian Rus', see Lev Tcherenkov and Stéphane Laederich, *The Proma*, vol. 1, *History, Language, and Groups* (Basel: Schwabe, 2004), xxviii, 4–5, 7, 95–99, 429, 442–445, 447, 448–450, 503, and 507–508. I use the word *gypsy* only when quoting sources of the Hungarian state that include

the word *cigány*, when quoting from other studies, or when the word appears in titles of books and articles.

18. According to Paul Robert Magocsi's assessment in 2011, a study of Subcarpathian Rus' "based on a multiethnic approach" had yet to appear. See his "Concluding Observations on the Symposium," *Nationalities Papers* 39, no. 1 (2011): 132.

19. For a penetrating historiographical analysis arguing that a central trend among historians of Jews accounts for a wall between their field and the study of the Holocaust, see David Engel, *Historians of the Jews and the Holocaust* (Stanford: Stanford University Press, 2010). See also Dan Michman, "The Integration of the Holocaust into Modern Jewish History: The Attempts of Leading Historians," in *The Holocaust in Jewish History: Historiography, Consciousness, and Interpretation* (Hebrew), ed. Dan Michman (Jerusalem: Yad Vashem, 2005), 45–67.

20. Studies of ancient Jewish societies have demonstrated the analytical advantages of "integrat[ing] the Jews into the history of the ancient eastern Mediterranean, allowing us to see how they were simultaneously like and unlike all other subjects. The Jews may thus be made to serve in some ways as exemplary—even in their difference—filling in part of a larger picture of the effects of Roman domination. . . . In other words, considering the wider political and social worlds in which ancient Jews lived can help explain why the evidence is the way it is . . . why the archaeology of Jewish Palestine in the second and third centuries seems so similar to that of the eastern Roman Empire in general." Seth Schwartz, *Imperialism and Jewish Society, 200 B.C.E. to 640 C.E.* (Princeton, NJ: Princeton University Press, 2001), 291–292. This methodological observation holds true for the modern era as well.

21. For a paradigmatic account in this vein see Donald Bloxham, *The Final Solution: A Genocide* (New York: Oxford University Press, 2009). And see the rather heated debate around the book, with critical reflections by Jürgen Matthäus, Martin Shaw, Omer Bartov, Doris Bergen, and Donald Bloxham's response, in "Review Forum," *Journal of Genocide Research* 13, no. 1–2 (2011): 107–152. Debórah Dwork and Robert Jan van Pelt, *Holocaust: A History* (New York: Norton, 2002), serves as an earlier landmark in situating the Holocaust within modern European history.

22. See A. Dirk Moses, "Conceptual Blockages and Definitional Dilemmas in the 'Racial Century': Genocides of Indigenous People and the Holocaust," *Patterns of Prejudice* 36, no. 4 (2002): 7–36; Robert M. Hayden, "Schindler's Fate: Genocide, Ethnic Cleansing, and Population Transfers," *Slavic Review* 55, no. 4 (1996): 727–748; Mark Mazower, "Violence and the State in the Twentieth Century," *American Historical Review* 107, no. 4 (2002): 1158–1178.

23. Christopher R. Browning, *Collected Memories: Holocaust History and Postwar Testimony* (Madison: University of Wisconsin Press, 2003), 37–85, presents a strong argument supporting the utilization of survivors' accounts in research on Holocaust history. See also Christopher R. Browning, *Remembering Survival: Inside a Nazi Slave-Labor Camp* (New York: Norton, 2010). Debórah Dwork, however, pioneered the recording, collection, and use of oral histories of Holocaust survivors with her groundbreaking book *Children with a Star: Jewish Youth in Nazi Europe* (New Haven, CT: Yale University Press, 1991). The literary scholar Lawrence Langer contributed greatly to this discussion with his *Holocaust*

Testimonies: The Ruins of Memory (New Haven, CT: Yale University Press, 1991). The work of anthropologist Victoria Sanford on testimonies of Maya survivors of the genocide in Guatemala in the early 1980s is exemplary in uncovering the overlapping qualities of testimonies as memory constructs, essential elements in historical reconstruction and understanding, and subaltern subjectivities. Testimonies thus undermine hegemonic narratives and open for survivors political spaces in the face of oppressive discourses of distortions and silences that in some places, as in Guatemala, rely on threats of renewed violence. See Victoria Sanford, "What Is an Anthropology of Genocide? Reflections on Field Research with Maya Survivors in Guatemala," in *Genocide: Truth, Memory, and Representation*, ed. Alexander Laban Hinton and Kevin Lewis O'Neil (Durham, NC: Duke University Press, 2009), 29–53 ("subaltern subjectivity" on p. 29, and "raw memories" on p. 34); and Victoria Sanford, *Buried Secrets: Truth and Human Rights in Guatemala* (New York: Palgrave Macmillan, 2003).

24. See, in particular, Omer Bartov, "Wartime Lies and Other Testimonies: Jewish-Christian Relations in Buczacz, 1939–1944," *East European Politics and Societies* 25, no. 3 (2011): 486–511; and Yehuda Bauer, *The Death of the Shtetl* (New Haven, CT: Yale University Press, 2009). On survivors' accounts of the Rwanda genocide, also concerning social relations before and during the genocide, see Samuel Totten and Rafiki Ubaldo, eds., *We Cannot Forget: Interviews with Survivors of the 1994 Genocide in Rwanda* (New Brunswick, NJ: Rutgers University Press, 2011).

25. See the following testimonies at the USC Shoah Foundation Institute for Visual History and Education: El'sbeta Gabor, interview no. 37402; Kalman Sabo, 36366; Danil Gerich, 36870; and Kalman Kish, 37384—all from Beregszász (today's Berehovo); Iurii Fenesh, 50135; Germina Beniak, 50134; Bozhena Buchko, 46674; and Iolana Tokar, 43593—all from Ungvár (Uzhhorod); and Iosif Teifel, 38740—from Munkács (Mukachevo).

26. The bibliography lists the collections of survivors' testimonies used in this study.

27. David Engel, "Away from a Definition of Antisemitism: An Essay in the Semantics of Historical Description," in *Rethinking European Jewish History*, ed. Jeremy Cohen and Moshe Rosman (Oxford: Littman Library of Jewish Civilization, 2009), 30–53.

28. David Nirenberg, *Communities of Violence: Persecution of Minorities in the Middle Ages* (Princeton, NJ: Princeton University Press, 1996), 4–5.

29. Saul Friedländer, *Nazi Germany and the Jews, 1939–1945: The Years of Extermination* (New York: HarperCollins, 2007).

30. Ibid., xvi–xvii.

31. Ibid., xvii.

32. See Saul Friedländer, *Nazi Germany and the Jews*, vol. 1, *The Years of Persecution, 1933–1939* (New York: Harper Perennial, 1998), chap. 3. For a thorough critical engagement with Friedländer's concept see A. Dirk Moses, "Redemptive Antisemitism and the Imperialist Imaginary," in *Years of Persecution, Years of Extermination: Saul Friedländer and the Future of Holocaust Studies*, ed. Christian Wiese and Paul Betts (London: Continuum, 2010), 233–254.

33. For a recent historiographical review of these debates see Dan Stone, *Histories of the Holocaust* (New York: Oxford University Press, 2010), 68–72, 222–242. See also the excellent analysis in Thomas Kühne, "Colonialism and the Holocaust: Continuities, Causations,

and Complexities," *Journal of Genocide Research* 15, no. 3 (2013): 339–362; and the essays in "Scholarly Forum on the Holocaust and Genocide," *Dapim: Studies on the Holocaust* 27, no. 1 (2013): 40–73.

34. Götz Aly, *"Final Solution": Nazi Population Policy and the Murder of European Jews* (London: Arnold, 1999); Karel C. Berkhoff, *Harvest of Despair: Life and Death in Ukraine Under Nazi Rule* (Cambridge, MA: Belknap, 2008); David Furber and Wendy Lower, "Colonialism and Genocide in Nazi-Occupied Poland and Ukraine," in *Empire, Colony, Genocide: Conquest, Occupation, and Subaltern Resistance in World History*, ed. A. Dirk Moses (Oxford: Berghahn, 2008), 372–401; Wendy Lower, *Nazi Empire-Building and the Holocaust in Ukraine* (Chapel Hill: University of North Carolina Press, 2005); Christian Gerlach, *Kalkulierte Morde: Die deutsche Wirtschafts- und Vernichtungspolitik in Weissrussland 1941 bis 1944* (Hamburg: Hamburger Edition, 1999); Christoph Dieckmann, *Deutsche Besatzungspolitik in Litauen, 1941–1944* (Göttingen: Wallstein, 2011).

35. Friedländer, *The Years of Extermination*, and, in a very different manner, Mark Mazower, *Hitler's Empire: Nazi Rule in Occupied Europe* (London: Allen Lane, 2008) both address almost exclusively the German-occupied territories in eastern Europe. Stone, *Histories of the Holocaust*, the latest large-scale survey of scholarship on the Holocaust, takes a German-centered perspective, also when discussing very briefly Hungary, Romania, and other Balkan states.

36. Timothy Snyder, *The Bloodlands: Europe Between Hitler and Stalin* (New York: Basic Books, 2010).

37. On Romania see Vladimir Solonari, *Purifying the Nation: Population Exchange and Ethnic Cleansing in Nazi-Allied Romania* (Washington, DC: Woodrow Wilson Center Press; Baltimore: Johns Hopkins University Press, 2010). On the Ustaša regime and the Independent State of Croatia see Alexander Korb, *Im Schatten des Weltkrieges: Massengewalt der Ustaša gegen Serben, Juden und Roma in Kroatien, 1941–1945* (Hamburg: Hamburger Edition, 2013). On the Balkans in general see Mark Biondich, *The Balkans: Revolution, War, and Political Violence since 1878* (New York: Oxford University Press, 2011). Mark Mazower's earlier work on Greece pioneered this direction. See his *Inside Hitler's Greece: The Experience of Occupation, 1941–1944* (New Haven, CT: Yale University Press, 1993). See also Mazower's locally focused but much more historically wide-ranging *Salonica, City of Ghosts: Christians, Muslims and Jews, 1430–1950* (New York: Vintage, 2006).

38. See Victoria J. Barnett, *Bystanders: Conscience and Complicity During the Holocaust* (Westport, CT: Greenwood Press, 1999), who drew on Gordon J. Horwitz, *In the Shadow of Death: Living Outside the Gates of Mauthausen* (New York: Free Press, 1990).

39. Political scientist Raul Hilberg coined this rigid typology, which retains its force. See his *Perpetrators, Victims, Bystanders: The Jewish Catastrophe, 1933–1945* (New York: HarperCollins, 1992). This tripartite division constitutes an example of the problems associated with decontextualized attempts to sort human behavior into neat types.

40. Ervin Staub, *The Roots of Evil: The Origins of Genocide and Other Group Violence* (New York: Cambridge University Press, 1989). See also Ervin Staub, "Transforming the Bystanders: Altruism, Caring, and Social Responsibility," in *Genocide Watch*, ed. Helen Fein (New Haven, CT: Yale University Press, 1992), 162–181.

41. Tim Cole, "Writing 'Bystanders' into Holocaust History in More Active Ways: 'Non-Jewish' Engagement with Ghettoization, Hungary 1944," *Holocaust Studies: A Journal of Culture and History* 11, no. 1 (2005): 55–74; and Ernesto Verdeja, "Moral Bystanders and Mass Violence," in *New Directions in Genocide Research*, ed. Adam Jones (London: Routledge, 2012), 153–168.

42. Jan T. Gross, *Neighbors: The Destruction of the Jewish Community in Jedwabne, Poland* (Princeton, NJ: Princeton University Press, 2001). And see Wendy Lower, "Pogroms, Mob Violence and Genocide in Western Ukraine, Summer 1941: Varied Histories, Explanations and Comparisons," *Journal of Genocide Research* 13, no. 3 (2011): 217–246. Lower discusses, among other issues, the far fewer instances of anti-Jewish communal violence in German-occupied central and eastern Ukrainian areas as compared to western parts. Diana Dumitru and Carter Johnson, "Constructing Interethnic Conflict and Cooperation: Why Some People Harmed Jews and Others Helped Them During the Holocaust in Romania," *World Politics* 63, no. 1 (2011): 1–42, confirmed this pattern when they found *no attacks at all* by Ukrainians against Jews in Romanian-controlled Transnistria, in contrast to their occurrence to the west in Bessarabia, mostly in summer 1941.

43. Joanna Bourke, *Fear: A Cultural History* (London: Virago, 2005), 289. See also Cheshire Calhoun and Robert C. Solomon, introduction to *What Is an Emotion? Classic Readings in Philosophical Psychology* (New York: Oxford University Press, 1984), 31–32.

44. Roger D. Petersen, *Understanding Ethnic Violence: Fear, Hatred, and Resentment in Twentieth-Century Eastern Europe* (Cambridge, UK: Cambridge University Press, 2002), 254.

45. Daniel Bar-Tal, Eran Halperin, and Joseph de Rivera, "Collective Emotions in Conflict Situations: Societal Implications," *Journal of Social Issues* 63, no. 2 (2007): 441–442. Similarly, "the role of emotion in international politics is relatively unexplored terrain." Khaled Fattah and K. M. Fierke, "A Clash of Emotions: The Politics of Humiliation and Political Violence in the Middle East," *European Journal of International Relations* 15, no. 1 (2009): 67–93, 69.

46. Colin Wayne Leach and Larissa Z. Tiedens, "Introduction: A World of Emotion," in *The Social Life of Emotions*, ed. Larissa Z. Tiedens and Colin Wayne Leach (Cambridge, UK: Cambridge University Press, 2004), 7.

47. Alon Confino, "Why Did the Nazis Burn the Hebrew Bible? Nazi Germany, Representations of the Past, and the Holocaust," *Journal of Modern History* 84, no. 2 (2012): 388.

48. Rosenwein called to "recognize various emotional styles, emotional communities, emotional outlets, and emotional restraints in *every* period," and "consider how and why these have changed over time." Barbara H. Rosenwein, "Worrying About Emotions in History," *American Historical Review* 107, no. 3 (2002): 821–845, 845 (emphasis in the text).

49. Petersen, *Understanding Ethnic Violence*.

50. I borrow "affective disposition" from Ronald Grigor Suny, "Thinking About Feelings: Affective Dispositions and Emotional Ties in Imperial Russia and the Ottoman Empire," in *Interpreting Emotions in Russia and Eastern Europe*, ed. Mark D. Steinberg and Valeria Sobol (DeKalb: Northern Illinois University Press, 2011), 102–127.

51. This formulation draws on Sara Ahmed, *The Cultural Politics of Emotions* (New York: Routledge, 2004). See also research on "intergroup emotions theory" in social psy-

chology, examining dynamic interactions between groups and the emotions involved in them. Diane M. Mackie and Eliot R. Smith, eds., *From Prejudice to Intergroup Emotions: Differentiated Reactions to Social Groups* (New York: Psychology Press, 2003), esp. chap. 7: Thierry Devos, Lisa A. Silver, Diane M. Mackie, and Eliot R. Smith, "Experiencing Intergroup Emotions," 111–130. In the conclusion to the volume the editors stress "the new research questions that arise once one conceptualizes prejudice in terms of discrete emotions rather than in terms of simple negative evaluations" (290).

52. The field of Ukrainian studies has dealt sparingly with Subcarpathian Rus', providing only scattered remarks and information in large-scale narratives of Ukrainian history. See Andrew Wilson, *The Ukrainians: Unexpected Nation* (New Haven, CT: Yale University Press, 2002); Serhy Yekelchyk, *Ukraine: Birth of a Modern Nation* (Oxford: Oxford University Press, 2007); Orest Subtelny, *Ukraine: A History* (Toronto: University of Toronto Press, 2000). Anna Reid's journalistic account, *Borderland: A Journey Through the History of Ukraine* (Boulder, CO: Westview Press, 1999), does not include a chapter on Subcarpathian Rus'. Indeed, it is dismissed as "somewhere in the middle of nowhere" (110–111). See also Anne Applebaum, "Across the Carpathians," in *Between East and West: Across the Borderlands of Europe* (New York: Pantheon, 1994), 232–245; Applebaum quotes Andy Warhol (born Andrew Warhola to parents who had immigrated to the United States from the Carpatho-Ruthenian village of Miková in northeastern Slovakia), who described the region as "nowhere" (241).

53. See, e.g., Mary Heimann, *Czechoslovakia: The State That Failed* (New Haven, CT: Yale University Press, 2007); and Mark Cornwall and R. J. W. Evans, eds., *Czechoslovakia in a Nationalist and Fascist Europe, 1918–1948* (New York: Oxford University Press, 2007).

54. See mainly Yeshayahu A. Jelinek, *The Carpathian Diaspora: The Jews of Subcarpathian Rus' and Mukachevo, 1848–1948* (New York: Columbia University Press, 2007); Ilana Rosen, *"In Auschwitz We Blew the Shofar": Carpatho-Russian Jews Remember the Holocaust* (Hebrew) (Jerusalem: Yad Vashem and the Avraham Harman Institute of Contemporary Jewry at the Hebrew University, 2004); and Dov Dinur, *The Holocaust of Subcarpathian Rus' Jews: Uzhorod* (Hebrew) (Jerusalem: Hebrew University, 1983).

55. Randolph L. Braham, *The Politics of Genocide: The Holocaust in Hungary*, 2 vols. (New York: Columbia University Press, 1994).

56. See Christian Gerlach and Götz Aly, *Das letzte Kapitel: Realpolitik, Ideologie und der Mord an den ungarischen Juden 1944/45* (Stuttgart: Deutsche Verlags-Anstalt, 2002). Gábor Kádár and Zoltán Vági, *Self-Financing Genocide: The Gold Train, the Becher Case and the Wealth of Hungarian Jews* (Budapest: Central European University Press, 2004), also stress the role of the Hungarian state, highlighting continuities before and after March 1944, but with very little reference to Subcarpathian Rus'.

57. See Howard Lupovitch, *Jews at the Crossroads: Tradition and Accommodation During the Golden Age of the Hungarian Nobility, 1729–1878* (New York: Central European University Press, 2007), 15–18. As Lupovitch has noted, this trend reflects the general stance of many Jews in Budapest toward Jews elsewhere in Hungary, especially in the northeastern parts of the country, including Subcarpathian Rus'. Such attitudes account for the sparse references to Subcarpathian Rus' Jews in the literature on Jews in Hungary, as, for instance,

in the 730-page book of Raphael Patai, *The Jews of Hungary: History, Culture, Psychology* (Detroit: Wayne State University Press, 1996).

While the last three years have seen the publication of several general surveys in Hungarian about Subcarpathian Rus', they address mainly the post-1945 period and fit into recent academic, public, and political discourses about Magyars who today live in lands formerly ruled by Hungary. See, e.g., Béla Baranyi, ed., *Kárpátalja* (Budapest: Dialóg Campus Kiadó, 2009); Fedinec Csilla and Vehes Mikola, eds., *Kárpátalja, 1919–2009: Történelem, Politika, Kultúra* (Budapest: MTA Etnikai-nemzeti Kisebbségkutató Intézete, 2010).

58. Tim Cole, *Traces of the Holocaust: Journeying In and Out of the Ghettos* (London: Continuum, 2011). For statistics and discussion on the number of victims of the Holocaust in Hungary see Braham, *The Politics of Genocide*, 2:1296–1300.

59. Paul A. Hanebrink, *In Defense of Christian Hungary: Religion, Nationalism, and Antisemitism, 1890–1944* (Ithaca, NY: Cornell University Press, 2006).

60. An important exception is Kinga Frojimovics, *I Have Been a Stranger in a Strange Land: The Hungarian State and Jewish Refugees in Hungary, 1933–1945* (Jerusalem: Yad Vashem, 2007). László Karsai, a central figure in the study of the Holocaust in Hungary, has recently argued that Hungary served as a safe haven for Jews before March 1944 owing to a "protective policy *vis-à-vis* the Jews [in which] humanitarian considerations played a role." See László Karsai, "The Jewish Policy of the Szálasi Regime," *Yad Vashem Studies* 40 (2012): 119–156, 121. Historians Zoltán Vági, László Csősz, and Gábor Kádár formulate the matter in a different way: "During the war, Hungarian Jews lived under continually deteriorating conditions. Tens of thousands perished in the Labor Service; others lost their jobs and social prestige. They were largely excluded from the universities and often humiliated by the public administration. Despite all of this, before the German occupation, one could see Jews in Hungary living a normal life compared to those in many other parts of Hitler's Europe." An example concerning Jews in Budapest follows this description, which omits the mass violence perpetrated by the Hungarian state in the borderlands before March 1944, even though the authors discuss these events in the book. See Zoltán Vági, László Csősz, and Gábor Kádár, *The Holocaust in Hungary: Evolution of a Genocide* (Lanham, MD: AltaMira Press, in association with the United States Holocaust Memorial Museum, 2013), xlvii (quote), 61.

61. The scholarship concerning the mass deportations of 1941 is limited and references many of the same sources. See Randolph L. Braham, "The Kamenets Podolsk and Délvidék Massacres: Prelude to the Holocaust in Hungary," *Yad Vashem Studies* 9 (1973): 133–156; Judit Fejes, "On the History of the Mass Deportations from Carpatho-Ruthenia in 1941," in *The Holocaust in Hungary: Fifty Years Later*, ed. Randolph L. Braham and Attila Pók (New York: Columbia University Press, 1997), 305–328; Frojimovics, *I Have Been a Stranger in a Strange Land*, 104–134. These accounts in English rely to a large extent on earlier work in Hungarian: Artur Geyer, "Az első magyarországi deportálás," *Új Élet Naptár, 1960–1961* (Budapest: MIOK, 1960), 75–82; Tamás Majsai, "A kőrösmezei zsidódeportálás 1941–ben," *A Ráday Gyűjtemény Évkönyve* IV–V (1984–1985), 59–86. See also Maria Ormos, *Egy magyar médiavezér: Kozma Miklós*, 2 vols. (Budapest: PolgART, 2000), which offers a biography of Miklós Kozma, the appointed governor (Kormányzói Biztos) of Kárpátalja (Subcarpathian Rus') from September 1940 until his death in December 1941.

62. See Holly Case, "The Holocaust and the Transylvanian Question in the Twentieth Century," in *The Holocaust in Hungary: Sixty Years Later*, ed. Randolph L. Braham and Chamberlain S. Brewster (New York: Columbia University Press, 2006), 17–40; Krisztián Ungváry, "Deportation, Population Exchange, and Certain Aspects of the Holocaust," in *The Holocaust in Hungary: A European Perspective*, ed. Judit Molnár (Budapest: Balassi Kiadó, 2005), 97–98. See also Krisztián Ungváry, "Vojvodina Under Hungarian Rule," in *Serbia and the Serbs in World War II*, ed. Sabrina P. Ramet and Ola Listhaug (Houndmills, Basingstoke: Palgrave Macmillan, 2011), 70–91.

Chapter 1

1. László Erno, "Hungarian Jewry: Settlement and Demography, 1735–38 to 1910," in *Hungarian-Jewish Studies*, vol. 1, ed. Randolph L. Braham (New York: World Federation of Hungarian Jews, 1966), 92–94, 99–101.

2. Yehuda Don and George Magos, "The Demographic Development of Hungarian Jewry," *Jewish Social Studies* 45, no. 3–4 (1983): 200n4; Erno, "Hungarian Jewry," 95–96, 101–102; Yeshayahu A. Jelinek, *The Carpathian Diaspora: The Jews of Subcarpathian Rus' and Mukachevo, 1848–1948* (New York: Columbia University Press, 2007), 13.

3. *The Scroll of the Beit Midrash* (Hebrew) (Munkács, 1904), 2. This unpublished document, composed by communal leaders, recounts the history of the Jewish community in Munkács until 1903. I thank Tuvia Klein for providing me a copy of the original.

4. Ibid., 3–5.

5. In 1910 Munkács Jews numbered 7,675, constituting almost 45 percent of the town's residents. *Kárpátalja Településeinek Vallási Adatai (1880–1941)* (Budapest: Központi Statisztikai Hivatal, 2000), 32–33. The basis of categorization is religion.

6. See the data, based on Hungarian statistics, concerning the increase in the number of Jews in the towns of Máramaros County between 1830 and 1880, in S. Y. Gross and Y. Joseph Hacohen, eds., *Maramorosh Book: One Hundred and Sixty Holy Communities in Their Life and Destruction* (Hebrew) (Tel Aviv: Maramorosh House, 1983), 267–455. In the small town of Ökörmező (Mizhhirya), for example, a community of 120 Jews in 1830, constituting about 10 percent of the population, more than doubled by 1880, when it numbered 269 (449).

7. Until 1918, 70–90 percent of the Carpatho-Ruthenian population in the region could not read or write in their own language. Paul Robert Magocsi, *The Shaping of a National Identity: Subcarpathian Rus', 1848–1948* (Cambridge, MA: Harvard University Press, 1978), 169, 15–16.

8. *Hungarian Ruthenia* (London: H. M. Stationary Office, 1920), 21. This small booklet, an original copy of which is located in the National Széchényi Library in Budapest, is based on official Hungarian publications such as the 8th volume (1914) of *Magyar Bánya-Kalaz*, the Hungarian Mines Handbook.

9. C. A. Macartney, "Ruthenia," in *Hungary and Her Successors: The Treaty of Trianon and Its Consequences, 1919–1937* (London: Oxford University Press, 1937), 201–202. See also Victor Karady, "Religious Divisions, Socio-Economic Stratification and the Modernization of Hungarian Jewry After the Emancipation," in *Jews in the Hungarian Economy, 1760–1945*, ed. Michael K. Silber (Jerusalem: Magnes Press of the Hebrew University, 1992), 167.

10. On the numerous *yeshivot* throughout the region, even in very small towns such as Ökörmező and Rahó (Rakhiv), see Avraham Fuchs's encyclopedic *The Yeshivot of Hungary in Their Glory and Destruction*, 2 vols. (Hebrew) (Jerusalem: published by the author, 1979, 1987).

11. One commentator, who generally expressed sympathy to the Hungarian state, wrote that "Ruthenia was really treated by the Magyars as a great deer-forest." Quoted in Macartney, "Ruthenia," 202.

12. On attempts at "magyarization" through the introduction of Hungarian into the liturgy of the Greek Catholic Church in the region, see Athanasius B. Pekar, *The History of the Church in Carpathian Rus'* (New York: Columbia University Press, 1992), 91–93.

13. Magocsi, *Shaping of a National Identity*, 63–75. See also Andrew C. Janos, *The Politics of Backwardness in Hungary, 1825–1945* (Princeton, NJ: Princeton University Press, 1982), 127: "In general, between 1869–1910, the rate of assimilation [to Hungarian culture] was highest among Germans whose proportion among the general population was down 21.6 percent. They were immediately followed by Slovaks (-21.0 percent). The Rumanians and the Serbs lagged behind with respective proportionate losses of 8.6 and 6.6 percent, while the proportions of [Caraptho-]Ruthenes remained stationary" (127n116). The data are based on Hungarian state sources and refer to the decrease in the number of people considered German, Slovak, Rumanian, and Serb as a result of assimilation. See also Robert Nemes, "Obstacles to Nationalization on the Hungarian-Romanian Language Frontier," *Austrian History Yearbook* 43 (2012): 28–44.

14. See Karady, "Religious Divisions," 170, 177; and Jelinek, *The Carpathian Diaspora*, 96, 102–103.

15. Magocsi, *Shaping of a National Identity*, 66–68, 73; Pekar, *The History of the Church in Carpathian Rus'*, 104–107. That Orthodoxy could claim no more than several hundred adherents among Carpatho-Ruthenians in the years just before World War I (Magocsi, *Shaping of a National Identity*, 179) did not assuage the Hungarian authorities.

16. These Hungarian apprehensions originated in 1849, when Russian army units arrived in the Carpathian region to help quash the Hungarian uprising against Vienna. See Magocsi, *Shaping of a National Identity*, 43–45.

17. Howard N. Lupovitch, *Jews at the Crossroads: Tradition and Accommodation During the Golden Age of the Hungarian Nobility, 1729–1878* (New York: Central European University Press, 2007), has dealt with the Jewish community in Miskolc but has commented more generally (15–18) on the antagonism of those who struggled to create and then document the "Golden Age" of Hungarian Jews—centered in Budapest—toward the Jews in the northeastern parts of Hungary who had arrived from Polish lands.

18. Quoted in Shimon Reinharz, "State of the Culture," in *Encyclopedia of the Jewish Diaspora*, vol. 7, *Karpatorus*, ed. Yehuda Erez (Hebrew) (Jerusalem: Encyclopedia of the Jewish Diaspora, 1959), 269–271.

19. The postcard, dated 7 July 1909, is in Yitzhak Livnat's private collection of Hungarian postcards, Israel.

20. Yekutiel Yehuda Greenwald, *Thousand Years of Jewish Life in Hungary* (Yiddish) (New York: Farish Press, 1945), 236.

21. Hugo Stransky, "The Religious Life in Slovakia and Subcarpathian Ruthenia," in *The Jews of Czechoslovakia: Historical Studies and Surveys*, vol. 2 (Philadelphia: Jewish Publication Society of America, 1971), 358–359; Yehuda Spiegel, "Ungvar," in *Jewish Towns: An Inventory of Jewish Communities Destroyed by the Despots and the Impure in the Last World War*, part 4, ed. Y. L. Hacohen Maimon (Hebrew) (Jerusalem: Mossad Harav Kook, 1949), 14–15.

22. On the bitter feuds that divided the Jews of Hungary during the nineteenth century, see Michael K. Silber, "The Emergence of Ultra-Orthodoxy: The Invention of a Tradition," in *The Uses of Tradition: Jewish Continuity in the Modern Era*, ed. Jack Wertheimer (New York: Jewish Theological Seminary of America, 1992), 23–84. The state approved the legal separation between different kinds of Jewish communities—Orthodox, Neolog, and Status Quo—in 1871, following the 1868–1869 Congress of Hungarian Jews. See also Michael K. Silber, "The Limits of Rapprochement: The Anatomy of an Anti-Hasidic Controversy in Hungary," *Studia Judaica* 3 (1994): 124–147.

Drawing on a new religious ideology (placing custom, *minhag*, and Jewish religious law, *halakhah*, on the same level) and struggling to control Jewish communities, the extreme ultra-Orthodox saw reformers of all kinds in effect as non-Jews, thereby opening the door to controversies in the Jewish world—centered on the question "who is a Jew?"—that erupt periodically until the present. Such positions led these extremists to vicious confrontations with Orthodox leaders, whom they viewed as too soft vis-à-vis the Reform movement. See also Jacob Katz, *A House Divided: Orthodoxy and Schism in Nineteenth-Century Central European Jewry* (Hanover, NH: Brandeis University Press, 1998).

23. See the important contribution by Rogers Brubaker and Frederick Cooper, "Beyond 'Identity'," *Theory and Society* 29, no. 1 (2000): 1–47. For local studies see Jeremy King, *Budweisers into Czechs and Germans: A Local History of Bohemian Politics* (Princeton, NJ: Princeton University Press, 2002); and Rogers Brubaker, Margit Feischmidt, Jon Fox, and Liana Grancea, *Nationalist Politics and Everyday Ethnicity in a Transylvanian Town* (Princeton, NJ: Princeton University Press, 2006). For scholarship dealing with national indifference in multiethnic, multilingual, and multireligious regions, see Pieter M. Judson, *Guardians of the Nation: Activists on the Language Frontiers of Imperial Austria* (Cambridge, MA: Harvard University Press, 2006); Tara Zahra, *Kidnapped Souls: National Indifference and the Battle for Children in the Bohemian Lands, 1900–1948* (Ithaca, NY: Cornell University Press, 2008); James E. Bjork, *Neither German nor Pole: Catholicism and National Indifference in a Central European Borderland* (Ann Arbor: University of Michigan Press, 2008); and Theodora Dragostinova, *Between Two Motherlands: Nationality and Emigration Among the Greeks of Bulgaria, 1900–1949* (Ithaca, NY: Cornell University Press, 2011). See also the special section on national indifference in *Austrian History Yearbook* 43 (2012), ed. Pieter M. Judson and Tara Zahra.

24. Dimitry Shumsky, *Between Prague and Jerusalem: The Idea of a Binational State in Palestine* (Hebrew) (Jerusalem: Zalman Shazar Center and Leo Baeck Institute, 2010), offers an exceptional contribution that situates Jews as part and parcel of a society characterized by national indifference. See also Tatjana Lichtenstein, "Racializing Jewishness: Zionist Responses to National Indifference in Interwar Czechoslovakia," *Austrian History Yearbook* 43 (2012): 75–97.

25. Israel Bartal and Scott Ury, "Between Jews and Their Neighbors: Isolation, Confrontation, and Influence in Eastern Europe," in *Polin: Studies in Polish Jewry*, vol. 24, *Jews and Their Neighbors in Eastern Europe since 1750*, ed. Israel Bartal, Antony Polonsky, and Scott Ury (Oxford: Littman Library of Jewish Civilization, 2012), 3–30, 4.

26. For an elaborate critique along these lines, centered on interethnic relations in the Austro-Hungarian sphere, see Shumsky, *Between Prague and Jerusalem*, esp. 11–12, 196–206, and 321–323.

27. According to Yehuda Erez, who worked in the region as a Zionist emissary from Palestine in the interwar period, "Apart from the rabbi, the area abounds with miracle-working rabbis who spread their dominion over people near and far and aspire to expand and enlarge it." See Yehuda Erez, "Through the Eyes of an Emissary from Palestine," in *Encyclopedia of the Jewish Diaspora*, vol. 7, *Karpatorus*, 233.

28. Ilana Rosen, "Saintly and Sympathetic Magic in the Lore of the Jews of Carpatho-Russia Between the Two World Wars," in *Demons, Spirits, Witches: Christian Demonology and Popular Mythology*, ed. Gábor Klaniczay and Éva Pócs (New York: CEU Press, 2006), 183–193.

29. Quoted in Raphael Mahler, "Hasidism and the Jewish Enlightenment," in *Essential Papers on Hasidism: Origins to Present*, ed. Gershon David Hundert (New York: New York University Press, 1991), 414.

30. According to a Joint Distribution Committee (JDC) worker in 1936, "For tuberculosis it is customary [among Jews] to drink horse urine. . . . Dr. Sternbach recounted many more of these beliefs." See an unsigned JDC memorandum from Mukačevo (the Czech name of Munkács), 3 August 1936, p. 1, JDC Archives, New York, file #186. In 1903, eight Jewish doctors and one Jewish pharmacist worked in the town. See *The Scroll of the Beit Midrash*, 5. On the JDC see note 53 of this chapter.

Folk customs, in general, animated daily life in Subcarpathian Rus'. A Polish Jew who had traveled in the region at the end of the nineteenth century, for example, described in his memoir how he quarreled with a local Jew because of the latter's belief in the power of coins that he had received from "tzadikim"—that is, "miracle rabbis." See Abraham Feuer, *The Memory of Abraham* (Hebrew) (New York: Accommodating Press, Printing and Publishers, 1924), 57–58.

31. See Pëtr Bogatyrëv, *Vampires in the Carpathians: Magical Acts, Rites, and Beliefs in Subcarpathian Rus'*, trans. Stephen Reynolds and Patricia A. Krafcik (New York: Columbia University Press, 1998), ix–xviii for a short biography of Bogatyrëv by Svetlana P. Sorokina.

32. Ibid., 76–77. Bogatyrëv did not mention the name of the village. It is likely that "diphtheria vaccination" refers to some sort of medical treatment, not only vaccination.

33. Ibid., 127–144, 146, quote on 127.

34. Ibid., 135–137.

35. Eugen Schoenfeld, *My Reconstructed Life* (Kennesaw, GA: Kennesaw State University Press, 2005), 10–11.

36. Many failed to find permanent employment. Dubbed *Luftmenschen*, literally people of air, they and their families subsisted on begging and odd jobs. See Jelinek, *The Carpathian Diaspora*, 27. Some Jews, mostly in the areas close to the Romanian border,

eked out a living by smuggling goods across the border. Jews continued such pursuits after World War I as well. See, e.g., testimony of Ya'akov Avraham Leibovich from Selo Slatina (the Czech name of Aknaszlatina), Yad Vashem Archives (YVA), O.3/12572, 3 (recorded in 2005); testimony of Aharon Rat from Velký Bočkov (Velyky Bychkiv), USC Shoah Foundation Institute for Visual History and Education, interview number 32662 (recorded in 1997), in which he related the illegal trade conducted by his family in contraband foodstuff from Sighet (the Romanian name for Máramarossziget), on the other side of the Iza River, in Romania.

37. In 1921 the proportion of agricultural workers among Jews in the region—26.9 percent—was the highest in Europe and perhaps in the whole world. See the report by the then well-known Jewish sociologist Salomon Goldelman, "Die Sozialökonomische Verfassung der Juden von Podkarpatska Rus," YIVO Archives, New York, RG 245.10, MKM 15.135 (n.d., probably from the late 1920s); "The Jews of Czechoslovakia," in *The Jewish Communities of Nazi-Occupied Europe*, prepared by the Research Institute on Peace and Post-War Problems (1944; New York: American Jewish Committee, 1982), 6; Arthur Ruppin, *The Sociology of the Jews*, vol. 1 (Hebrew) (Tel Aviv: Shtiebel Publications, 1935), 116, 121–123, 166–167.

38. *Pressburger Zeitung* 78 (1841), 416, as translated to English in Michael K. Silber, "A Jewish Minority in a Backward Economy: An Introduction," in Silber, *Jews in the Hungarian Economy*, 12.

39. This literary genre comprises answers of rabbis to questions addressed to them.

40. See, e.g., Shimon Reinharz, "Rabbi Moshe Schick," in *Encyclopedia of the Jewish Diaspora*, vol. 7, *Karpatorus*, 412, concerning *responsa* of Rabbi Moshe Schick (1807–1879) of Huszt.

41. In 1921, 88.9 percent of the population in Subcarpathian Rus' lived in villages and small towns with fewer than ten thousand inhabitants. Joseph Rothschild, *East Central Europe Between the Two World Wars* (Seattle: University of Washington Press, 1974), 92. In 1930 that figure stood at 83.5 percent and for Jews at 64.5 percent. See *Kárpátalja Települészeinek Vallási Adatai (1880–1941)*, 19.

42. Testimony of Samuel Muller, USC Shoah Foundation, 23869.

43. Naftali Deutsch, *A Holocaust Survivor: In the Footsteps of His Past: A Fascinating Chronicle of a Jewish Boy's Miraculous Survival from Five Concentration Camps* (Hebrew) (Jerusalem: Yad Vashem, 2010), 24–25.

44. See, e.g., testimony of Katherine Bodek, USC Shoah Foundation, 13482 (Poroskő/Poroshkovo); testimony of Gloria Lyon, USC Shoah Foundation, 25639 (Nagybereg/Beregi); testimony of Clara Ilales, YVA, O.3/12365, 3 (Bilke/Bilki).

45. In 1930, 11,313 Jews lived in Mukačevo (44 percent of the population), 7,357 in Užhorod (28 percent), 5,680 in Berehovo (Berehovo) (30 percent), and 3,619 in Sevluš (Vynohradovo) (38 percent). See *Kárpátalja Települészeinek Vallási Adatai (1880–1941)*, 38–39, 89, 102, and 120. See also Ezra Mendelsohn, *The Jews of East Central Europe Between the World Wars* (Bloomington: Indiana University Press, 1983), 143.

46. Testimony of Abraham Klein, USC Shoah Foundation, 24703.

47. YVA, O.3/11957, 4 (recorded in 2001). See also testimony of Tova Weinstock, ibid.,

O.3/11473, 4. For Mukačevo see also, e.g., testimony of Dvorah Lavi, ibid., O.3/6436, 2; testimony of Esther Konsans, ibid., O.3/5145, 2; and testimony of Edita Moskowitz, ibid., O.3/10064, 3.

48. In 1921, 40 percent of the region's Jews were under the age of fifteen, perhaps the highest figure of its kind in Europe at the time. See Ruppin, *Sociology of the Jews*, 1:43–52. This data finds corroboration in most of the testimonies of Holocaust survivors from the region, who grew up in large families. Benjamin Kaufman from Drahovo (Drahovo), for instance, whose family consisted of parents and eight children (even though his mother gave birth twelve times!), spoke of "families [in my town] with two to fifteen children." YVA, O.3/12500, 4. On especially high birthrates among Carpatho-Ruthenians—forty-six per thousand in 1920—see *Hungarian Ruthenia*, 2–3, 4–5.

49. Magocsi, *Shaping of a National Identity*, 66, 77; Macartney, "Ruthenia," 202.

50. Jelinek, *The Carpathian Diaspora*, 34. For example, Rose Pinkasovic Zelkovitz (born Ruchel Lea Pinkasovic in 1923) recounted that her father, Solomon Pinkasovic, left for the United States in 1899, followed by all four of his brothers. When he returned in 1907, he had saved enough money to build "a beautiful house" in Alsókálocsa (Kolochava), as well as open a grocery store and become a local grain dealer. A distant cousin of hers, Gershon Pinkasovic, had also worked in the United States, where he lived from 1910 to 1926. See Rose Pinkasovic Zelkovitz, *From the Carpathian Mountains to the New Jersey Seashore: A Holocaust Survivor's Memoir*, ed. Maryann McLoughlin (Galloway, NJ: Holocaust Resource Center, Richard Stockton College of New Jersey, 2004), 3–4. On a Jewish family that had also returned from the United States to the region in the interwar period, see the 1999 memoir of Regina Godinger Hoffman, "A Void in My Heart," ed. Stanley M. Hoffman, Archives of the United States Holocaust Memorial Museum, 1999.A.0099, 1.

51. Translated and quoted in Livia Rothkirchen, "Deep-Rooted yet Alien: Some Aspects of the History of the Jews in Subcarpathian Ruthenia," *Yad Vashem Studies* 12 (1977): 162–163.

52. Graydon A. Tunstall, *Blood on the Snow: The Carpathian Winter War of 1915* (Lawrence: University Press of Kansas, 2011), 7, 12. See also Paul Robert Magocsi, *Historical Atlas of Central Europe* (Seattle: University of Washington Press, 2002), 121–123, and map 37 on page 122.

53. See Yehuda Bauer, *My Brother's Keeper: A History of the American Jewish Joint Distribution Committee, 1929–1939* (Philadelphia: Jewish Publication Society of America, 1978), 6–18, on the circumstances that brought the JDC into being and a brief overview of its activities during World War I and the immediate postwar period.

54. Consul General of the United States in Budapest (signature illegible) to Albert Lucas, Secretary of the JDC, 16 Sept. 1916, JDC Archives, file #111.

55. Shmuel Hacohen Weingarten, ed., *Memorial Book for the Jewish Community of Nagyszőllős and Its Surroundings* (Hebrew) (private publication, 1976), 69–70. See Spiegel, "Ungvar," 39–41, on Jews who fled from Ungvár when Russian units infiltrated beyond the Uzhok pass toward the town. In Majdánke (Maydan) thirty Jewish families fled the village during the war. See Zvi Kaspi, *Maydan* (Yiddish) (Tel Aviv: private publication, n.d.), 14. See also Aryeh Sole, *Light in the Mountains: Hebrew-Zionist Education in Carpatho-Russia*

from 1920 to 1944 (Hebrew) (Tel Aviv: World Association of Subcarpathian Jews and Hebrew Schools, 1986), 20.

56. Macartney, "Ruthenia," 218; Zdenek L. Suda, *Zealots and Rebels: A History of the Communist Party of Czechoslovakia* (Stanford, CA: Hoover Institution Press, 1980), 29–30. For the fighting in the region after October 1918 see Magocsi, *Historical Atlas of Central Europe*, 127, and map 38 on page 126 therein.

57. Magocsi, *Shaping of a National Identity*, 91, 93; Lajos Horváth, *Hucul Köztársaság, nyugat-ukránok és ideiglenes román megszállás, 1918–1921* (Nyírtelek: Gidófalvy Péter, 2007).

58. On reports of anti-Jewish violence by Czech soldiers see Spiegel, "Ungvar," 42. Martin Wein, "Czech Nation-Building, Czechoslovakia, and the Jews, 1897–1948," manuscript, 139, also lists violence of Czech soldiers against Jews, including several cases of murder, in Beregújfalu (Novoye Selo) in Bereg County (May 1919), Velk? Vít'az in eastern Slovakia (June 1919), and Michalovce, also in eastern Slovakia (August 1919). (My thanks to Martin Wein for allowing me to read his manuscript.) Sole, *Light in the Mountains*, 20–21, and Jelinek, *The Carpathian Diaspora*, 118, mention anti-Jewish violence and killings of Jews by Ukrainian rioters, who probably belonged to units of the Western Ukrainian Republic. Magocsi, *Shaping of a National Identity*, 73–74, cites accounts of violence perpetrated by Hungarian soldiers against Carpatho-Ruthenian farmers because of their real or imagined support of Russia. Finally, some soldiers of the Russian army, who had temporarily penetrated the battle lines, attacked Jews. See the accounts of Morris Cohen, collected by workers of the JDC in Ťačová (Tyachiv) (9 August 1922); Mendel Katzwer, Leibe Roth, and Rose Weiss (Nižní Verecki [Nyzhni Vorota], 18 August 1922), in JDC Archives, file #196. See also, in general, Jelinek, *The Carpathian Diaspora*, 117–119, 128.

59. Eleanor Perényi, *More Was Lost* (New York: Helen Mark Books, 2001), 14. This memoir, written by the wife of Baron Perényi's son, Sziga, was originally published in 1946. Baron Perényi went on to organize the first counterrevolutionary coup against the Kun regime, which failed completely. Rothschild, *East Central Europe Between the Two World Wars*, 151.

60. See, e.g., the accounts of Herman Rosenfield and Martin Klein, collected by workers of the JDC in Chust (the Czech name of Huszt) (8 August 1922); and Isidore Gross (Berehovo, 10 August 1922), in JDC Archives, file #196. See also Jelinek, *The Carpathian Diaspora*, 136.

61. Magocsi, *The Making of a National Identity*, 77–102. This and the following paragraphs draw mostly on Magocsi's work.

62. On the formation and function of the national councils see also Paul Robert Magocsi, "The Ruthenian Decision to Unite with Czechoslovakia," *Slavic Review* 34, no. 2 (1975): 360–381.

63. Macartney, "Ruthenia," 216, 249; Oscar [Oszkár] Jászi, "The Problem of Sub-Carpathian Ruthenia," in *Czechoslovakia: Twenty Years of Independence*, ed. Robert J. Kerner (Berkeley: University of California Press, 1940), 204; Magocsi, *Shaping of a National Identity*, 96–97, 101, 220–221.

64. Magocsi, *Shaping of a National Identity*, 100.

65. See "Synopsis, Report by Dr. Leon Wechsler [director of the Vienna office of the JDC] on Czecho-Slovakia," April-May 1920, JDC Archives, file #126.

66. "Report on Conditions in Czecho-Slovakia," following the trip of Dr. Julius Goldman [director of the JDC in Europe] and Leon Wechsler, 31 April 1920, 12, JDC Archives, file #126.

67. D. M. Olkon, JDC representative in Mukačevo, to Dr. Julius Goldman, 20 August 1920, JDC Archives, file #127.

68. Magocsi, *Shaping of a National Identity*, 191–194.

Chapter 2

1. The heated exchange around Mary Heimann's *Czechoslovakia: The State That Failed* (New Haven, CT: Yale University Press, 2009) offers a window on the major issues that frame the debate about interwar Czechoslovakia in the past twenty years. See also Tara Zahra, *Kidnapped Souls: National Indifference and the Battle for Children in the Bohemian Lands, 1900–1948* (Ithaca, NY: Cornell University Press, 2008).

2. Andrea Orzoff, *Battle for the Castle: The Myth of Czechoslovakia in Europe, 1914–1948* (New York: Oxford University Press, 2009).

3. Such intersections question Eurocentric abstract notions of progress, according to which capitalism, nationalism, and secularism appear inevitably in every society. My analysis in this chapter highlights the encounter with modern trends of a *specific* society in a *particular* time and situation, whereby the deep-seated traditions that shaped life in Subcarpathian Rus' became an *integral* part of modernity in the region. Thus, perceptions of time, place, and human relations changed as "modern" and "nonmodern" currents intermeshed. On these theoretical concerns see Dipesh Chakrabarty, *Provincializing Europe: Postcolonial Thought and Historical Difference* (Princeton, NJ: Princeton University Press, 2000).

4. Paul Robert Magocsi, *The Shaping of a National Identity: Subcarpathian Rus', 1848–1948* (Cambridge, MA: Harvard University Press, 1978), 199–204, 211–213. As a rule, whenever the Czechoslovak state encountered a conflict between the vested interests of the Czech nation (defined in ethnic terms) and the pressures of other groups, its leaders protected the former at the expense of the latter, thereby striking a blow against the ideals of democracy that stood at the heart of the Czech national narrative. This process, which had begun immediately with the establishment of the state, also held true for tensions within the Czech group, first and foremost concerning the rights of women. See Melissa Feinberg, *Elusive Equality: Gender, Citizenship, and the Limits of Democracy in Czechoslovakia, 1918–1950* (Pittsburgh: University of Pittsburgh Press, 2006).

5. C. A. Macartney, "Ruthenia," in *Hungary and Her Successors: The Treaty of Trianon and Its Consequences, 1919–1937* (London: Oxford University Press, 1937), 225.

6. Heimann, *Czechoslovakia*, 69.

7. Elaine Rusinko, *Straddling Borders: Literature and Identity in Subcarpathian Rus'* (Toronto: University of Toronto Press, 2003), 16, and, in detail, chap. 5, 296–406.

8. Paul Robert Magocsi, *Shaping of a National Identity*, 207–209; Hans Ballreich, *Karpatenrussland: Ein Kapital tschechischen Nationalitätenrechts und tschechischer Nationalitätenpolitik* (Heidelberg: Carl Winter, 1938), 63–69. Highlighting the power of the vice-governor in contrast to the largely symbolic post of governor, one commentator noted

that the "Governor . . . is housed, appropriately enough, in the local museum." Quoted in Macartney, "Ruthenia," 224.

9. See, e.g., Yitzhak Gershuni, ed., *Tapuach: A Collection of Names and Details on the History of the Jewish Community of Tetsh* (Hebrew) (private publication, 1994), 373. Tetsh is the Yiddish name of Ťačová (Tyachiv).

10. Moshe Moskovitz, *Jews of a Different Sort: From a Small Village in Carpatho-Russia Through a Road of Hurdles to Israel* (Hebrew) (private publication, 1997), 20.

11. Alex Gross, *Yankele: A Holocaust Survivor's Bittersweet Memoir* (Lanham, MD: University Press of America, 2001), 4. Palanok is part of today's Mukachevo.

12. See, e.g., Peretz Litman, *The Boy from Munkacs: A Story of a Survivor* (Hebrew) (private publication, 1996), 28; testimony of Irene Buchman from Bilky (Belki), USC Shoah Foundation Institute for Visual History and Education, interview number 3316. In 1932, less than 11 percent of the localities in the region enjoyed electricity. Zora P. Pryor, "Czechoslovak Economic Development in the Interwar Period," in *A History of the Czechoslovak Republic, 1918–1948*, ed. Victor S. Mamatey and Radomír Luža (Princeton, NJ: Princeton University Press, 1973), 212.

13. As historian Carlile A. Macartney has commented, "the 'public works' undertaken by the Republic in Ruthenia consist largely of offices into which the Ruthenes penetrate no farther than the waiting-rooms, or motor roads along which only Czech cars circulate." Macartney, "Ruthenia," 226.

14. Pryor, "Czechoslovak Economic Development," 213.

15. Aryeh Sole, "Subcarpathian Ruthenia: 1918–1938," in *The Jews of Czechoslovakia: Historical Studies and Surveys*, vol. 1 (Philadelphia: Jewish Publication Society of America, 1968), 128.

16. Yekutiel Yehuda Greenwald, *Thousand Years of Jewish Life in Hungary* (Yiddish) (New York: Farish Press, 1945), 245–246; Gershuni, *Tapuach*, 370, 372, 374, and 381–382.

17. Joseph Eden (Einczig), *The Jews of Kaszony, Subcarpathia* (New York: published by the author, 1988), 1. The title uses a short form of the town's Hungarian name, Mezőkászony. See also Joseph Eden's testimony in USC Shoah Foundation, 2880.

18. See comments of the proprietor Isak Feiler and the merchant Hermann (last name illegible) in "minutes of meeting of the preliminary conference held on August 10, 1922, with the local committee [of the JDC]," Nižní Verecki (Nyhzni Vorota), JDC Archives, New York, file #196. See also Yeshayahu A. Jelinek, *The Carpathian Diaspora: The Jews of Subcarpathian Rus' and Mukachevo, 1848–1948* (New York: Columbia University Press, 2007), 133.

19. On agricultural protection in Czechoslovakia from 1925 onward see Pryor, "Czechoslovak Economic Development," 204, 208.

20. Macartney, "Ruthenia," 235, 237.

21. Infant mortality rates are a sensitive health indicator for the general population. See, e.g., testimonies of Zipora Pardes, Yad Vashem Archives (YVA), O.3/10026, 2 (Mukačevo); Alter Gadish, ibid., O.3/5475, 4 (Mukačevo); Adela Kreuzer, USC Shoah Foundation, 19245 (Ganiče [Hanychi]); Sam Moskovitz, ibid., 18040 (Dubové [Dubove]).

22. An earlier attempt by the JDC to establish a Jewish hospital in Mukačevo in the immediate postwar period failed because the Czech authorities confiscated the site of

the planned hospital—the Kohner Castle, formerly owned by a wealthy Jewish family—and disagreements between the JDC and the Jewish community's *chevra kadisha*. See Aryeh Sole, "Between the Two World Wars," in *Encyclopedia of the Jewish Diaspora*, vol. 7, *Karpatorus*, ed. Yehuda Erez (Hebrew) (Jerusalem: Encyclopedia of the Jewish Diaspora, 1959), 148. A dispute between the *chevra kadisha* and Dr. Bohuslav Albert, the Red Cross representative in Subcarpathian Rus' and the director of the town's general hospital, hindered the plan in 1924. See the lengthy correspondence between May 1923 and March 1924 of Harry Gell, JDC's reconstruction representative in Czechoslovakia; Dr. Linhardt and his successor, Dr. Haering, who managed the Smichov warehouse of the Red Cross in Prague; Dr. Golub, the director of the JDC's medico-sanitary department in Warsaw (whence medical supplies were sent to Prague); Dr. Ze'ev Sternbach, a Zionist activist in Mukačevo who served as a medical adviser for the JDC; Dr. Bernhard Kahn, the director of the JDC in Europe; and Dr. Alice Masaryk, President of the Czechoslovak Red Cross, in the Central Archives for the History of the Jewish People (CAHJP), Jerusalem, Hungary Files, Inv. 145, #48 (Medical Supplies).

23. Macartney, "Ruthenia," 235. More broadly, on the collapse of international trade in Czechoslovakia in the early 1930s see Victor S. Mamatey, "The Development of Czechoslovak Democracy, 1920–1938," in *A History of the Czechoslovak Republic, 1918–1945*, ed. Victor S. Mamatey and Radomír Luža (Princeton, NJ: Princeton University Press, 1973), 142–143.

24. USC Shoah Foundation, 26142 (recorded in 1997).

25. Macartney, "Ruthenia," 236.

26. Daniel A. Miller, "Colonizing the Hungarian and German Border Areas During the Czechoslovak Land Reform, 1918–1938," *Austrian History Yearbook* 34 (2003): 303–317. Land reform also offered opportunities to settle Czech and Slovak re-emigrants and provide them with economic resources.

27. Magocsi, *Shaping of a National Identity*, 213.

28. Dr. Julius Goldman, director of the JDC in Europe, to Felix M. Warburg, head of the JDC, 19 July 1920, JDC Archives, file #126. On the initial stages of the JDC's work in the region see also Herman Dicker, *Piety and Perseverance: Jews from the Carpathian Mountains* (New York: Sepher-Hermon Press, 1981), 33–39.

29. "Synopsis, Report by Dr. Leon Wechsler on Czecho-Slovakia," April-May 1920, JDC Archives, file #126.

30. "Report on Conditions in Czecho-Slovakia," following the trip of Dr. Julius Goldman and Leon Wechsler, 31 April 1920, 14–16, 24–25, JDC Archives, file #126.

31. "First Report of the Czecho-Slovakian Branch of the Joint Distribution Committee of the American Funds for Jewish War Sufferers for the Months of July and August 1920," by Leon Wechsler, 8 Oct. 1920, 19, JDC Archives, file #127. A report on relief work of the JDC in Czechoslovakia during 1919 concluded that the Prague committee of the JDC "seems to have acted upon the Talmudic principle that one's own poor come first." JDC Archives, file #126. Considering the derogatory perceptions of east European Jews in the eyes of Prague's Jewish leaders, this should come as no surprise. See Martin Wein, "Czech Nation-Building, Czechoslovakia, and the Jews, 1897–1948," manuscript, 117–118, 237–240. I thank Martin Wein for allowing me to read his manuscript.

32. Moshe Ussoskin, "Jewish Cooperatives in Czechoslovakia: A Chapter of the Jewish History in Czechoslovakia Between the Two World Wars" (1970), 7, in YVA, M.72, JM/19.640, reel 22, folder 540, frames 865–897, here 872. In addition to regular loans of up to five thousand Czechoslovak koruna (around $150 in the 1920s and $240 after 1934) with 8 percent interest over an eighteen-month period, the JDC also distributed "blanco credit"—sums that the organization's leaders treated, in effect, as subventions rather than loans. See report by Bernhard Kahn, 3 August 1936, 13, in YVA, M.72, JM/19.639, reel 21, folder 534, frame 979. See also the report "Der Joint in der Podkarpatska Rus and der Slovakei" (30 Nov. 1937), 3–4, in YVA, M.72, JM/19.639, reel 21, folder 534, frames 956–962, here 958–959.

On Prague's economic measures, see Joseph Rothschild, *East Central Europe Between the Two World Wars* (Seattle: University of Washington Press, 1974), 106–107; and Pryor, "Czechoslovak Economic Development," 197.

33. Report of activities of the JDC in Czechoslovakia, 19 April 1937, YVA, M.72, JM/19.639, reel 21, folder 534, frames 972–974, here 972.

34. Henrietta K. Buchman, Secretary of the Committee on Cultural Affairs of the JDC, to Dr. Stephen S. Wise, President of the American Jewish Congress, 4 Jan. 1940, in YVA, M.72, JM/19.776, reel 50, folder 709, frames 915–916; Aryeh Sole, *Light in the Mountains: Hebrew-Zionist Education in Carpatho-Russia from 1920 to 1944* (Hebrew) (Tel Aviv: World Association of Subcarpathian Jews and Hebrew Schools, 1986), 129, 131.

35. On the embezzlement of around $20,000, in part from Jewish loan associations, by Mr. Lillienfeld, the JDC representative in Czechoslovakia in the 1930s, see the correspondence from November 1935 to February 1936, in YVA, M.72, JM/19.639, reel 21, folder 534, frames 989, 994–995, 996–999, and 1000–1005. See the report on Jewish loan associations in Czechoslovakia in 1936, in YVA, M.72, JM/19.640, reel 22, folder 540, frames 953–955, concerning embezzlement by the manager of the Jewish loan association in Bilky.

36. See, e.g., testimony of Yaakov Fischgrund, in Gershuni, *Tapuach*, 433; and references in Aharon Moshe K. Rabinowitz, "The Jewish Party," in *The Jews of Czechoslovakia: Historical Studies and Surveys*, vol. 2 (Philadelphia: Jewish Publication Society of America, 1971), 270–271, 285–287, 288, 294, 300, 302, 306.

37. Karola Aykler, along with her children and her father, a prominent Magyar who had lived in the region before World War I, were denied Czechoslovak citizenship; thus, the children could not enroll in schools. See Susan M. Papp, *Outcasts: A Love Story* (Toronto: Dundurn Press, 2009), 23. Indeed, thousands of Magyars—mostly families of people who had held official posts under Hungarian rule before World War I—left the region following its annexation to Czechoslovakia. See Wein, "Czech Nation-Building," 163.

38. Kurt R. Grossman, "Refugees to and from Czechoslovakia," in *Jews of Czechoslovakia*, 2:565–581. Grossman served as executive secretary of the National Coordinating Committee, set up in 1933 to assist refugees in Czechoslovakia. See also the study on Manfred Georg, a Jewish refugee from Germany who founded the monthly *Jüdische Revue* in Mukačevo, which appeared between June 1936 and November 1938. Daniel Müller, *Manfred Georg und die Jüdische Revue: Eine Exilzeitschrift in der Tschechoslowakei, 1936–1938* (Konstanz: UVK Medien, 2000).

39. See, e.g., testimonies of Iurii Fenesh, USC Shoah Foundation, 50135 (Užhorod [Uzhhorod]); Iolana Tokar, ibid., 43593 (Užhorod).

40. David M. Crowe, *A History of the Gypsies of Eastern Europe and Russia* (New York: St. Martin's Griffin, 1996), 46–47. Germina Beniak, née Tokar, who was born in 1922 in the Roma camp in Užhorod, stated that Roma manufactured and supplied the bricks to construct the school building. See her testimony in USC Shoah Foundation, 50134.

41. Czechoslovak Law No. 117 of 19 July 1927 made Roma identity cards with fingerprints mandatory for those above the age of fourteen, required wandering Roma to carry special licenses, and forbade the entry of Roma to certain areas and places, such as holiday resorts. See Crowe, *History of the Gypsies*, 45. Almost all the testimonies by Roma examined in this study mention life in a Roma camp in interwar Subcarpathian Rus'.

42. Macartney, "Ruthenia," 239n2.

43. Macartney, "Ruthenia," 238–240; Magocsi, *Shaping of a National Identity*, 194–195. For an overview of political parties in interwar Czechoslovakia see Rothschild, *East Central Europe*, 95–100. The fifth major party was the National Democratic Party.

44. Magocsi, *Shaping of a National Identity*, 197, 213–214, 216–217; Macartney, "Ruthenia," 238–240.

45. Magocsi, *Shaping of a National Identity*, 219; Rothschild, *East Central Europe*, 99–100.

46. On the arrest and torture of Domokos Aykler, as well as the searches conducted in his home in Sevluš (Vynohradovo), see Papp, *Outcasts*, 50–52, 54–55. Hokky, a close friend of Aykler, smuggled him out of the country after his release from prison in September 1938. See ibid., 53–54, 58–61.

47. See, e.g., the rabidly anti-Czech Charles J. Hokky, *Ruthenia: Spearhead Toward the West* (Gainesville, FL: Danubian Research and Information Center, 1966), which contains mostly exaggerated and, in some cases, fantastic allegations.

48. Rothschild, *East Central Europe*, 98; Magocsi, *Shaping of a National Identity*, 195.

49. Zdenek L. Suda, *Zealots and Rebels: A History of the Communist Party of Czechoslovakia* (Stanford, CA: Hoover Institution Press, 1980), 16; Magocsi, *Shaping of a National Identity*, 90–91.

50. Suda, *Zealots and Rebels*, 40, 46–47; Magocsi, *Shaping of a National Identity*, 195. For the party platform of the regional secretariat Subcarpathian Rus' of the Czechoslovak Communist Party of the Third International (in Czech), which presents an extreme agenda, see CAHJP, CS/79/4.

51. See the election poster "in the name of the Jewish workers" of the Joint Organization of Merchants and Workers in Užhorod, calling on the "Jewish proletariat" to vote for the Communist Party in the general elections of March 1924, in the private collection of Rabbi Meir Frankel in Brooklyn, NY. I thank Meir Frankel, a central figure in the Munkács Hasidic community in Brooklyn, for inviting me so generously to use his private archive. This poster, like many others, was published in both Yiddish and Hungarian. See also the election poster of the Jewish Section of the Communist Party addressed to "Jews, workers, and poor people," most probably related to the local elections in 1923, in CAHJP, CS/79/2.

52. Sole, "Subcarpathian Ruthenia," 136; Rabinowicz, "The Jewish Party," 283, 289, also 326–327.

53. See the election posters of the Jewish Party for the general elections of March 1924, campaigning against the Jewish Democratic Party, in the private collection of Meir Frankel.

54. See the election bulletin of the Jewish Economic Party, *Jidische Wahlstimme*, Užhorod, 13 Nov. 1925, which agitated mainly against the Jewish Party, in the National Library of Israel, Manuscripts and Archives Department (NL, MAD), Hebrew University of Jerusalem, V. 2799; and see the election posters of the Jewish Party against the Jewish Economic Party in ibid., V. 2112/2. On the Jewish Economic Party see also Marie Chrova, "Jewish Politics in Central Europe: The Case of the Jewish Party in Interwar Czechoslovakia," in *Jewish Studies at the Central European University: Yearbook*, vol. 2 (1999–2000).

55. See the election poster of the Jewish Republican Party, in Labor and Hechalutz Movement Archive (LHMA), Pinchas Lavon Institute, Tel Aviv, VII, 37-437-3.

56. Sole, "Subcarpathian Ruthenia," 135–136; Gustav Fleischmann, "The Religious Congregation, 1918–1938," in *Jews of Czechoslovakia*, 1:306–307. On the growing strength of the right-wing faction in the Agrarian Party see Orzoff, *Battle for the Castle*, 96, 97–98, 133, 177. The formation in December 1935 of a Ukrainophile faction in the Agrarian Party in Subcarpathian Rus' echoed this tendency. Magocsi, *Shaping of a National Identity*, 232. References to the anti-Jewish aspects of the Agrarian Party appear in many of the election posters of the Jewish Party. See, e.g., the accusation in 1925 that "several rabbis had been bought with antisemitic money," in NL, MAD, V. 2112/2. See also the warning to Jews in 1928 not to lend their support to parties that would strengthen the "anti-Jewish front," mostly the Agrarian Party, and not to vote for "people, who have sold their Jewish name to parties that are our haters," in CAHJP, HU/51.

On alliances between Jews and political parties with anti-Jewish agendas in Hungary and Romania at the time see Bela Vago, "The Attitude Towards the Jews as a Criterion of the Left-Right Concept," in *Jews and Non-Jews in Eastern Europe, 1918–1945*, ed. Bela Vago and George L. Mosse (Jerusalem: Israel Universities Press, 1974), 21–49.

57. Macartney, "Ruthenia," 224, 239–240; Rothschild, *East Central Europe*, 98, 102n9, 105; Suda, *Zealots and Rebels*, 65.

58. See the table titled "Statisztikai kimutatás az 1924. évi podkárpátszká-ruszi parlamenti választásokról, kerületenként" (statistical summary, by districts, of the Parliament election results in Subcarpathian Rus' in 1924), Archive of the Memorial Museum of Hungarian-Speaking Jewry, Safed, H46011781.

59. Jiří Sláma, "Die Parlamentswahlen im Jahre 1935 in Karpatorussland," *Bohemia* 29 (1988): 34–49; Macartney, "Ruthenia," 240.

60. The diary is in LHMA, III, 38-437-4B. On Birobidzhan see Yehuda Bauer, *My Brother's Keeper: A History of the American Jewish Joint Distribution Committee, 1929–1939* (Philadelphia: Jewish Publication Society of America, 1978), 90–97; and Robert Weinberg, *Stalin's Forgotten Zion: Birobidzhan and the Making of a Soviet Jewish Homeland, an Illustrated History, 1928–1996* (Berkeley: University of California Press, 1998).

61. See the letter of Hechalutz Organization in Czechoslovakia to the Jewish Agency in Jerusalem, 25 May 1936, Central Zionist Archives (CZA), Jerusalem, S6/3677. Another

letter—from the Zionist Organization in Czechoslovakia to the Jewish Agency in Jerusalem (3 May 1936)—stressed "the enormous power of communism" in the region (ibid.). These tactics would become common practice by communist parties in eastern Europe in the period immediately after World War II. See Jan T. Gross, "Social Consequences of War: Preliminaries to the Study of Imposition of Communist Regimes in East Central Europe," *East European Politics and Societies* 3, no. 2 (1989): 198–214, esp. 208–213.

62. Quoted in Yehuda Spiegel, "The Elections to the Czechoslovak Parliament in 1935," in *Encyclopedia of the Jewish Diaspora*, vol. 7, *Karpatorus*, 264, and, for related events, see 263, 266–267. See also Rabinowicz, "The Jewish Party," 269, 272, 292; and Jelinek, *The Carpathian Diaspora*, 156–157.

63. The rise of modern Jewish Orthodox politics began half a century earlier, in late nineteenth-century Galicia. Jewish Orthodox leaders at the time realized the need to respond to the liberal secular system in Austro-Hungary, which emerged as part of the *Kulturkampf* in Europe, the struggle between the modern state and religious authorities, and which strengthened Galician Jewish liberals. The kind of politics that evolved employed a lot of religious language. Hence, in the elections to the Jewish community of Lemberg in 1877, Jewish Orthodox leaders stressed that even coming to an election meeting signified "a great mitzvah pertaining to the whole of Israel and to our holy religion." See Rachel Menkin, "Politics and Orthodoxy: The Case of Galicia," in *Orthodox Judaism: New Perspectives*, ed. Yosef Salmon, Aviezer Ravitzky, and Adam S. Ferziger (Hebrew) (Jerusalem: Magnes Press, 2006), 447–469, esp. 454–455 (the quote from an election poster), 463.

64. Poster in the name of the *yeshivot* in Subcarpathian Rus' and Slovakia, NL, MAD, V. 2112/2, printed in Avraham Fuchs, *The Yeshivot of Hungary in Their Glory and Destruction*, vol. 1 (Hebrew) (Jerusalem: published by the author, 1979), 504.

65. See article from a bulletin of the Jewish Party, probably related to the provincial elections of 1928, in CAHJP, HU/51. See also the election poster of the Jewish Party against the Jewish Democratic Party in 1924, which labels the latter "Jews' persecutors," in the private collection of Meir Frankel.

66. NL, MAD, V. 2112/2.

67. CAHJP, CS/79/10.

68. See election poster beginning and ending with the well-known "save me from my brother Esau" (Genesis 32:11), in NL, MAD, V. 2112/2.

69. See election poster of the Agrarian Party for the general elections of March 1924, in CAHJP, HU/51. The poster added another layer of exclusion, stating that most Zionists lacked the right to vote in Czechoslovakia, as many of them were actually Russian and Polish Jews who had been expelled from their countries.

70. Magocsi, *Shaping of a National Identity*, 178–181, 179.

71. Macartney, "Ruthenia," 231. See also Athanasius B. Pekar, *The History of the Church in Carpathian Rus'* (New York: Columbia University Press, 1992), 100–101, 109, 111–112, 116–118.

72. Magocsi, *Shaping of a National Identity*, 181, 182.

73. On Agudath Yisrael see Gershon C. Bacon, *The Politics of Tradition: Agudat Yisrael in Poland, 1916–1939* (Jerusalem: Magness Press, 1996).

74. For the protocol of the meeting and its decision see the Religious Zionist Archive, Jerusalem, file 7/6. See also David Gelb, *The History of Our Rabbi* (Hebrew) (Mukačevo: Grafia, 1938), 71–72, sec. 148. This book is a partisan biography of Rabbi Shapira; Alan L. Nadler, "The War on Modernity of R. Hayim Elazar Shapira of Munkacs," *Studia Judaica* 3 (1994): 102–106; and Aviezer Ravitzky, *Messianism, Zionism and Jewish Religious Radicalism* (Hebrew) (Tel Aviv: Am Oved, 2006), 62–66.

75. See, e.g., the failure to found a branch of Agudath Yisrael in Sevluš, owing to the influence of the region's ultra-Orthodox leaders, in Shmuel Hacohen Weingarten, ed., *Memorial Book for the Jewish Community of Nagyszöllös and Its Surroundings* (Hebrew) (private publication, 1976), 77–78.

76. On Rabbi Shapira's religious ideology, particularly his Messianism, see Nadler, "War on Modernity," esp. 100, 107–110, and 112–113. Rabbi Shapira calculated the Messiah's appearance to the fall of 1941. On the rise of Hasidism as a political as well as spiritual movement see Glenn Dynner, *Men of Silk: The Hasidic Conquest of Polish Jewish Society* (New York: Oxford University Press, 2006).

77. "cheder oder gymnasya," *Yiddishe Zeitung*, 9 Sept. 1927. This newspaper served as Rabbi Shapira's mouthpiece in Mukačevo. See Avigdor Dagan, "The Press," in *Jews of Czechoslovakia*, 1:529. On Rabbi Shapira's general tendency to refer to his opponents as "non-Jews" see Nadler, "War on Modernity," 118.

78. Nadler, "War on Modernity," 95–96, 96n14.

79. Translated in Michael K. Silber, "The Emergence of Ultra-Orthodoxy: The Invention of a Tradition," in *The Uses of Tradition: Jewish Continuity in the Modern Era*, ed. Jack Wertheimer (New York: Jewish Theological Seminary of America, 1992), 74n111. Both Rabbi Schick and Rabbi Haim Sofer also banned marriages between Orthodox and Reform Jews, relying on Rabbi Moses Sofer's declaration about the Hamburg synagogue reformers in 1819, according to which "we should not give our daughters to their sons" (ibid., 74n110).

80. Nadler, "War on Modernity," 117; see also 93, 97.

81. Gelb, *The History of Our Rabbi*, 89, sec. 184.

82. Shmuel Hacohen Weingarten, "The Munkacs-Belz Polemics," in *Encyclopedia of the Jewish Diaspora*, vol. 7, *Karpatorus*, 226–232.

83. For "Belz pigs," where Rabbi Shapira used the Hebrew *hazirim* to replace *hasidim*, see Weingarten, "The Munkacs-Belz Polemics," 230. By using the word *pigs* here and in other contexts, Rabbi Shapira aimed to establish the deceptive nature of his opponents' "Jewishness": just as pigs exhibit an external sign of a kosher animal in Judaism—cloven hoof—but are not kosher. See Nadler, "War on Modernity," 102n31. For the second quote, where the language highlights the ferocity of this episode, see the election poster of the Jewish Republican Party, in LHMA, VII, 37-437-2.

84. The ordinances of the *beit midrash* of the Belzer Hasidim in Mukačevo demonstrate their strict ultra-Orthodox position, particularly their negative stance regarding Reform Judaism. I thank Tuvia Klein for providing me with a copy of the ordinances.

85. The agreement ("Friedensvereinbarung") that ended the split was signed on 11 March 1934. I thank Tuvia Klein for providing me with a copy of this document. The previous year, Rabbi Shapira successfully concluded a battle with another Hasidic leader, the

Spinka rebbe, Rabbi Yitzchak Eizik Weiss, who had also arrived in Mukačevo at the beginning of World War I as a refugee. In 1933 he left the town and moved to Sevluš. Weingarten, *Memorial Book*, 110–111.

86. Shmuel Hacohen Weingarten, "Early Zionist Activity," in *Encyclopedia of the Jewish Diaspora*, vol. 7, *Karpatorus*, 322; testimony of Chaya Gilor, YVA, O.3/11435, 2 (Mukačevo); Mordechai Berkowitch, *We Shall Remember: The Experiences of a Boy from Subcarpathian Rus' in the Period of the Holocaust* (Hebrew) (private publication, 2002), 23. See also Jelinek, *The Carpathian Diaspora*, 113–115.

87. See collective testimony, Moreshet Archive, Givat Haviva, Israel, A/1023.2; Avraham Ben-David, "Hashomer Haztair," in *Encyclopedia of the Jewish Diaspora*, vol. 7, *Karpatorus*, 351–360.

88. Antman Shalom, "The Movement in Czechoslovakia," in *Religious Zionism*, ed. Yitzhak Rephael and S. Z. Shragai (Hebrew) (Jerusalem: Mosad Harav Kook, 1977), 2:393; Yehoshua Halevi, *The History of Betar in Czechoslovakia* (Hebrew) (Tel Aviv: Organization of the Alumni of Betar in Czechoslovakia, 1960), 22–23, 29, 31, 309. See also Weingarten, *Memorial Book*, 116.

89. Menahem Frank and Yehiel Tenne, eds., *Hechalutz Hatzair in Subcarpathian Rus': A Collection* (Hebrew) (Lohamei Haghettaot: Ghetto Fighters' House and Hakibbutz Hameuchad, 1984), 12, 21; Yehuda Erez, "'Hechalutz' and 'Hechalutz Hatzair'," in *Encyclopedia of the Jewish Diaspora*, vol. 7, *Karpatorus*, 337–338.

90. On Kugel see Wein, "Czech Nation-Building," 251–254.

91. YVA, O.3/6491, 26 (recorded in 1990). On the clash between Hechalutz Hatzair and Hashomer Hatzair, for example, see Frank and Tenne, *Hechalutz Hatzair in Subcarpathian Rus'*, 95.

92. Frank and Tenne, *Hechalutz Hatzair in Subcarpathian Rus'*, 98.

93. Spiegel, "Elections to the Czechoslovak Parliament," 261.

94. Ilana Rosen, "Hasidism Versus Zionism as Remembered by Carpatho-Russian Jews Between the Two World Wars," in *Jewishness: Expression, Identity, and Representation*, vol. 1, ed. Simon J. Bronner (Oxford: Littman Library of Jewish Civilization, 2008), 213–238.

95. See the testimony of Zvia Weiser (Tomer) in Frank and Tenne, *Hechalutz Hatzair in Subcarpathian Rus'*, 31. See also testimony of Shmu'el Vyzer from Vyšný Bystrý (Verkhniy Bystryy), who recounted "very bitter arguments" at home after one of his brothers, formerly a student at the *yeshiva* of Rabbi Shapira in Mukačevo, decided to become a Zionist. See USC Shoah Foundation, 21374.

96. See, e.g., testimony of Aharon Golan, YVA, O.3/8736, 5–7 (Chust). See also testimony of Moshe Zairi, ibid., O.3/7667, 2–3, 7 (Sevluš), who saw no contradiction between his religious and secular education. A Zionist, he continued to dress like an orthodox Jew and observe religious precepts that, he believed, in no way contradicted his membership in Betar.

97. Testimony of Avraham Perri, in Rosen, "Hasidism Versus Zionism," 221, and 224–226, 231–232 for Rosen's analysis.

98. YVA, O.3/10935, 2 (recorded in 1998). See also, e.g., testimonies of Ilan Mordechai, ibid., O.3/12672, 10 (Iza [Iza]); Frank Colb, ibid., O.3/12710, 19 (Bilky); Yaakov Avraham

Leibovich, ibid., O.3/12572, 6 (Selo Slatina). All of them specifically mentioned the role of rabbis in prohibiting Zionist activities.

99. For example, a letter from the Organization of Hechalutz Hatzair in Czechoslovakia (20 Nov. 1934) mentions a membership of six hundred in Subcarpathian Rus'. More than a year later (21 March 1936), Elyakim Berlfin, who worked in the movement's central branch in Mukačevo, wrote to Shlomo Lipski, a Zionist emissary from Palestine, that the local branch numbered only twenty-five people. Both letters are in LHMA, III, 42-437-2. While Betar seemed to have enjoyed considerable support among Jewish youth in the region, even if we take at face value the estimate of one of its leaders in the area, Yehuda Udi (Weissberger), the movement had only twenty-two hundred members at its peak—a small minority in a region where almost half of the one hundred thousand Jews were under the age of fifteen (see Chapter 1n48). See Yehuda Udi, "Betar," in *Encyclopedia of the Jewish Diaspora*, vol. 7, *Karpatorus*, 367. Also, the Hebrew education system in the region appealed only to a very small minority of 3.5 percent. Jelinek, *The Carpathian Diaspora*, 217.

100. On Hechalutz Hatzair see Frank and Tenne, *Hechalutz Hatzair in Subcarpathian Rus'*, 75, 82.

101. See, e.g., testimony of Fircha Kestenbaum, YVA, O.3/7123, 6 (Chust).

102. Yeshayahu A. Jelinek, "Jewish Youth in Carpatho-Rus': Between Hope and Despair (1920–1938)," *Shvut* 7, no. 23 (1998): 151–152, 154–155.

103. Magocsi, *Shaping of a National Identity*, 105–129.

104. Ibid., 170, 172. Yehudit Ferber, who was born in 1920 in Sevluš, studied in a Carpatho-Ruthenian high school in Berehovo (Berehovo) with teachers from Kyiv and Lwów. See her testimony in the USC Shoah Foundation, 15194.

105. Magocsi, *Shaping of a National Identity*, 123, 138–141, 156–157, 205, 317–318.

106. Ibid., 308–309. On Karabelesh see also Rusinko, *Straddling Borders*, 345–363.

107. Ivan Pop, "Revai, Iuliian," in *Encyclopedia of Rusyn History and Culture*, ed. Paul Robert Magocsi and Ivan Pop, rev. and exp. ed. (Toronto: University of Toronto Press, 2005), 414.

108. Ivan Pop, "Shtefan, Avhustyn," in *Encyclopedia of Rusyn History and Culture*, ed. Paul Robert Magocsi and Ivan Pop, rev. and exp. ed. (Toronto: University of Toronto Press, 2005), 457; Magocsi, *Shaping of a National Identity*, 325.

109. Magocsi, *Shaping of a National Identity*, 173, 422n35.

110. Quoted in ibid., 144; see also 153, 413n96, 413n97. On the languages of newspapers in Subcarpathian Rus' see ibid., 141. Elaine Rusinko has posited that "by 1938, it was clear that the Ukrainian language . . . showed democratic dynamism in Subcarpathian Rus', as compared to Russian, which, fairly or not, had by now earned an elitist reputation." Rusinko, *Straddling Borders*, 337; see also 313, 361–362.

111. Magocsi, *Shaping of a National Identity*, 227–233.

112. YVA, O.3/11792, 6 (recorded in 2000).

113. Ari Halpert stayed in the region after World War II, and he lived in Uzhhorod, where I interviewed him on 1 September 2010. He died in June 2012.

114. USC Shoah Foundation, 21374.

115. Avraham Fuchs, *I Shall Talk and Testify: The History of the Karpatorus Community*

of Shandrif (Hebrew) (Jerusalem: private publication, 2001), 14. Shandrif was the town's name in Yiddish.

116. USC Shoah Foundation, 16631 (recorded in 1996).

117. Aranka Siegal, *Upon the Head of the Goat: A Childhood in Hungary, 1939–1944* (London: J. M. Dent and Sons, 1981), 15.

118. Wein, "Czech Nation-Building," 213–214; Harm Ramkema, "Poverty, Diversity and Conflict: Some Remarks on Subcarpathian Jewry," *Carpatho-Rusyn American* 17, no. 2 (1994): 4–7.

119. Livia Rothkirchen, "Deep-Rooted yet Alien: Some Aspects of the History of the Jews in Subcarpathian Ruthenia," *Yad Vashem Studies* 12 (1977): 167. One could find, for example, copies of Czech and Carpatho-Ruthenian translations of *Mein Kampf*. See Sole, "Between the Two World Wars," 218–219.

120. YVA, M.72, JM/19.639, reel 21, folder 534, frame 955. Another commentator observed in 1937 that "anti-Semitism [among Carpatho-Ruthenians shows] . . . at present only faint signs." See Macartney, "Ruthenia," 246.

121. Quotes from an election poster, in CAHJP, CS/79/6.

122. See the July 1942 report of the Territorial Subcommittee of the Advisory Committee on Post-War Foreign Policy of the US State Department, in *Wartime American Plans for a New Hungary: Documents from the U.S. Department of State, 1942–1944*, ed. Ignác Romsics (New York: Columbia University Press, 1992), 177, which notes with regard to the interwar years: "The numerous Jewish element would also have been reluctant, on the whole, to join the New Hungarian state [*sic*] with its copies of the Nürnberg laws." On the anti-Jewish nature of the Hungarian state and society after World War I see Paul A. Hanebrink, *In Defense of Christian Hungary: Religion, Nationalism, and Antisemitism, 1890–1944* (Ithaca, NY: Cornell University Press, 2006), 47–163. See also Jelinek, *The Carpathian Diaspora*, 188–190.

123. In the 1935 general elections the pro-Nazi Henlein Party received 1,535 votes in the region—a substantial number of adult votes out of a population of about fourteen thousand local Germans. See Macartney, "Ruthenia," 240; Sláma, "Die Parlamentswahlen im Jahre 1935," 36. On the Henlein Party and on Pan-Germanism accompanied by anti-Jewish positions among Germans in former Austro-Hungarian lands see Rothschild, *East Central Europe*, 75, 126–129, and J. W. Bruegel, "The Germans in Pre-War Czechoslovakia," in *A History of the Czechoslovak Republic, 1918–1948*, ed. Victor S. Mamatey and Radomír Luža (Princeton, NJ: Princeton University Press, 1973), 182–183. See also testimonies about the animosity between Jews and Germans in the region: Jean Greenstein (Sevluš), USC Shoah Foundation, 3721; Shmuel Givoni, Moreshet Archive, A. 1543, 4 (Mukačevo); Bella Fleischmann, ibid., A. 1503, 5 (Mukačevo).

124. David Engel, "Away from a Definition of Antisemitism: An Essay in the Semantics of Historical Description," in *Rethinking European Jewish History*, ed. Jeremy Cohen and Moshe Rosman (Oxford: Littman Library of Jewish Civilization, 2009), 30–53.

125. Alon Confino's recent analysis of the analytical category *ideology* in Holocaust studies has yielded a related assertion: "It [the term *ideology*] has become such a catch-all notion about motivations in the Third Reich that it is difficult to discriminate between

ideology, on the one hand, and ways to think outside, alongside, against, underneath, and above it." See Alon Confino, *Foundational Pasts: The Holocaust as Historical Understanding* (New York: Cambridge University Press, 2012), 122.

126. Engel, "Away from a Definition of Antisemitism," 53.

127. For this methodological observation see Rogers Brubaker and Frederick Cooper, "Beyond 'Identity'," *Theory and Society* 29, no. 1 (2000): 1–47, esp. 17, 24, 26.

128. In a JDC report (3 Jan. 1922) on the region Dr. Emanuel Frankel commented that "the actual czechian [sic] persons in power show them [Jews] a special mistrust. The Jews are considered as the adherents of the magyar (Hungarian) Regime [sic] and are classified at least as half Hungarians (so called 'Magyarons')" (3). See JDC Archives, file #186. See also Jelinek, *The Carpathian Diaspora*, 126–134.

129. A report on Subcarpathian Rus', August 1921, signed by J. Rieur, 2, JDC Archives, file #186.

130. Jelinek, *The Carpathian Diaspora*, 151–152. An example of Jews' preference for Czech schools comes from the Czech school in the small town of Nižni Verecki: besides one Czech girl, all the students were Jews. See testimony of Fircha Hermal, YVA, O.3/8782, 1. See also Rebecca Barkai-Rappaport, *Horrible Years: A Diary* (Hebrew) (Tel Aviv: Traklin, 1986), 5, where the author described the Czech school in Seredně (Seredneye), near Užhorod: "Most of the students were Jews and a minority of Czechs."

In 1930, there was one Czech elementary school for every 212 Czechs, while the corresponding figure for Carpatho-Ruthenians stood at 997. Macartney, "Ruthenia," 233. The number of Czech schools in the region increased from 22 in 1920 to 188 in 1938. Magocsi, *Shaping of a National Identity*, 169, 212.

131. A report of the Union of Jewish Schools for Subcarpathian Rus' to Dr. Cyrus Adler, 29 March 1927, 2, JDC Archives, file #192. See also Weingarten, *Memorial Book*, 135–136. Among 19,395 Jewish elementary students (defined by religion) in the 1935–1936 school year, 61 percent studied in Czech schools, and only 24 percent attended Carpatho-Ruthenian institutions. Jelinek, *The Carpathian Diaspora*, 217.

132. A report by Dr. Spiegel to the JDC office in Vienna, 21 July 1923, 3, JDC Archives, file #192.

133. Jelinek, *The Carpathian Diaspora*, 151–152, 188, 198–200, 229. See also Henry Abramson, "Collective Memory and Collective Identity: Jews, Rusyns and the Holocaust," *Carpatho-Rusyn American* 17, no. 3 (1994): 4–7.

134. Magocsi, *Shaping of a National Identity*, 211–233, has described the emerging "legacy of discontent" between Carpatho-Ruthenians and the Czechoslovak government. Magocsi, however, has not considered the effects of this discontent on interethnic relations in the region. For another analysis of Jewish life in interwar Czechoslovakia centered on problems of loyalty, see Rebekah Klein-Pejšová, *Mapping Jewish Loyalties in Interwar Slovakia* (Bloomington: Indiana University Press, 2015).

135. Abram de Swaan, "Widening Circles of Disidentification," *Theory, Culture and Society* 14, no. 2 (1997): 108.

136. Catherine Lutz and Geoffrey M. White, "The Anthropology of Emotions," *Annual Review of Anthropology* 15 (Oct. 1986): 431.

137. Sara Ahmed, *The Cultural Politics of Emotions* (New York: Routledge, 2004).

138. Daniel Bar-Tal, Eran Halperin, and Joseph de Rivera, "Collective Emotions in Conflict Situations: Societal Implications," *Journal of Social Issues* 63, no. 2 (2007): 443.

139. Isaiah Trunk, introduction to part 2 of *Jewish Responses to Nazi Persecution: Collective and Individual Behavior in Extremis* (New York: Stein and Day, 1979), 66.

140. It is very doubtful, for example, that the Bulgarian authorities planned and implemented the deportation of Jews from western Thrace and eastern Macedonia (more than eleven thousand people) to German hands in March 1943—almost all of them were killed upon their arrival at the Treblinka death camp—because of anti-Jewish hatreds, especially as recent research has demonstrated the dominant pro-Jewish positions that permeated Bulgarian society at the time. See, e.g., Stephen Reicher et al., "Saving Bulgaria's Jews: An Analysis of Social Identity and the Mobilization of Social Solidarity," *European Journal of Social Psychology* 36, no. 1 (2006): 49–72. Estonia provides another example. See Anton Weiss-Wendt, *Murder Without Hatred: Estonians and the Holocaust* (Syracuse, NY: Syracuse University Press, 2009).

141. Bar-Tal, Halperin, and de Rivera, "Collective Emotions in Conflict Situations," 448.

142. N. T. Feather and Rebecca Sherman, "Envy, Resentment, Schadenfreude, and Sympathy: Reactions to Deserved and Undeserved Achievement and Subsequent Failure," *Personality and Social Psychology Bulletin* 28, no. 7 (2002): 953–961.

Chapter 3

Material used in Chapter 3 was first published in *Polin: Studies in Polish Jewry*, vol. 26, *Jews and Ukrainians*, ed. Yohanan Petrovsky-Shtern and Antony Polonsky (Oxford: Littman Library of Jewish Civilization, 2014), published on behalf of the Institute for Polish-Jewish Studies and the American Association of Polish-Jewish Studies.

1. Ivan Olbracht, *Nikola the Outlaw*, trans. Marie K. Holeček (Evanston: Northwestern University Press, 2001), 16–17. Original Czech language edition titled *Nikola Šuhaj loupežník* (Praha: Sfinz, 1933).

2. The name *Carpatho-Ukraine*, in use since the mid-1920s by the Communist Party in Subcarpathian Rus' and by local Ukrainian nationalists, had no previous history. See Ivan Pop, "Carpatho-Ukraine," in *Encyclopedia of Rusyn History and Culture*, ed. Paul Robert Magocsi and Ivan Pop, rev. and exp. ed. (Toronto: University of Toronto Press, 2005), 61. Even though the official name of the autonomous region remained *Subcarpathian Rus'*, *Carpatho-Ukraine* is used here because the leaders of the autonomous regime employed it in all their proclamations and publications, and the government in Prague authorized it as an alternative name.

3. Mary Heimann, *Czechoslovakia: The State That Failed* (New Haven, CT: Yale University Press, 2007), 87.

4. Ibid.

5. This neglect characterizes other relevant scholarship. Paul Robert Magocsi, the foremost specialist on the history of Subcarpathian Rus', devoted limited attention to the Carpatho-Ukrainian stage. See Paul Robert Magocsi, *The Shaping of a National Identity: Subcarpathian Rus', 1848–1948* (Cambridge, MA: Harvard University Press, 1978), 237–246;

see also Paul Robert Magocsi, *A History of Ukraine* (Toronto: University of Toronto Press, 1996), 614–616. Yeshayahu Jelinek's account of the history of Subcarpathian Rus' Jews likewise afforded this period of time only a marginal place. Yeshayahu A. Jelinek, *The Carpathian Diaspora: The Jews of Subcarpathian Rus' and Mukachevo, 1848–1948* (New York: Columbia University Press, 2007), 236–240. Livia Rothkirchen hardly treated this topic at all in her comprehensive article on Jewish life in Subcarpathian Rus'. See Livia Rothkirchen, "Deep-Rooted yet Alien: Some Aspects of the History of the Jews in Subcarpathian Ruthenia," *Yad Vashem Studies* 12 (1977): 147–191. Ilana Rosen's literary analyses of survivors' accounts provided by Jews from the region pay little attention to the Carpatho-Ukrainian phase. See Ilana Rosen, *"In Auschwitz We Blew the Shofar": Carpatho-Russian Jews Remember the Holocaust* (Hebrew) (Jerusalem: Yad Vashem and the Avraham Harman Institute of Contemporary Jewry at the Hebrew University, 2004). And my contribution on the Jewish community of Khust focused much more on the period of Hungarian rule followed by the German occupation. See Raz Segal, "The Jews of Huszt Between the World Wars and in the Holocaust," *Yalkut Moreshet: Holocaust Documentation and Research* 4 (2006): 80–119.

Several figures who had played central roles in Carpatho-Ukraine wrote accounts that espouse ideological standpoints about this episode but offer few scholarly insights. See, e.g., Vincent Shandor, *Carpatho-Ukraine in the Twentieth Century: A Political and Legal History* (Cambridge, MA: Harvard University Press, 1997); and Augustin Stefan, *From Carpatho-Ruthenia to Carpatho-Ukraine* (New York: Carpathian Star Publishing, 1954). Ivan Pop has commented that these and similar texts constitute "a kind of amalgam that includes an undifferentiated compilation of historical facts, memoirs by marginal participants in the events of 1938 and 1939, and an apologia by politically motivated publicists." See Ivan Pop, "Historiography," in Magocsi and Pop, *Encyclopedia of Rusyn History and Culture*, 174. Pop's view also applies to Peter G. Stercho, *Diplomacy of Double Morality: Europe's Crossroads in Carpatho-Ukraine, 1919–1939* (New York: Carpathian Research Center, 1971).

Finally, the subject has triggered much highly biased and polemical work. According to one commentator, "the political and intellectual climate in post-1991 independent Ukraine, pervaded as it is by a kind of nationalist euphoria, on the one hand, and by the continuing influence of Marxism (mixed at times with post-Communist ideas), on the other, has not encouraged the development of impartial scholarly research. . . . A good example of such research [is] the numerous studies about autonomous Carpatho-Ukraine" (Pop, "Historiography," 178).

6. Paul Robert Magocsi, *Ukraine: An Illustrated History* (Seattle: University of Washington Press, 2007), 266. Jews in Carpatho-Ukraine numbered almost 66,000 (13 percent), Magyars 26,000 (5 percent), and Czechs and Slovaks 17,500 (3 percent). See Shandor, *Carpatho-Ukraine in the Twentieth Century*, 84.

7. One contemporary commentator noted that the budget of Carpatho-Ukraine showed a deficit of two million pounds. See Alexander Henderson, *Eyewitness in Czecho-Slovakia* (London: George G. Harrap, 1939), 285. Another source estimated that "the mere maintenance of the province as a part of the Czech state is now costing the Prague government between $50,000 and $100,000 [equivalent to $750,000–$1,500,000 today] a day." George F. Kennan, "Report on Conditions in Ruthenia" (March 1939), in *From Prague After*

Munich: Diplomatic Papers, 1938–1940 (Princeton, NJ: Princeton University Press, 1968), 68–69.

8. The memoir of Vincent Shandor, who served as the representative of Carpatho-Ukraine in Prague, discusses the chaos that prevailed among Carpatho-Ukraine's leading figures. This was most evident in the disorganization that characterized the paramilitary Carpathian Sich and its conflicts with the Khust cabinet. See Shandor, *Carpatho-Ukraine in the Twentieth Century*, 165–187. On the carelessness and neglect of the Carpatho-Ukrainian leadership regarding economic issues see Kennan, "Report on Conditions in Ruthenia," 65.

9. Henderson, *Eyewitness in Czecho-Slovakia*, 250–254; Kennan, "Report on Conditions in Ruthenia," 63; Stefan, *From Carpatho-Ruthenia to Carpatho-Ukraine*, 38; Shandor, *Carpatho-Ukraine in the Twentieth Century*, 71–74, 94, 100n60; see also Magocsi, *Shaping of a National Identity*, 239.

10. Kennan, "Report on Conditions in Ruthenia," 65; see also the *New York Times*, 7 Jan., 9 Jan., and 12 Jan. 1939.

11. Magocsi, *Shaping of a National Identity*, 243.

12. For testimonies about this battle between Czech and Carpathian Sich forces see, e.g., Aharon Golan, Yad Vashem Archives (YVA), O.3/8736, 9; and Zvi Manshel, ed., *The Jewish Community of Khust and Its Environs, Memorial Book* (Hebrew) (Rehovot: Organization of the Khust Community and Its Environs, 2000), 137, 451–452.

13. Michael Winch, *Republic for a Day: An Eyewitness Account of the Carpatho-Ukraine Incident* (London: Robert Hale, 1939); headline of article by Anne O'Hare McCormick, in the *New York Times*, 17 March 1939.

14. The efforts of local leaders from 1848 until the present to attain political autonomy attest to this long-term tension. See Paul Robert Magocsi and Ivan Pop, "Autonomy," in Magocsi and Pop, *Encyclopedia of Rusyn History and Culture*, 22–23. On the literary production that emerged in the process, see Elaine Rusinko, *Straddling Borders: Literature and Identity in Subcarpathian Rus'* (Toronto: University of Toronto Press, 2003).

15. Albert S. Kotowski, "'Ukrainisches Piemont'? Die Karpatenukraine am Vorabend des Zweiten Weltkrieges," *Jahrbücher für Geschichte Osteuropas* 49 (2001): 67–95. This article draws on the records of the German legation in Khust. See also Orest Subtelny, *Ukraine: A History* (Toronto: University of Toronto Press, 2000), 451.

16. See telegrams from the German Foreign Office to German embassies in Paris, London, Rome, Warsaw, Washington, Tokyo, Brussels, Belgrade, Bucharest, and Bern and to the German consulate in Geneva, 10 Oct. 1938; a report from the German embassy in Prague to the German Foreign Office, 23 Oct. 1938; and a report on Carpatho-Ukraine, 12 Nov. 1938—all in YVA, TR.2/JM/2026. These documents address Polish-Hungarian relations, especially with regard to the prospect of a joint Polish-Hungarian border following Hungarian occupation of Carpatho-Ukraine, and the impact of the friendly stance in Slovakia and Carpatho-Ukraine toward Germany on the position of the Czecho-Slovak government vis-à-vis Berlin. See also Stephen D. Kertesz, *Diplomacy in a Whirlpool: Hungary Between Nazi Germany and Soviet Russia* (Notre Dame, IN: University of Notre Dame Press, 1953), 38–45.

17. Rogers Brubaker, *Nationalism Reframed: Nationhood and the National Question in the New Europe* (Cambridge, UK: Cambridge University Press, 1996), 18–22. See also the

insightful analysis of Max Bergholz, "Sudden Nationhood: The Microdynamics of Intercommunal Relations in Bosnia-Herzegovina After World War II," *American Historical Review* 118, no. 3 (2013): 679–707.

18. Brubaker, *Nationalism Reframed*, 19–21.

19. Yekutiel Yehuda Greenwald, *Thousand Years of Jewish Life in Hungary* (Yiddish) (New York: Farish Press, 1945), 235.

20. Testimony of Malkah Baldor, USC Shoah Foundation Institute for Visual History and Education, interview number 26048. See also testimonies of Dina Drezner, ibid., 30181 (Hanychi); Michael Jackson, ibid., 26142 (Torun'); and Aharon Rat, ibid., 32662 (Velyky Bychkiv).

21. YVA, O.3/12365, 4.

22. Ibid., O.3/12500, 5.

23. Kennan, "Report on Conditions in Ruthenia," 64. Almost all primary and secondary sources note these Ukrainian nationalists. See, e.g., testimony of Yafah Rat, USC Shoah Foundation, 32552 (Velyky Bychkiv); and Henderson, *Eyewitness in Czecho-Slovakia*, 282.

24. Testimony of Eva Slomovits, USC Shoah Foundation, 24130. See also Shandor's reference to "[Carpathian] Sich members from the highland villages." Shandor, *Carpatho-Ukraine in the Twentieth Century*, 175.

25. The argument here acknowledges the complex history of relations between Jews and Ukrainians, in which anti-Jewish positions and violence figured among other aspects. Nevertheless, episodes of large-scale violence against Jews had happened in Ukrainian lands, whence many recruits of the Carpathian Sich came. See, e.g., Henry Abramson, *A Prayer for the Government: Ukrainians and Jews in Revolutionary Times, 1917–1920* (Cambridge, MA: Harvard University Press, 1999).

26. Rabbi Yehoshua Greenwald, "Eye of Tear," preface to *The Grace of Yehoshua* (Hebrew) (New York: Schlesinger Bros., 1948), 5, accessed through the software "The History of the Holocaust in Prefaces to Rabbinical Literature," developed by the Center for Holocaust Research, Jerusalem College, Israel. See also testimony of Aharon Golan, YVA, O.3/8736, 9, in which he related cases of Jews' beards cut off and robbery of Jews.

27. Testimonies of Martin Pearl, USC Shoah Foundation, 1768 (Hanychi); Yafah Rat, ibid., 32552 (Velyky Bychkiv); Irene Buchman, ibid., 3316 (Bilki). In relation to this violence Jelinek mentions Khust, Bushtyno, Novobarovo, and Nyzhnya Apsha. See Jelinek, *The Carpathian Diaspora*, 237.

28. Testimonies of Dov Golani, YVA, O.3/8438, 10; Yisrael Rosenfeld, ibid., O.3/5603, 7; Henia Moskowitz, ibid., O.3/10158, 2, in which she spoke of anti-Czech violence as well (on anti-Czech violence in mid-March see also the *New York Times*, 17 March 1939); Rose Gelb, USC Shoah Foundation, 10374 (Drahovo); Yosef Fridman, ibid., 22182 (Torun'). See also the entry on Velyky Bychkiv, in *Maramorosh Book: One Hundred and Sixty Holy Communities in Their Life and Destruction*, ed. S. Y. Gross and Y. Joseph Hacohen (Hebrew) (Tel Aviv: Maramorosh House, 1983), 284.

29. Segal, "The Jews of Huszt," 86. On the Jews expelled to no-man's-land see "News from all over the World by the Jewish Telegraphic Agency, New York," vol. 5, no. 43, 23 Jan. 1939, YVA, M.72, JM/19.640, reel 22, folder 541, frames 1066–1067. Autonomous Slovakia

and Hungary also forced some Jews over these borders. See Eduard Nižňanský, "Die Deportation der Juden in der Zeit der autonomen Slowakei im November 1938," *Jahrbuch für Antisemitismusforschung* 7 (1998): 20–45; Dov Dinur, *Chapters in the History of Subcarpathian Rus' Jewry* (Hebrew) (Jerusalem: Hebrew University, 1983), 87.

30. Testimony of Esther Offer, USC Shoah Foundation, 21141. See also testimony of Juri Klein, in *The Jewish Community of Khust and Its Environs*, ed. Zvi Manshel (Hebrew) (Rehovot: Organization of the Khust Community and Its Environs, 2000), 200; and testimony of Yaakov Fischgrund about deportations from Tyachiv, in *Tapuach: A Collection of Names and Details on the History of the Jewish Community of Tetsh*, ed. Yitzhak Gershuni (Hebrew) (private publication, 1994), 434–435.

31. See, e.g., the case of János Szimocskó, town magistrate of Tur'i Remety in 1938, who on 3 December of that year petitioned for the "annexation of Túrjaremete [Tur'i Remety] by Hungary," a move that landed him in prison for the next three months. See his letter to Miklós Kozma, the Hungarian governor of the region in 1940–1941, 25 May 1941, Magyar Országos Levéltár (National Archives of Hungary, MOL), K429, cs. 40, 2210.

Carpatho-Ruthenians who objected to the Ukrainian-oriented government of Carpatho-Ukraine also faced persecution, including imprisonment in Dumen, a detention camp near Rakhiv. See Kennan, "Report on Conditions in Ruthenia," 64–65; Magocsi, *Shaping of a National Identity*, 242, 244, 448–449n43, 450n56; see also Paul Robert Magocsi and Ivan Pop, "Dumen," in Magocsi and Pop, *Encyclopedia of Rusyn History and Culture*, 106–107.

32. Tivadar Kováts to Miklós Kozma, n.d., probably April 1941, MOL, K429, cs. 37, 1254; see also a letter from Tivadar Kováts, 27 March 1941, ibid., 1255. For another case of cooperation between a Jew, Béla Friedman Farago, and a Magyar, István Aykler, see Susan M. Papp, *Outcasts: A Love Story* (Toronto: Dundurn Press, 2009), 66.

33. Manshe, *Jewish Community of Khust*, 137, 451–452; Shandor, *Carpatho-Ukraine in the Twentieth Century*, 178–187.

34. See, e.g., testimonies of Dov Golani, YVA, O.3/8438, 11; Irena Naomi-Gross, ibid., O.3/8496, 4; Zelig Komornik, USC Shoah Foundation, 38620 (Sokirnitsa); and Abraham Himmel, ibid., 25962. Himmel mentioned Polish forces involved in a massacre in Nyzhni Veretski [today's Nyzhni Vorota], which was not impossible in view of Polish incursions into Carpatho-Ukraine. See also Pop, "Carpatho-Ukraine," which mentions "a bloody tragedy at Krasne Pole near the village of Roskosovo just west of Khust" (62).

35. Greenwald, "Eye of Tear," 5. He used the word *Ukrainians* to refer to Carpatho-Ruthenians.

36. Aranka Siegal, *Upon the Head of the Goat: A Childhood in Hungary, 1939–1944* (London: J. M. Dent and Sons, 1981), 5–6.

37. Testimony of Eva Slomovits, USC Shoah Foundation, 24130 (Zarichchya).

38. Testimony of Aharon Rat, USC Shoah Foundation, 32662.

39. Magocsi, *Shaping of a National Identity*, 450n60, mentions estimates of more than four thousand. See also Shandor, *Carpatho-Ukraine in the Twentieth Century*, 223; Shandor adduces a Czech estimate of around five thousand. One letter from late March 1939 describes "Hungarian 'mopping up' patrols." Irving N. Linnell, American Consul General in Prague, to the American Chargé d'Affairs in Berlin, in Kennan, *From Prague After Munich*,

90. On executions in Solotvyno see Shandor, *Carpatho-Ukraine in the Twentieth Century*, 189n25, 204. On execution in Velyky Bychkiv of another group of Carpathian Sich prisoners along with two local Carpatho-Ruthenians see ibid., 204–205. Shandor recounted numerous other cases of killings that occurred in Boroniava, Khust, Nyzhni Veretski, Perechyn, Vynohradovo, Tyachiv, and Volové [today's Mizhhirya], mostly of Carpathian Sich men but also of civilians. He also reported about farmers who had seen many corpses in the Tisza River. See ibid., 221, 228. Shandor relied on accounts of Carpatho-Ruthenians present in the region at the time, and although I was not able to verify all cases or numbers, Jews' testimonies leave no doubt that the Hungarian occupying forces indeed perpetrated such acts.

40. See "Vortrag über die russinische Frage," a speech by Miklós Kozma, 23 May 1939, MOL, K429, cs. 28/3; "A ruszin probléma," 24 April 1939, ibid.; and "Az ukrán kérdés Kárpátalján," 12 Jan. 1941, ibid., cs. 35, 547.

41. "Vortrag über die russinische Frage," 20–25, 28–30. Nothing, of course, stood farther from Ukrainian nationalists than Pan-Slavism. The Hungarian authorities' incorrect perception drew on anxieties that originated in 1849, when Russian army units arrived in the Carpathian region to help quash the Hungarian uprising against Vienna. See Magocsi, *Shaping of a National Identity*, 43–45.

42. Special report by Kozma, then head of the Hungarian News Agency (Magyar Távirati Iroda), 16 Jan. 1939, MOL, K429, cs. 28/4.

43. See "Szovjetoroszországba és egyéb helyekre, Kárpátaljáról történő kiszökésekre adatok" (Data on escapes from Subcarpathia to Soviet Russia and other locations), n.d., probably late 1940, in MOL, K429, cs. 34. See also Paul Robert Magocsi, "Magyars and Carpatho-Rusyns: On the Seventieth Anniversary of the Founding of Czechoslovakia," *Harvard Ukrainian Studies* 14, no. 3/4 (1996): 450.

44. According to Yisrael Rosenfeld, many Jews hung anything containing the Hungarian national colors out of their windows. YVA, O.3/5603, 7. For survivors' testimonies that describe Jews' initial reaction to the Hungarian occupation as "liberation," see, e.g., Rose Gelb, USC Shoah Foundation, 10374 (Drahovo); Aharon Rat, ibid., 32662 (Velyky Bychkiv); and Michael Jackson, ibid., 26142 (Torun').

45. An article in the 19 March 1939 *New York Times* reported that "Hungarian painting crews and workmen were following the occupation army. Workmen were removing public signs in the Slovak and Ukrainian languages and replacing them with signs in Hungarian. Painters were splashing Hungarian colors of red, white and green on highway markers. Trucks brought flags to decorate buildings of occupied cities."

46. MOL, K149-1942-6-24860. The Ukrainian versions of place names in this passage are Khust, Solotvyno, and Svaliava.

47. Ibid., K774-1944.

48. See the decision of the Court of the Head of Staff of the Royal Hungarian Army as Court of Justice, no. H.227/42, Munkács, 22 July 1942, Hajdú-Bihar County Archives, Debrecen, RG VI. 1/a, Fascicle 1, doc. 3914/1943. I thank László Csősz for bringing this court case to my attention.

49. Charles King, *Extreme Politics: Nationalism, Violence, and the End of Eastern Europe* (New York: Oxford University Press, 2010), 74.

50. For the opposite view see Magocsi, "Magyars and Carpatho-Rusyns," 440–441, 450. Magocsi argues that most Carpatho-Ruthenians in Carpatho-Ukraine were loyal to the federated Czecho-Slovak state. Magocsi used data about the number of Carpatho-Ruthenians in the Czechoslovak army formations in the Soviet Union during World War II to demonstrate the presumed loyalty of Carpatho-Ruthenians to Czechoslovakia. Yet the figures he cited and later partly revised (see Paul Robert Magocsi, "Czechoslovak Army Corps," in Magocsi and Pop, *Encyclopedia of Rusyn History and Culture*, 82) are based on sources that exclude the accounts of Jews who had also served in these military units. Their testimonies paint a different picture. For research based on Jews' perspectives see Erich Kulka, *Jews in Svoboda's Army in the Soviet Union: Czechoslovak Jewry's Fight Against the Nazis During World War II* (Lanham, MD: University Press of America, 1987). At any rate both in the case of Jews and in the case of Carpatho-Ruthenians, service in the Czechoslovak forces during World War II stemmed from a variety of motives, not least the wish to escape the daily misery of the Gulag camps, whence many recruits came; the inference that joining the Czechoslovak army at the time expressed primarily loyalty to an idea of a Czechoslovak state calls for, at the very least, research of a significant number of personal accounts by Carpatho-Ruthenians.

51. Subtelny, *Ukraine*, 451.

52. Magocsi, *Shaping of a National Identity*, 91, 93; see also Lajos Horváth, *Hucul Köztársaság, nyugat-ukránok és ideiglenes román megszállás, 1918–1921* (Nyírtelek: Gidófalvy Péter, 2007).

53. See brief biographical information on these people in Magocsi, *Shaping of a National Identity*, 292–294, 309–310.

54. A good example is Voloshyn. He supported the pro-Hungarian option in November 1918, but he quickly came to favor Czechoslovakia. In 1938 he became the leader of Carpatho-Ukraine. See Magocsi, *Shaping of a National Identity*, 321–322.

55. Precisely such considerations, and not grand revolutionary visions, ensured the strength of the Czechoslovak Communist Party in the region during the interwar years. See Zdenek L. Suda, *Zealots and Rebels: A History of the Communist Party of Czechoslovakia* (Stanford, CA: Hoover Institution Press, 1980), 3.

56. See Maria Todorova, "The Trap of Backwardness: Modernity, Temporality, and the Study of Eastern European Nationalism," *Slavic Review* 64, no. 1 (2005): 140–164.

57. This approach, very common in the literature on Carpatho-Ruthenians, marked the policies of both Czech and Hungarian authorities concerning the region. The historian Hugh Seton-Watson, for example, while dismissing Carpatho-Ukraine with a few sentences, wrote of Ukrainian nationalists speaking to "dazed peasants from the mountains, who hardly understood one word in ten." See Hugh Seton-Watson, *Eastern Europe Between the Wars, 1918–1941* (New York: Harper Torchbooks, 1967), 395.

58. See Larry Wolff, *Inventing Eastern Europe: The Map of Civilization on the Mind of the Enlightenment* (Stanford: Stanford University Press, 1994).

59. This question has received short shrift in the existing literature. Magocsi, for instance, has stated that "because of its pronounced anti-Hungarian stance, the Ukrainophile orientation spread rapidly, especially among the younger generation," but no detailed exposition follows. See Magocsi, *Shaping of a National Identity*, 246.

Chapter 4

Chapter 4 is derived in part from my article "Beyond Holocaust Studies: Rethinking the Holocaust in Hungary," *Journal of Genocide Research* 16, no. 1 (2014): 1–23, available online: *www.tandfonline.com/toc/cjgr20/16/1#.VaLIiekVjIU*.

1. Paul Robert Magocsi, *The Shaping of a National Identity: Subcarpathian Rus', 1848–1948* (Cambridge, MA: Harvard University Press, 1978), 247. Even though the strip of land occupied by Hungary in November 1938, following the First Vienna Accord, became an integral part of Hungary, the next two chapters continue to treat it together with the former Carpatho-Ukraine and refer to them as Subcarpathian Rus'. After the annexation of northern Transylvania by Hungary in August 1940, Ugocsa County and Máramaros County were enlarged to their pre–World War I dimensions through the addition of the parts of those counties that had come under Romanian rule between 1919 and 1940. For the administrative division of Kárpátalja into three districts see Mihály Benedek, ed., *A Magyar Királyi Csendőrség Zsebkönyve* (Budapest: A Csendőrségi Lapok Kiadása, 1944), 451–452.

2. According to Eleanor Perényi, daughter-in-law of Baron Perényi, "[Baron Perényi], in a fit of righteous sentimentality on the part of the Prime Minister, who was a friend of his, had been appointed Governor of Ruthenia. He was much too old for all the work, but he had prestige." See Eleanor Perényi, *More Was Lost* (New York: Helen Mark Books, 2001), 246. The memoir was originally published in 1946.

3. Alon Confino, "A World Without Jews: Interpreting the Holocaust," *German History* 27, no. 4 (2009): 531–559. See also Confino's contribution to "Forum: Cultural History and the Holocaust," *German History* 31, no. 1 (2013): 61–85, 65; and Alon Confino, *A World Without Jews: The Nazi Imagination from Persecution to Genocide* (New Haven, CT: Yale University Press, 2014).

4. See Confino's application of his framework to his recent study of the history of Israel/Palestine in 1948: Alon Confino, "Miracles and Snow in Palestine and Israel: Tantura, a History of 1948," *Israel Studies* 17, no. 2 (2012): 25–61.

5. See table 23 in Joseph Rothschild, *East Central Europe Between the Two World Wars* (Seattle: University of Washington Press, 1974), 155.

6. For a summary of the history of that period in Hungary see ibid., 138–157. Rothschild claims that "passionate revisionism was the general—indeed, the virtually universal—response of Hungarian society to Trianon" (157). See also Holly Case, *Between States: The Transylvanian Question and the European Idea During World War II* (Stanford: Stanford University Press, 2009), 66.

7. Donald Bloxham, *The Final Solution: A History* (New York: Oxford University Press, 2009), charts the emergence and consequences of this European process.

8. On the forced and violent transfers of 1.2 million Christians and half a million Muslims, in part following an agreement between Turkey and Greece in 1923, see Mark Mazower, *Dark Continent: Europe's Twentieth Century* (London: Penguin, 1999), 61–62.

9. Krisztián Ungváry, "Deportation, Population Exchange, and Certain Aspects of the Holocaust," in *The Holocaust in Hungary: A European Perspective*, ed. Judit Molnár (Budapest: Balassi Kiadó, 2005), 91–92; Christian Gerlach and Götz Aly, *Das letzte Kapitel: Realpolitik, Ideologie und der Mord an den ungarischen Juden 1944/45* (Stuttgart: Deutsche

Verlags-Anstalt, 2002), 425–429. On the history of Magyar-German relations see Case, *Between States*, 35–39.

10. See Ungváry, "Deportation, Population Exchange," 95–96. On Werth's position regarding Carpatho-Ruthenians see also Loránt Tilkovszky, *Revízió és Nemzetiségpolitika Magyarországon (1938–1941)* (Budapest: Akadémiai Kiadó, 1967), 236–237.

11. Case, *Between States*, 186.

12. On the political consensus in Hungary about "Greater Hungary," which transcended divisions between the Right and the Left, see ibid., 223.

13. See the postcards in Yitzhak Livnat's private collection of Hungarian postcards, which show, for instance, Horthy Square and Horthy Street in Munkács, formerly Masaryk Square and Masaryk Street in interwar Mukačevo. Livnat's collection also includes examples of the new stamps with the word *visszatért*, meaning returned or back.

14. USC Shoah Foundation Institute for Visual History and Education, interview number 21374.

15. Deportáltakat Gondozó Országos Bizottság (National Committee for Attending Deportees: DEGOB), protocols 277 and 279. DEGOB, a Jewish organization founded in Budapest in March 1945 to help survivors, also collected testimonies, which are available anonymously online at www.degob.hu. See also testimony of Sheindy Levi, Yad Vashem Archives (YVA), O.3/6578, 3–4.

16. For the reports and correspondence on this case see Gosudarstvennyi arkhiv Zakarpatskoi oblasti (the State Archives of the Transcarpathian Province: GaZo), Berehovo, fond 185, opis 1, delo 149.

17. For similar cases in Hungarian-occupied northern Transylvania, mostly against Romanians, see Case, *Between States*, 138–140.

18. See a report to the Minister of the Interior (Jan. 1943), citing Decree 10.621/7 res-1939 of the Minister of the Interior (10 June 1939), translated in Kinga Frojimovics, *I Have Been a Stranger in a Strange Land: The Hungarian State and Jewish Refugees in Hungary, 1933–1945* (Jerusalem: Yad Vashem, 2007), 163–164.

19. Kinga Frojimovics, "Who Were They? The Characteristics of the Religious Currents of Hungarian Jewry on the Eve of Its Destruction" (Hebrew), *Yad Vashem Studies* 35, no. 1 (2007): 147–148. See also Yeshayahu A. Jelinek, *The Carpathian Diaspora: The Jews of Subcarpathian Rus' and Mukachevo, 1848–1948* (New York: Columbia University Press, 2007), 234, 257–261.

20. Jolly Zeleny, for example, related that her family's Christian domestic became the owner of her father's shop in Ungvár (Uzhhorod). USC Shoah Foundation, 5890. And Mordechai Hoffman's father trusted non-Jewish acquaintances, who took over his timber business and gave him most of the profits. YVA, O.3/10102, 7.

21. YVA, M.72, JM/19.639, reel 21, folder 534, frame 842.

22. It is instructive that István Bethlen, Hungary's prime minister between 1921 and 1931, opposed the Second Anti-Jewish Law (May 1939) because he feared that ethnic Germans would most likely take control of the economic positions that the law would force Jews to relinquish. He also objected to the idea of a "Jewish constituency" (par. 5 of the proposed law) for general elections, which, he explained, could create a precedent that the German

minority in Hungary could use. See Nathaniel Katzburg, *Hungary and the Jews: Policy and Legislation, 1920–1943* (Ramat Gan: Bar-Ilan University Press, 1981), 123–125. See also Jelinek, *The Carpathian Diaspora*, 259. On the growing political strength and influence of ethnic Germans in Hungary from late 1938 see Randolph L. Braham, *The Politics of Genocide: The Holocaust in Hungary*, 2 vols. (New York: Columbia University Press, 1994), 1:161–164. This issue points to meanings of the anti-Jewish legislation that extended beyond the country's Jewish population. This was neither the first nor the last time that ethnic Germans in Hungary drew the attention of Hungarian leaders in the context of discussions and policies dealing with the ethnonational character of the desired Hungarian state.

23. Katzburg, *Hungary and the Jews*, 114–157. The law proclaimed that "one who himself, or at least one of his parents, or at least two of his grandparents were at the time of the entry into force of the present Law members of the Jewish religious community, or have been such previous to the entry into force of the Law, shall be regarded as a Jew, as shall also descendants of such persons born after the entry into force of the Law." Translated and quoted in ibid., 139.

24. GaZo, fond 94, opis 1, delo 849.

25. Translated and quoted from Deputy Kálmán Bocsáry's introduction of the bill by the government in the Lower House (30 June 1941), in Katzburg, *Hungary and the Jews*, 173. Indeed, the final version of the law, which also forbade extramarital relations, stated explicitly that such contact would involve a Jew and "a decent non-Jewish woman *of Hungarian nationality*" (ibid., 179, emphasis added). Here, too, the law dealt with the boundaries of the ethnonational Magyar community.

26. GaZo, fond 272, opis 1, delo 324.

27. Very few extramarital relations between Jews and Magyars have surfaced in the sources. A notable exception is the relationship between Hedy Weisz, a Jewish woman from Nagyszőllős, and Tibor Aykler, a Magyar from a prominent family in town, recounted in Susan M. Papp, *Outcasts: A Love Story* (Toronto: Dundurn Press, 2009). See also the correspondence in summer 1942 between the investigation department of the Kassa Gendarmerie District, the lord lieutenant (*főispán*) of Ugocsa County, and his subprefect, about the relationship between Gabriella Szántó, a woman who had converted from Judaism to Christianity in 1936 and served in 1942 as a town clerk in Verbőcz (Verbovets'), and László Vásárhelyi, a Magyar and the town's head notary. GaZo, fond 259, opis 2, delo 117. The file contains no documents about the outcome of the investigation.

28. See Katzburg, *Hungary and the Jews*, 191–200.

29. The Public Administration Committee of Bereg County to the Prime Minister, 6 March 1941, GaZo, fond 94, opis 1, delo 3822. The file also includes the decision by the Municipal Committee of Borsod County (18 Dec. 1941) to second the request of Bereg County that, in turn, was supported by the Public Administration Committee of Ungvár (18 Feb. 1942).

30. Eleanor Perényi recounted in her memoir that she and her husband had helped their Jewish neighbor by concluding a deal to buy his property without "exchang[ing] a cent of money." Perényi, *More Was Lost*, 89–93, 229.

31. This law thus demonstrated clearly the assertion of legal scholar Philip Allott: "Law

establishes possible futures for society, in accordance with society's theories, values, and purposes." See Philip Allott, "The Concept of International Law," in *The Role of Law in International Politics: Essays in International Relations and International Law*, ed. Michael Byers (Oxford: Oxford University Press, 2000), 69, quoted and discussed in Jens Meierhenrich, *The Legacies of Law: Long-Run Consequences of Legal Developments in South Africa, 1652–2000* (New York: Cambridge University Press, 2008), 15.

32. Frojimovics, *I Have Been a Stranger*, 58, 73–74, 83–84. See also "News from All over the World by the Jewish Telegraphic Agency, New York," vol. 5, no. 43, 23 Jan. 1939, YVA, M.72, JM/19.640, reel 22, folder 541, frames 1066–1067.

33. On the establishment of the KEOHK in 1931 and its organizational structure see Frojimovics, *I Have Been a Stranger*, 23–33.

34. GaZo, fond 281, opis 1, delo 641.

35. See ibid., with a list (1 April) of forty-one families and altogether a bit more than two hundred people; and see a second, undated list, which includes all seventy-one families, in ibid., fond 45, opis 3, delo 69. On 1 April the Public Notary Office in Radvánc informed the chief constable in Ungvár that thirty-one of the people listed "did not present themselves despite the summons they had received." The file contains four additional summonses that the chief constable issued on 3 April. See ibid., fond 281, opis 1, delo 641. A total of 699 Jews lived in the town in 1930. See *Kárpátalja Településeinek Vallási Adatai (1880–1941)* (Budapest: Központi Statisztikai Hivatal, 2000), 101.

36. See, e.g., the Abraham Spiegel collection, Archives of the United States Holocaust Memorial Museum (USHMM), 2004.546; the two township residence certificates (1 August 1941 and 10 Feb. 1942), signed by a judge and a notary, regarding Lebovics Sándor of Nagydobrony (Velikaya Dobron'), in the Archive of the Memorial Museum of Hungarian-Speaking Jewry (MMHSJ), Safed, Israel, D.8985 and D.8984.

37. MMHSJ, D.8563, emphasis in the original.

38. Magyar Országos Levéltár (National Archives of Hungary, MOL), K249, cs. 38, 1653. This document is quoted in slightly different translations in Frojimovics, *I Have Been a Stranger*, 106; and in Maria Ormos, *Egy magyar médiavezér: Kozma Miklós*, 2 vols. (Budapest: PolgART, 2000), 2:758.

39. Kinga Frojimovics has argued that "the mass expulsion of Ukrainians [i.e., Carpatho-Ruthenians] and gypsies was not carried out in the end." Frojimovics, *I Have Been a Stranger*, 106n186. Ormos wrote more cautiously that "as far as we are concerned, but do not know for certain—Roma and [Carpatho-]Ruthenians did not make the [deportation] list." Ormos, *Egy magyar médiavezér*, 2:758. The analysis in this chapter presents a more complex picture.

40. See Bárdossy's letter (3 July) and Kozma's reply (10 July), in MOL, K249, cs. 38, 1653. On the cultural and educational efforts of Basilian Fathers in Subcarpathian Rus' in spreading Ukrainian orientation and irredentism during the interwar period, see Magocsi, *Shaping of a National Identity*, 183–184, 186, 228. On the expulsion of Basilian Fathers and Basilian Sisters from Ungvár immediately after the Hungarian occupation in November 1938, and the confiscation of their printing shop, see Athanasius B. Pekar, *The History of the Church in Carpathian Rus'* (New York: Columbia University Press, 1992), 141–142, 134–136.

41. The reference is to a designated area along the border with east Galicia, to which the Hungarian authorities paid particular attention. See "Zsidóktól mentesitett határmenti terület déli határának megállapitása és kiutasitandó, avagy internálandó zsidók jegyzéke" (Establishment of the southern boundary of the Jew-free border area and list of Jews to be expelled or interned), Ungvár, 25 July 1941, in YVA, JM/10963, published in English translation in Judit Fejes, "On the History of the Mass Deportations from Carpatho-Ruthenia in 1941," in *The Holocaust in Hungary: Fifty Years Later*, ed. Randolph L. Braham and Attila Pók (New York: Columbia University Press, 1997), 321–326.

42. Quoted in Ormos, *Egy magyar médiavezér*, 2:758.

43. MOL, K149-1941-6-12103, quoted in János Bársony, "The Hungarian Pharrajimos, the Unexplored Territories of the Roma Holocaust and Its Aftereffect," in *The Holocaust in Hungary: A European Perspective*, ed. Judit Molnár (Budapest: Balassi Kiadó, 2005), 406. Árpád Siménfalvy's use of *megtisztitsa* (cleanse) indicates that he agreed with Kozma.

44. Decree 192/res/1941. VIII/b from Sándor Siménfalvy to heads of primary police authorities, titled "Enumeration of Foreigners [Külhonosok] Obliged to Leave the Country," Budapest, 12 July 1941, printed in Gábor Tóth, *"As Eltávolítás Haladéktalanul Végrehajtandó": Deportálások Kárpátalján A Második Világháború Idején* (Ungvár: KMMI-Füzetek, 2009). The decree speaks of "külföldi állampolgárok" (foreign citizens).

45. Fejes, "On the History of the Mass Deportations," 307.

46. Shmuel Hacohen Weingarten, ed., *Memorial Book for the Jewish Community of Nagyszőllős and Its Surroundings* (Hebrew) (private publication, 1976), 180–181.

47. István I. Mócsy, *The Uprooted: Hungarian Refugees and Their Impact on Hungary's Domestic Politics, 1918–1921* (New York: Columbia University Press, 1983).

48. Frojimovics, *I Have Been a Stranger*, 107, 110; Ormos, *Egy magyar médiavezér*, 2:758. Whether the mass deportations of summer 1941 originated with Kozma's plans or designs by authorities in Budapest, and the extent to which the periphery and the core pushed for their implementation, remains unclear. However, that the Hungarian prime minister should sign a letter to Kozma, dated 3 July 1941, with the handwritten words "your true follower," indicates clearly that these men saw eye to eye on such cardinal matters. See MOL, K249, cs. 38, 1653.

49. YVA, O.3/11224, 5–6. The whole family managed to survive together for a few months, evading German mass murder campaigns in east Galicia and hostile Ukrainians, and they eventually managed to slip across the border back into Subcarpathian Rus'. Ibid., 6–10.

50. Frojimovics, *I Have Been a Stranger*, 126, referring to a decree by Sándor Siménfalvy.

51. This is a common assertion raised both in memoirs and subsequently in scholarship, but while such pleas no doubt reached Hungarian leaders, no clear evidence shows that they prompted action on the part of the latter.

52. Klaus-Michael Mallmann, "Der qualitative Sprung im Vernichtungsprozess: Das Massaker von Kamenez-Podolsk Ende August 1941," *Jahrbuch für Antisemitismusforschung* 10 (2001): 243, 249.

53. Giorgio Agamben, *Homo Sacer: Sovereign Power and Bare Life* (Stanford: Stanford University Press, 1998), esp. 126–135.

54. "A Magyar Szent Koronához visszacsatolt felvidéki és visszatért kárpátaljai területek

lakosságának állampolgárságára vonatkozó rendelkezések kiegészitése" (Supplement of the decrees on the citizenship of people living in the returned Subcarpathian areas and the reannexed Felvidék areas of Hungary), YVA, JM/10963. This decree stemmed from Decree 3800/1941 ME on the Hungarian-Slovak citizenship agreement.

55. See, e.g., references to such occurrences in villages in the area of Ósándorfalva (Alexandrovka), in Avraham Fuchs, *I Shall Talk and Testify: The History of the Karpatorus Community of Shandrif* (Hebrew) (Jerusalem: private publication, 2001), 23. Shandrif was the Yiddish name of the town.

56. See lists in MMHSJ, H.472.21756. The Hungarian authorities created these lists during the mass deportations in the spring and early summer of 1944, recording the material possessions and property of Jewish deportees in obsessive detail. In some cases other information—also regarding the 1941 deportations—was recorded as well.

57. Čičarovce in present-day Slovakia.

58. MMHSJ, H.472.21655.

59. Frojimovics, *I Have Been a Stranger*, 115. Concerning the destruction of entire Jewish communities in the summer of 1941, see ibid., 114–115, 121–122.

60. The Yugoslav lands that Hungary occupied in April 1941, as it joined Nazi Germany's attack in the Balkans; these included the Bácska and the Baranya regions.

61. For the violence of the Hungarian army against Romanians in Transylvania see Rogers Brubaker, Margit Feischmidt, Jon Fox, and Liana Grancea, *Nationalist Politics and Everyday Ethnicity in a Transylvanian Town* (Princeton, NJ: Princeton University Press, 2006), 76–80; and Case, *Between States*, 101–102. The quote referring to the Délvidék is a translation of a Hungarian government decision of 28 April 1941, immediately after the Hungarian occupation of the area, stipulating that those groups must leave the country within three days. See Braham, *The Politics of Genocide*, 1:199. Complete unanimity existed between regional and central authorities, as on 25 April a local order used almost identical language. Ungváry, "Deportation, Population Exchange," 97–98. See also Enikő A. Sajti, *Hungarians in the Voivodina, 1918–1947* (New York: Columbia University Press, 2003), 236–237.

62. Sajti, *Hungarians in the Voivodina*, 234–249, 342–402; Ungváry, "Deportation, Population Exchange," 98; Yossef Lewinger, "The Holocaust in the Regions Occupied by Hungary," in *History of the Holocaust: Yugoslavia*, ed. Menachem Shelah (Hebrew) (Jerusalem: Yad Vashem, 1990), 341–368.

63. Homi Bhabha, "Of Mimicry and Man: The Ambivalence of Colonial Discourse," *October* 8 (Spring 1984): 125–133, 127, 132, emphases in text.

64. Imre Kertész, *Fatelessness*, trans. Tim Wilkinson (London: Vintage, 2006), 139, emphasis added. On the autobiographical dimensions of Kertész's work, particularly this novel, see, e.g., Leon I. Yudkin, *Literature in the Wake of the Holocaust* (Paris: Suger Press, 2003), 188–192. See also the insightful reading offered by Ruth Franklin, *A Thousand Darknesses: Lies and Truth in Holocaust Fiction* (New York: Oxford University Press, 2011), 121–140.

65. Naftali Deutsch, *A Holocaust Survivor: In the Footsteps of His Past: A Fascinating Chronicle of a Jewish Boy's Miraculous Survival from Five Concentration Camps* (Hebrew) (Jerusalem: Yad Vashem, 2010), 28. See also Aranka Siegal, *Upon the Head of the Goat: A Childhood in Hungary, 1939–1944* (London: J. M. Dent and Sons, 1981), 7.

66. Report of the Royal Hungarian Border Area Police Captaincy in Ungvár, 9 August 1941, in YVA, JM/10963.

67. Raz Segal, "The Jews of Huszt Between the World Wars and in the Holocaust," *Yalkut Moreshet: Holocaust Documentation and Research* 4 (2006): 92, citing survivors' testimonies and memoir accounts (111n66).

68. See Braham, *The Politics of Genocide*, 1:205–214; Randolph L. Braham, "The Kamenets Podolsk and Délvidék Massacres: Prelude to the Holocaust in Hungary," *Yad Vashem Studies* 9 (1973): 133–156; Mallmann, "Der qualitative Sprung im Vernichtungsprozess"; and, most recently, George Eisen and Tamás Stark, "The 1941 Galician Deportation and the Kamenets-Podolsk Massacre: A Prologue to the Hungarian Holocaust," *Holocaust and Genocide Studies* 27, no. 2 (2013): 207–241.

69. Magocsi, *Shaping of a National Identity*, 249, 452n85. Magocsi relied on a postwar Soviet investigation report from December 1945, according to which 112,500 Jews and 70,895 Carpatho-Ruthenians were deported from the region between 1941 and 1944; 114,982 of them perished in concentration camps. Since the number of Jews—most of whom were indeed murdered in German concentration and death camps—fits reliable estimates, the number of Carpatho-Ruthenians may also be viewed as reliable. But in the latter case "concentration camps" refers in almost all instances to Hungarian internment camps.

70. Vincent Shandor, *Carpatho-Ukraine in the Twentieth Century: A Political and Legal History* (Cambridge, MA: Harvard University Press, 1998), 247.

71. See a report of the Royal Hungarian Border Area Police Captaincy of Ungvár, covering the period from June to September 1942, MOL, K149-1942-6-24860.

72. Magocsi, *Shaping of a National Identity*, 249.

73. See Ágnes Ságvári, "The Holocaust in Carpatho-Ruthenia" (1999), an unpublished summary of events together with lists of relevant archival documents, in www.zsido.hu/tortenelem/holocaust.htm.

74. See the correspondence between the Public Security Department (Közbiztonsági Osztálya) of the Ministry of the Interior and the Ungvár Captaincy of the Hungarian Police, from 21 Feb. 1940 until 20 July 1943 (quote in the letter dated 1 Oct. 1942), in MOL, K149-1943-8-12230.

75. Magocsi, *Shaping of a National Identity*, 248.

76. Quoted in Elaine Rusinko, *Straddling Borders: Literature and Identity in Subcarpathian Rus'* (Toronto: University of Toronto Press, 2003), 413.

77. Magocsi, *Shaping of a National Identity*, 110–114, 248–249, esp. 113–114.

78. The gendarmerie unit of Csap to the Chief Constable of Ungvár, 24 June 1940, GaZo, fond 281, opis 1, delo 630.

79. László Karsai, "Zentrale Aspekte des Völkermordes an den ungarischen Roma," in *Ungarn und der Holocaust: Kollaboration, Rettung und Trauma*, ed. Brigitte Mihok (Berlin: Metropol, 2005), 103–114.

80. Chief Constable of the town of Ungvár to the Subprefect of Ung County, 10 Dec. 1940, GaZo, fond 45, opis 2, delo 257. The subject of this letter is stated as "Solution to the Gypsy question [Cigánykérdés rendezése]."

81. Vel'ké Kapušany in today's Slovakia.

82. Chief Constable of Nagykapos to the Subprefect of Ung County, 10 Dec. 1940, GaZo, fond 45, opis 2, delo 257. See also testimony of Karoly Lendvai from Szentgál, in another part of wartime Hungary, who described "an Arrow Cross guard" who had screamed at him, "Rot, you Jew-Gypsy." See Donald Kenrick and Grattan Puxon, *Gypsies Under the Swastika* (Hatfield: University of Hertfordshire Press, 1995), 104.

83. Resolution of the legal committee of Nyitra-Pozsony County, 27 May 1941, GaZo, fond 45, opis 2, delo 257. The quotes in the Hungarian text: "cigánykérdés általában . . . nem kivánatos elemek."

84. Frojimovics, *I Have Been a Stranger*, 76–77n142.

85. GaZo, fond 185, opis 1, delo 61.

86. Ibid., fond 281, opis 1, delo 630.

87. The gendarmerie unit of Mezőkászony to the Chief Constable of Beregszász, 3 June 1939, ibid., fond 185, opis 1, delo 61.

88. The gendarmerie unit of Ungvár to the Chief Constable of the town, 25 May 1940, ibid., fond 281, opis 1, delo 630.

89. USC Shoah Foundation, 36366. See also testimony of El'sbeta Gabor, ibid., 37402 (Beregszász).

90. USC Shoah Foundation, 5316.

91. Ibid., 43087.

92. See above, p. 72, and reference in note 43 of this chapter.

93. See, e.g., the resolution of the semiannual meeting of the legal committee of Ung County, 16 April 1941, GaZo, fond 45, opis 2, delo 257, and the testimony of Kalman Sabo, whose father was sent to a labor camp in 1943. USC Shoah Foundation, 36366 (Beregszász).

94. See Subprefect of Ugocsa County to the Chief Constable of Nagyszőllős, 9 May 1942, referring to the former's decree of 14 March 1942; see also the report of the Chief Constable of Nagyszőllős to the Subprefect of Ugocsa County, 28 May 1942, and the Chief Constable of Halmi (Halmeu in today's Romania) to the Subprefect of Ugocsa County, 25 May 1942. GaZo, fond 258, opis 1, delo 568.

95. See, e.g., the orders of the Subprefect of Bereg County to the Chief Constables of Vásárosnamény, Munkács, and Beregszász, and to the Mayors of Munkács and Beregszász, 29 June 1942, GaZo, fond 258, opis 1, delo 568 (food tickets); orders of the Chief Constable of Beregszász to all public notaries, 13 Oct. 1942, ibid., fond 576, opis 8, delo 19 (food-ration coupons and curfew). Allegations that Roma ruined and stole crops served as justification for the curfew.

96. Paul A. Hanebrink, *In Defense of Christian Hungary: Religion, Nationalism, and Antisemitism, 1890–1944* (Ithaca, NY: Cornell University Press, 2006), 47–163.

97. Mallmann, "Der qualitative Sprung im Vernichtungsprozess," 243, 249.

98. On the German decision to begin murdering all the Jews in German-occupied Soviet territories and not only Jewish men of military age, see Peter Longerich, *Holocaust: The Nazi Persecution and Murder of the Jews* (New York: Oxford University Press, 2010), chap. 13.

99. On 26 October 1941 a Hungarian-German ministerial committee reached an agreement: Jews who had been deported from Hungary and managed to escape back into the

country, should be interned in Hungary and not deported again. See Kassa Gendarmerie District to Miklós Kozma, 28 Oct. 1941, YVA, JM/10963.

100. Many of the senior officers in the Hungarian army resembled top military commanders of other armies that took active parts in mass violence. Mass killings in German-controlled colonies in southwest Africa in the early twentieth century; in Indonesian-occupied East Timor throughout the last third of the twentieth century; and in the genocide in Guatemala in the early 1980s provide some examples. See chapters by Isabel Hull, John G. Taylor, and Greg Grandin, in *The Specter of Genocide: Mass Murder in Historical Perspective*, ed. Robert Gellately and Ben Kiernan (Cambridge, UK: Cambridge University Press, 2003).

101. Jelinek, *The Carpathian Diaspora*, 269–271; Braham, *The Politics of Genocide*, 1:283–293. Nothing came of these efforts, in part because the relevant authorities in Berlin refused to set their deportation process in motion for only some of the Jews in Hungary.

102. While extremists vociferously raised ideas to deport Jews or imprison them in ghettos and labor camps, the conservative Right never lost sight of the "Jewish Question" in the frame of "Greater Hungary" but preferred to weigh possible steps in light of broader economic, political, and military constraints and developments. See Katzburg, *Hungary and the Jews*, 229.

103. See a report titled "The Jewish Question in Carpathia," submitted to Kozma in October 1940, which also raised the possibility of ghettoization. "A zsidókérdés kárpátáljan," in MOL, K429, cs. 34, 2.d.73.

104. On the German diplomatic pressure on the Hungarian leadership concerning the inclusion of the Jews of Hungary in the "final solution," see Braham, *The Politics of Genocide*, 1:237–257. For a recent account of the evolution of the "final solution" see Longerich, *Holocaust*, esp. part 4.

105. MOL, K150, 1942, I/31-h.

106. Jelinek, *The Carpathian Diaspora*, 261–262.

107. GaZo, fond 144, opis 1, delo 348.

108. Ibid.

109. Translated and reproduced as document 2-3, in Zoltán Vági, László Csősz, and Gábor Kádár, *The Holocaust in Hungary: Evolution of a Genocide* (Lanham, MD: AltaMira Press, in association with the United States Holocaust Memorial Museum, 2013), 31–32, original in Hajdú-Bihar County Archives, Debrecen, RG IV.B. 1406/b., box 284, doc. 16.978/1942.

110. Tamás Majsai, "The Deportation of Jews from Csikszereda and Margit Slachta's Intervention on Their Behalf," in *Studies on the Holocaust in Hungary*, ed. Randolph L. Braham (New York: Columbia University Press, 1990), 113–163. The town's present Romanian name is Miercurea Ciuc.

111. Translated in Majsai, "Deportation of Jews," 147. See also the letter of Lipót Török to Margit Slachta (c. 1942), in ibid., 158–159.

112. Ibid., 149. The Slovak government began to expel Jews into Germans' hands (to the Lublin District and Auschwitz) in March 1942, and by July it had deported fifty-four thousand people, two-thirds of the country's Jewish population. The Slovak and German

authorities deported an additional four thousand Jews to Auschwitz in September and October. See Leni Yahil, *The Holocaust: The Fate of European Jewry, 1932–1945* (New York: Oxford University Press, 1990), 352–354, 401.

113. Majsai, "Deportation of Jews," 161. On continued deportations in 1942 and 1943 see Frojimovics, *I Have Been a Stranger*, 134–135, 140–171.

114. Testimony of Sam Moskowitz, USC Shoah Foundation, 18040. See also the testimony of Aharon Rat, whose mother and two sisters hid in Nagybocskó (Velyky Bychkiv), their hometown, and he and his brother fled to the mountains. USC Shoah Foundation, 32662.

115. After escaping to the mountains from Alsóapsa (Nyzhnya Apsha) during the deportations of summer 1941, returning to his village, and evading a search conducted by Hungarian gendarmes, Menhaem Vayg headed to Budapest. USC Shoah Foundation, 22581. Eliezer Hershkowitz and his two brothers from Keselymezö (Koshel'ovo) moved in 1942 to Budapest, where, "unlike in my hometown, I earned money and I could send some money to my parents in order to help them." YVA, O.3/12846, 14.

116. The discriminatory labor service of Jews in the Hungarian army stemmed from an illegal procedure. On 2 December 1940 the military authorities decided to separate Jews in labor units from non-Jews. This move required an ex post facto executive decree in April 1941, which, in effect, changed the legislation about labor service in paragraphs 87 and 230 of Law 2 of 1939, especially as the latter contained no reference to the segregation of Jews and, indeed, applied to non-Jews as well as Jews. Law 14 (31 July 1942) provided legal legitimacy for the decree. Katzburg, *Hungary and the Jews*, 202–205. Recruitment in Subcarpathian Rus' was often announced via large posters. See, e.g., the "draft announcements" from Perecseny (Perechin), Nov. and Dec. 1942, in GaZo, fond 118, opis 1, delo 648.

117. DEGOB, 183.

118. Gerhard L. Weinberg, *A World at Arms: A Global History of World War II* (New York: Cambridge University Press, 2005), chap. 8, esp. 455–456.

119. Political scientist Stathis Kalyvas's insight about civil wars is helpful here: "It is the convergence of local motives and supralocal imperatives that endows civil war with its particular character and leads to joint violence that straddles the divide between the political and the private, the collective and the individual." See Stathis N. Kalyvas, "The Ontology of 'Political Violence': Action and Identity in Civil Wars," *Perspectives on Politics* 1, no. 3 (2003): 475–494, 487.

120. In March 1943, for example, the commander of Sonderkommando 4a ordered the shooting of all Hungarian Jews encountered by his unit. See Nuremberg Document 3012-PS, in *Judenverfolgung in Ungarn* (Frankfurt am Main: United Restitution Organization, 1959), 140.

121. This man now faced a second phase of lethal hardships, as a new unit in which he served fell into the hands of Arrow Cross men in Sombathely in January 1945. "They lined us up and beat us with everything they could find: clubs, rubber truncheons, and broom sticks. . . . We were [then] set off, of course on foot, to Austria." There he built fortifications until "we were handed over to a Gestapo officer. He was a man-eater. Then we were transported to Mauthausen." A subsequent death march brought him to Gunskirschen, where US forces freed him in May 1945.

122. USC Shoah Foundation, 21374.

123. Ibid., 7144. On the confiscation of vineyards see also DEGOB, 282 (Beregszász).

124. On problems with the supply of food see Ödön Zsegora, parliamentary representative for the Nagybocskó District, to Miklós Kozma, 30 Sept. 1941, MOL, K429, cs. 39. Aranka Siegal, for example, stated that "the half kilo of butter a week the seven of us were entitled to was hardly ever available, and it was almost impossible to get milk or eggs." Siegal, *Upon the Head*, 76. Moshe Zairi from Nagyszőllős stressed that "the negative economic implications of the war hit everyone, not only Jews." YVA, O.3/7667, 11.

125. USC Shoah Foundation, 18040.

126. Hungarian Police Report, Munkács, June 1942, translated in Mária Schmidt, "Provincial Police Reports: New Insights into Hungarian Jewish History, 1941–1944," *Yad Vashem Studies* 19 (1988): 238. On the construction of victims of mass violence as "enemies," see Martin Shaw, *War and Genocide: Organized Killing in Modern Society* (Cambridge, UK: Polity, 2003).

127. USC Shoah Foundation, 5316.

128. See, e.g., the testimony of Menahem Vayg about the painful encounter of his father with gendarmes. USC Shoah Foundation, 22581 (Alsóapsa).

129. See the ten depositions submitted in the investigation conducted by the Central Committee of Liberated Jews in the American Occupied Zone in Germany against Jan Bodko, a Magyar from Huszt, who, as part of his work in the gendarmerie's investigation department in the region, tortured and murdered victims suspected of assisting refugees or to force them to surrender their property and money to him. In one of the depositions Jene Roth stated that Bodko, whom he knew as a client in his barbershop, tortured non-Jews as well as Jews. Fischel Liebermann, who suffered four days of beatings by Bodko in 1941, knew him as a neighbor when they were both adolescents. Sara Einhorn, Julia Katz, and Josef Roth also mentioned that they knew Bodko for many years before the war. Bodko was arrested by US military authorities on 16 October 1947 in the displaced persons camp in Deggendorf, on his way to Venezuela, after survivors identified him. See YVA, M.21.1/231.

130. MMHSJ, A.1474.01.92.

131. USC Shoah Foundation, 13482 (Poroskő [Poroshkovo]).

132. Ibid., 3721.

133. Ibid., 24130 (Zarichchya).

134. Ibid., 47358 (Nagyszőllős).

135. See, e.g., the testimony of Maurice Katz, who recounted the shelter for refugees in the attic of his family's house in Ungvár. USC Shoah Foundation, 6828. In Munkács several young Jews set up the organization "For the Relief of Our People," which provided refugees with food and clothing, found places to hide them in the town temporarily, and arranged for their journey to Budapest. See Raz Segal, *Days of Ruin: The Jews of Munkács During the Holocaust* (Jerusalem: Yad Vashem, 2013), 37. See also Frojimovics, *I Have Been a Stranger*, 139–140, 161–163. The Hungarian authorities uncovered this activity in 1942. See the report of the Royal Hungarian Border Area Police Captaincy of Ungvár (for June until September 1942), which notes the arrest of thirty-nine people allegedly connected to this organization.

MOL, K149-1942-6-24860. See also the descriptions of the organized assistance to refugee Jews in Beregszász, in Siegal, *Upon the Head*, 63–67, 109–111, 113.

136. The unimaginability of genocide bears exploration. Philip Gourevitch observed this phenomenon in the context of the genocide in Rwanda in 1994, commenting that "what fascinates me most in existence [is] the peculiar necessity of imagining what is, in fact, real." See Philip Gourevitch, *We Wish to Inform You That Tomorrow We Will Be Killed with Our Families: Stories from Rwanda* (New York: Farrar, Straus and Giroux, 1998), 7.

137. Confino, "A World Without Jews."

138. Eviatar Zerubavel, "The Social Sound of Silence: Toward a Sociology of Denial," in *Shadows of War: A Social History of Silence in the Twentieth Century*, ed. Efrat Ben-Ze'ev, Ruth Ginio, and Jay Winter (Cambridge, UK: Cambridge University Press, 2010), 32–44.

139. See "Szovjetoroszországba és egyéb helyekre, Karpátaljáról történő kiszökésekre adatok" (Data on escapes from Subcarpathia to Soviet Russia and other locations), n.d., probably late 1940, in MOL, K429, cs. 34. Many survivors mention this movement in their accounts. Zvi Ferber escaped the Hungarian occupation to the Soviet Union in 1939 only to be arrested and deported to a forced labor camp. He eventually managed to join the Czechoslovak army units in the Soviet Union in 1944. See YVA, O.59/17. Esther Beck's brother crossed the border to the Soviet Union in 1940 together with a few other young men. He, too, was arrested and sent to the Gulag. USC Shoah Foundation, 7279 (Repinné). See also testimony of Frank Colb, YVA, O.3/12710, 19 (Bilke [Belki]).

140. The files of the gendarmerie's investigation department in Subcarpathian Rus' tell the story. They are located in GaZo and part of them in MMHSJ. Some of the documents have been published in *For a Better World: Life and Death of User Oszkár Eizikovics*, ed. Eli Netzer (Hebrew) (Kibbutz Dalia: Ma'arechet, 2005). On Borkaniuk, who was executed in Budapest in October 1942, see Magocsi, *Shaping of a National Identity*, 291–292. The report of the Royal Hungarian Border Area Police Captaincy of Ungvár, covering the period between June and September 1942, also mentions the capture of the cell, stating that a court of high-ranking military officers "sentenced 6 persons, among them 3 Jews, to death by hanging, and 137 to prison terms of altogether 877 years and 8 months." MOL, K149-1942-6-24860.

141. In Nagyszőllős, a Soviet agent who parachuted near the town in early 1944, set up a small resistance group among several Jews and non-Jews (Magyars as well as Carpatho-Ruthenians). Their initial activities quickly came to the attention of the Hungarian authorities. Very few survived their subsequent ordeals in captivity. See Weingarten, *Memorial Book*, 131–133, 183.

142. YVA, O.3/8782, 2, 8.

143. Testimony of Aharon Rat, USC Shoah Foundation, 32662.

144. Yitzhak Gershuni, ed., *Tapuach: A Collection of Names and Details on the History of the Jewish Community of Tetsh* (Hebrew) (private publication, 1994), 375.

145. Helen Fein, *Accounting for Genocide: National Responses and Jewish Victimization During the Holocaust* (New York: Free Press, 1979), 314–316.

146. Braham, "Kamenets Podolsk and Délvidék Massacres"; Gerlach and Aly, *Das letzte Kapitel*.

147. Counterfactual analysis offers one way to address this issue. See, e.g., the insightful examination in Julian Jackson, *The Fall of France: The Nazi Invasion of 1940* (New York: Oxford University Press, 2003), chap. 5.

148. Tim Cole's illuminating social history of the Holocaust in Hungary, for example, deals almost exclusively with Hungary within the pre-1938 borders but in the post-March 1944 period. See Tim Cole, *Traces of the Holocaust: Journeying In and Out of the Ghettos* (London: Continuum, 2011).

149. Frojimovics, *I Have Been a Stranger*, 57.

150. See Braham, *The Politics of Genocide*, 1:237–257.

151. A. Dirk Moses, "Raphael Lemkin, Culture, and the Concept of Genocide," in *The Oxford Handbook of Genocide Studies*, ed. Donald Bloxham and A. Dirk Moses (New York: Oxford University Press, 2012), 19–41.

152. Magocsi, *Shaping of a National Identity*, 43–45.

Chapter 5

1. Christian Gerlach and Götz Aly, *Das letzte Kapitel: Realpolitik, Ideologie und der Mord an den ungarischen Juden 1944/45* (Stuttgart: Deutsche Verlags-Anstalt, 2002), 91–114, esp. 98–99, 104–105; György Ránki, "The Germans and the Destruction of Hungarian Jewry," in *The Holocaust in Hungary: Forty Years Later*, ed. Randolph L. Braham and Bela Vago (New York: Columbia University Press, 1985), 83, 86.

Reporting on the political situation in Hungary, Edmund Veesenmayer of the German Foreign Office wrote (10 Dec. 1943): "The Jew is enemy no. 1. These 1.1 million Jews [overestimating the number of Jews in Hungary, which was no more than eight hundred thousand, including Christians whom the state saw as Jews according to the anti-Jewish legislation] are all saboteurs against the Reich.... Tackling the Jewish question thoroughly should be the order of the day for a variety of reasons. Settling this question is a prerequisite for involving Hungary in the Reich's defensive and existential struggle." Translated and reproduced as document 2-17, in Zoltán Vági, László Csősz, and Gábor Kádár, *The Holocaust in Hungary: Evolution of a Genocide* (Lanham, MD: AltaMira Press, in association with the United States Holocaust Memorial Museum, 2013), 68–69, original in Nuremberg Documents NG-5560.

2. On Eichmann, his subordinates, and their role in Hungary see David Cesarani, *Becoming Eichmann: Rethinking the Life, Crimes, and Trial of a "Desk Murderer"* (Cambridge, MA: Da Capo Press, 2007), esp. chap. 6; Hans Safrian, *Eichmann's Men* (New York: Cambridge University Press, 2010), esp. chap. 10; and Randolph L. Braham, *The Politics of Genocide: The Holocaust in Hungary*, 2 vols. (New York: Columbia University Press, 1994), 1:413–417.

3. Roger D. Petersen, *Understanding Ethnic Violence: Fear, Hatred, and Resentment in Twentieth-Century Eastern Europe* (New York: Cambridge University Press, 2002), 62.

4. Sara Ahmed, *The Cultural Politics of Emotions* (New York: Routledge, 2004), 55.

5. Braham, *The Politics of Genocide*, 1:423–425, 430, 434, 438. On Baky and Endre see also Miklós Lackó, *Arrow-Cross Men, National Socialists, 1935–1944* (Budapest: Akadémiai Kiadó, 1969), 16, 36–37.

6. On Ferenczy see Jenő Lévai, *Black Book on the Martyrdom of Hungarian Jewry* (Zurich: Central European Times, 1948), 107–108.

7. Affidavit of Dieter Wisliceny, Bratislava, 11 June 1947, NG-1823, 3, in *The Holocaust: Selected Documents in Eighteen Volumes*, ed. John Mendelsohn, vol. 8, *Deportation of the Jews to the East: Stettin, 1940, to Hungary, 1944* (New York: Garland, 1982), 231–236, 233.

8. Aladár R. Vozáry, *Így történt! 1944. Március 19.–1945. Január 18.* (Budapest: Halász Könyvkiadóvállalat, 1945), 13–14.

9. Shmuel Hacohen Weingarten, ed., *Memorial Book for the Jewish Community of Nagyszőllős and Its Surroundings* (Hebrew) (private publication, 1976), 180. An undated and unsigned memorandum, drafted immediately after the German invasion by a person who knew the local and regional officials quite well and who most likely worked in the office of the region's governor, evaluated some of the senior Hungarian officials in Ung County and recommended whether they should continue to serve or be replaced. Jewish relatives, friends, and connections disqualified a person. Cooperation with the Czech authorities during the interwar years most likely meant removal. Carpatho-Ruthenian origin or an approach considered too positive regarding Carpatho-Ruthenians might prove harmful. Corruption and negligence might also lead to dismissal. Finally, personal power struggles clearly surfaced between the lines, particularly between József Eperjessy, the head of the local branch of the extreme right Party of Hungarian Renewal, and the conservative rightists behind the memorandum. It seems that Eperjessy objected to their preference for Sándor Molnár as lord lieutenant instead of Árpád Siménfalvy, and therefore they accused Eperjessy of pro-Czech leanings in the 1920s and 1930s and of employing a Jew. According to the first paragraph of the document, Siménfalvy's Jewish friends and connections necessitated his replacement. See Magyar Országos Levéltár (National Archives of Hungary: MOL), K774-1944. It is clear that personal rivalry also framed Siménfalvy's case, whose activity in the service of "Greater Hungary," as we saw in the previous chapter, attested to his worldview and commitment to it.

10. See the letter from the German SS Einsatzkommando in Kassa to the Gendarmerie District VIII (Kassa), 1 April 1944, and the minutes of a meeting in Ungvár (2 April) between Colonel Győző Tölgyessy, the commander of the Gendarmerie District VIII (Kassa), and Géza Halász, councilor in the Ministry of the Interior, in MOL, K774-1944. See also László Karsai, "Jewish Deportations in Carpatho-Ruthenia in 1944," *Acta Historica* 101 (1995): 37–49, 39–40.

11. The Jewish council of Ungvár to the office of the mayor of Ungvár, 7 April 1944, Gosudarstvennyi arkhiv Zakarpatskoi oblasti (State Archives of the Transcarpathian Province: GaZo), fond 94, opis 2, delo 2016. The stamp at the bottom of the letter included the German title of the Jewish council: Ältestenrat der Juden. See also the attached document, titled "The Structure and Task Assignment of the Jewish Council," which provides the names of council members (four people), the heads of the six departments (public kitchen, public welfare, council office, registration office, official journal and complaints, and refugee affairs), and the people working in each department.

12. Vozáry, *Így történt!* 14–15; Weingarten, *Memorial Book*, 183; the telegram from Edmund Veesenmayer, now German Plenipotentiary in Hungary, to Karl Ritter, Ambassador

for Special Assignments, German Foreign Office, 3 April 1944, in Randolph L. Braham, *The Destruction of Hungarian Jewry: A Documentary Account* (New York: Pro Arte for the World Federation of Hungarian Jews, 1963), 2:543–544.

13. Braham, *The Politics of Genocide*, 1:577–578.

14. See the Archive of the Memorial Museum of Hungarian-Speaking Jewry (MMHSJ), Safed, Israel, E.7289, H.472.17335.

15. See his letter in Yad Vashem Archives (YVA), O.15H/77.

16. Decree 6163/1944. res. of the Hungarian Ministry of the Interior concerning the concentration of Jews in camps, signed by László Baky, Budapest, 7 April 1944, in Ilona Benoschofsky and Elek Karsai, eds., *Vádirat A Nácizmus Ellen: Dokumentumok a magyarországi zsidóüldözés történetéhez*, vol. 1, *1944 március 19–1944 május 15: A német megszállástól a deportálás megkezdéséig* (Budapest: A Magyar Izraeliták Országos Képviselete Kiadása, 1958), 124–127.

17. Braham, *The Politics of Genocide*, 1:580.

18. Ibid., 581.

19. Ibid., 439, 585, 590.

20. See Decree 162/1944, in MOL, K774-1944; and in GaZo, fond 53, opis 3, delo 7.

21. MMHSJ, H.472.14883.

22. See Veesenmayer to Ritter, telegram, 18 April 1944, NG-5594, in Braham, *The Destruction of Hungarian Jewry,* 2:547–548.

23. Braham, *The Politics of Genocide*, 1:581.

24. See, e.g., the testimonies of Alter Gadish, YVA, O.3/5474, 13; Bella Fleischmann, Moreshet Archive, Givat Haviva, Israel, A.1503, 4; Vozáry, *Így történt!* 13, 29; and testimony in Deportáltakat Gondozó Országos Bizottság (National Committee for Attending Deportees: DEGOB), protocol 123. DEGOB, a Jewish organization founded in Budapest in March 1945 to help survivors, also collected testimonies, which are available anonymously online at *www.degob.hu*. See also Raz Segal, *Days of Ruin: The Jews of Munkács During the Holocaust* (Jerusalem: Yad Vashem, 2013), 76, and sources in 76n7.

25. Braham, *The Politics of Genocide*, 1:613–614. This decree went into effect two days later.

26. See their report in MOL, K774-1944.

27. On the geographic dimensions of the Holocaust, the urban changes brought about by ghettoization, and the perceptions and interventions of non-Jews as it happened, see Tim Cole, *Holocaust City: The Making of a Jewish Ghetto* (New York: Routledge, 2003); and "Debating the Ghetto: Newspapers from Szeged" and "Placing the Ghetto: Maps from Tolna County," chaps. 3 and 4 respectively in Tim Cole, *Traces of the Holocaust: Journeying In and Out of the Ghettos* (London: Continuum, 2011), 41–55, 56–70.

28. See the daily report from Huszt, 3 May, in Kinga Frojimovics and Judit Molnár (eds.), *Makor: Gettómagyarország 1944. A Központi Zsidó Tanács iratai* (Budapest: Magyar Zsidó Levéltár, 2002), 80. These reports resulted from the efforts of the central Jewish council in Budapest to gather information about the conditions of ghettoization across the country. Much of the information most likely came from Jews in the labor battalions of the Hungarian army, who could move around the country with legal permits.

29. See the daily reports from Beregszász, 1 May and 8 May, in Frojimovics and Molnár, *Makor,* 57.

30. Vozáry, *Így történt!* 30.
31. Ibid., 37.On the reduction of the ghetto area in Munkács see also Segal, *Days of Ruin*, 83–84.
32. "Memories of Noah Yakobovich from Ghetto Selish," in Weingarten, *Memorial Book*, 185. Selish was the Yiddish name of the town. See also the testimony of Jean Greenstein, who was arrested and taken to the synagogue (USC Shoah Foundation Institute for Visual History and Education, interview number 3721).
33. Testimony of Eitan Porat, YVA, O.3/9578, 9. See also testimony of Pessia Elberg, ibid., O.3/7750, 10–11.
34. Elaine Scarry, *The Body in Pain: The Making and Unmaking of the World* (New York: Oxford University Press, 1985), 29.
35. Segal, *Days of Ruin*, 84, 86.
36. See the memorandum of the region's ministerial councilor (illegible signature), Ungvár, 17 April 1944, in MOL, K774-1944.
37. See letters from the mayor of Munkács to the notary of Bereg County, 27 April 1944, and the notary of Bereg County to the region's governor, 28 April 1944, in MOL, K774-1944.
38. See the daily report from Ilosva, 25 May 1944, in Frojimovics and Molnár, *Makor*, 81.
39. Naftali Deutsch, *A Holocaust Survivor: In the Footsteps of His Past: A Fascinating Chronicle of a Jewish Boy's Miraculous Survival from Five Concentration Camps* (Hebrew) (Jerusalem: Yad Vashem, 2010), 34–36.
40. USC Shoah Foundation, 18040.
41. See László Ferenczy's report to the Minister of the Interior, 29 May 1944, in MMHSJ, H.000. MUNKA.
42. USC Shoah Foundation, 18040. See also testimony in DEGOB, 1277.
43. S. Y. Gross and Y. Joseph Hacohen, eds., *Maramorosh Book: One Hundred and Sixty Holy Communities in Their Life and Destruction* (Hebrew) (Tel Aviv: Maramorosh House, 1983), 275.
44. See, e.g., testimonies of Ivona Hecht, YVA, O.3/8007, 12; Zuri Gintzler, ibid., O.3/8040, 4; and those in DEGOB, 28, 153, 696.
45. See, e.g., testimonies in DEGOB, 180, 279.
46. Susan M. Papp, *Outcasts: A Love Story* (Toronto: Dundurn Press, 2009), 145.
47. Braham, *The Politics of Genocide*, 1:577–578.
48. MMHSJ, H.472.21625.
49. Ibid., H.472.21669.
50. USC Shoah Foundation, 15110.
51. DEGOB, 1110.
52. Ibid., 174. See also testimony 1217 in ibid.; and the testimony of Mordechai Martin Hoffman, YVA, O.3/10102, 12. On such cruel interrogations in the Sajovitz and Kallus brick factories on the outskirts of Munkács, to which the authorities expelled around twenty thousand Jews from villages and towns in Bereg County, see Segal, *Days of Ruin*, 79–80.
53. Politikatörténeti Intézet Levéltár, Budapest (Archive of the Institute of Political History: PIL), 941/3, 4 ő.e., originally in GaZo, fond 94, opis 6, delo 153. As the first seventeen

names on the list show, by early May the authorities had already begun to seek able non-Jews to take over the businesses.

54. See the list, dated 17 May 1944, in PIL, 941/3, 6 ő.e., originally in GaZo, fond 160, opis 1, delo 4421.

55. See the list, dated 2 June 1944, in PIL, 941/3, 8 ő.e.

56. MMHSJ, H.472.21756.

57. See the report, dated 19 May 1944, in YVA, M.52, 732, originally in GaZo, fond 160, opis 1, delo 4421.

58. On a ransom of one million pengős in Beregszász see the testimonies in DEGOB, 282, 443, and 1091 (the latter mentioned the help of non-Jews in donating to the sum); the testimony of Esther Asael (Greenwald), YVA, O.3/4422, 14; and Aranka Siegal, *Upon the Head of the Goat: A Childhood in Hungary, 1939–1944* (London: J. M. Dent and Sons, 1981), 128–130. On a ransom of one million pengős in Ungvár see the testimony in DEGOB, 1743; and Dov Dinur, *The Holocaust of Subcarpathian Rus' Jews: Uzhorod* (Hebrew) (Jerusalem: Hebrew University of Jerusalem, 1983), 13 (who mentioned the generosity of a Greek Catholic priest).

59. Vozáry, *Így történt!* 14.

60. See Braham, *The Politics of Genocide*, 1:553–556. The definitive study on the mass robbery of Jews in Hungary during World War II is Gábor Kádár and Zoltán Vági, *Self-Financing Genocide: The Gold Train, the Becher Case and the Wealth of Hungarian Jews* (Budapest: Central European University Press, 2004).

61. See testimonies in DEGOB, 153, 696, and 1135. See also Raz Segal, "The Jews of Huszt Between the World Wars and in the Holocaust," *Yalkut Moreshet: Holocaust Documentation and Research* 4 (2006): 101.

62. USC Shoah Foundation, 13482. Another survivor from Ungvár used the exact same word: "It is impossible to describe how awful our departure was. It is also awful to remember it" (DEGOB, 3313).

63. DEGOB, 153. See also, e.g., testimony 1087 in ibid.

64. MMHSJ, H.472.9706, printed in Weingarten, *Memorial Book*, 187–90.

65. On twelve suicide attempts (of which one, Lajosné Fried who jumped from the third floor, proved fatal) at the beginning of the ghettoization process in Ungvár, see the report of the police chief, Thurzó György, to the governor of the region, Vilmos Pál Tomcsányi, 22 April 1944, in MOL, K774-1944. On suicide in Munkács see Vozáry, *Így történt!* 37. On suicide before ghettoization in Mezőkászony (Koson) see Joseph Eden (Einczig), *The Jews of Kaszony, Subcarpathia* (New York: published by the author, 1988), 47. On a case of suicide in the synagogue of Nagybocskó (Velyky Bychkiv), where the Jews waited for three days before their expulsion to the ghetto in Mátészalka, see the testimony of Aharon Rat, USC Shoah Foundation, 32662. And on a person who committed suicide in the ghetto in Beregszász, see the testimony in DEGOB, 282.

66. I thank Tuvia Klein for providing me with copies of the letters in his possession. For the quote see letter number 5, probably from May 1944; see also letters 2 (26 April) and 3 (probably April).

67. Eugen Schoenfeld, *My Reconstructed Life* (Kennesaw, GA: Kennesaw State Univer-

sity Press, 2005), 68–69. Benjamin Kaufman's mother took food with her when her family left Drahovo (Drahovo) for the ghetto in Szeklence: "kosher, not kosher, it mattered only to take some food." See his testimony in YVA, O.3/12500, 17. On the purchase and consumption of pork by Jews in the ghettos in Subcarpathian Rus', see, for instance, the testimony of Aharon Rat, USC Shoah Foundation, 32662.

68. Amos Goldberg, *Trauma in First Person: Diary Writing During the Holocaust* (Hebrew) (Or Yehuda: Kinneret, Zmora-Bitan, Dvir; Beer Sheva: Heksherim Institute, Ben-Gurion University of the Negev, 2012). See also Amos Goldberg, "If This Is a Man: The Image of Man in Autobiographical and Historical Writing During and After the Holocaust," *Yad Vashem Studies* 33 (2005): 381–429.

69. USC Shoah Foundation, 40835.

70. While the category of gender has received attention in the study of the Holocaust in Hungary, we still lack a thorough examination of sexual violence in Hungary during World War II, also concerning the destruction of the Jewish communities. See Tim Cole, "A Gendered Holocaust? The Experience of 'Jewish' Men and Women in Hungary, 1944," in *The Holocaust in Hungary: Sixty Years Later*, ed. Randolph L. Braham and Brewster S. Chamberlin (New York: Columbia University Press, 2006), 43–61.

71. Siegal, *Upon the Head*, 132, 136–137.

72. Testimony of Ahuvah Schechter, YVA, O.3/12248, 9. See also the testimonies of three female survivors in DEGOB, 2824.

73. See Regina Mühlhäuser, "Between 'Racial Awareness' and Fantasies of Potency: Nazi Sexual Politics in the Occupied Territories of the Soviet Union, 1942–1945," in *Brutality and Desire: War and Sexuality in Europe's Twentieth Century*, ed. Dagmar Herzog (Houndmills, Basingstoke: Palgrave Macmillan, 2009), 197–220. See also David Raub Snyder, *Sex Crimes Under the Wehrmacht* (Lincoln: University of Nebraska Press, 2007), 135–148, 190–200.

74. Gross and Hacohen, *Maramorosh Book*, 223. See also the testimony of Abraham Himmel from Alsóverecke (Nyzhni Veretski [today's Nyzhni Vorota]), who recalled a Carpatho-Ruthenian midwife who was close to his family before March 1944 but abused his mother and spit in her face during the deportation of Jews from the town. USC Shoah Foundation, 25962.

75. DEGOB, 1448.

76. David Gur, "Missions of the Zionist Youth Movements in Hungary to the Provincial Cities in 1944," *Yalkut Moreshet: Holocaust Documentation and Research* 2 (2004): 77–85.

77. Menahem Frank and Yehiel Tenne, eds., *Hechalutz Hatzair in Subcarpathian Rus': A Collection* (Hebrew) (Lohamei Haghettaot: Ghetto Fighters' House and Hakibbutz Hameuchad, 1984), 142–144.

78. USC Shoah Foundation, 3721.

79. YVA, O.3/6578, 12–13. On such disbelief in Munkács see Segal, *Days of Ruin*, 99–101, 115–116.

80. See part of the testimony of Zvi Prizant, in *Chust and Vicinity: A Memorial Book of the Community*, ed. Zvi Manshel (Rehovot: Organization of Chust and Vicinity, 2002), 474–478, 477.

81. Ibid., 477.

82. Yehoshua Greenwald, *The Grace of Yehoshua* (Hebrew) (New York: Schlesinger Bros., 1948), part 20, quoted in Avraham Fuchs, *The Holocaust in Rabbinic Sources* (Hebrew) (private publication, 1995), 222.

83. See Helena Rosenfeld's testimony in YVA, M-1/E, 354. See also the testimony of Morris Muller, who used forged identity documents to escape from the ghetto in Huszt to Budapest (USC Shoah Foundation, 5316).

84. Christian Gerlach, "The Decision-Making Process for the Deportation of Hungarian Jews," in *The Holocaust in Hungary: A European Perspective*, ed. Judit Molnár (Budapest: Balassi Kiadó, 2005), 473–481, 476.

85. Christian Gerlach and Götz Aly trace the extended interaction of German and Hungarian authorities in Hungary after March 1944, which brought about the deportations of more than half a million Jews from Hungary in the spring and summer. They posit that this case of genocide followed no predetermined order and evolved in several stages that depended on a dynamic military, political, and economic context. See Gerlach and Aly, *Das letzte Kapitel*, 249–274. László Karsai, by contrast, interprets the evidence in a way that points to a fundamental decision in early April to deport all Jews from Hungary. See László Karsai, "The Last Chapter of the Holocaust," *Yad Vashem Studies* 34 (2006): 293–329. Most recently, Zoltán Vági, László Csősz, and Gábor Kádár argued that four main decisions marked a multiphase process, which led to a final German-Hungarian agreement on 22 April concerning the deportations of all Jews from Hungary. See Vági, Csősz, and Kádár, *The Holocaust in Hungary*, li–lv.

86. See telegram NG-2233 in Braham, *The Destruction of Hungarian Jewry*, 1:356. The specific details in the telegram—numbers and names of territories—pertain only to Hungary's borderland regions, while the ghettoization in Trianon Hungary ("Landesinnern"— the inner lands, without indicating deportation zones, schedules, or numbers of projected deportees) and Budapest appear at the end of the first paragraph more as a desired possibility than a finalized program.

87. See the telegram of Veesenmayer to the German Foreign Office, 11 May 1944, in Braham, *The Destruction of Hungarian Jewry*, 1:373. And see the discussion in Gerlach and Aly, *Das letzte Kapitel*, 259–262.

88. See table 19.1, in Braham, *The Politics of Genocide*, 1:674.

89. Braham, *The Politics of Genocide*, 1:663; Gerlach and Aly, *Das letzte Kapitel*, 251–252.

90. Cesarani has asserted that after Eichmann's office (IVB4 of the RSHA, the Reich Security Main Office) "had lost its monopoly over the 'Jewish Question'" in 1943, he welcomed the opportunity afforded by the German invasion of Hungary: "Eichmann travelled to Hungary with most of his men and personally directed the deportations. For the first time he commanded his own Sonderkommando in the field." See Cesarani, *Becoming Eichmann*, 12–13.

91. See his letters in MOL, K774-1944.

92. See the official memorandum about the meeting, by the chief of the Ungvár police, in YVA, JM/10963, quoted in Karsai, "Jewish Deportations," 45.

93. Braham, *The Politics of Genocide*, 1:585, 667. László Ferenczy's report of 29 May leaves no doubt that he knew exactly what deportations meant, as he commented that

"after the selection in Auschwitz, the Jews will immediately be transported by trains to the various working sites." See Ferenczy's report to the Minister of the Interior, 29 May 1944, in MMHSJ, H.ooo. MUNKA. See also Braham, *The Politics of Genocide*, 1:681, 2:833.

94. According to a report of the Hungarian police in Munkács in late May 1944, "the transportation [from Munkács] started on May 11." See an English translation of part of the report in Mária Schmidt, "Provincial Police Reports: New Insights into Hungarian Jewish History, 1941–1944," *Yad Vashem Studies* 19 (1988): 264. At any rate, since deportation trains passed through Kassa on 14 May, the still common reference to the beginning of deportations from Hungary on 15 May is misleading. See the list in appendix 6 in Braham, *The Politics of Genocide*, 2:1403–1405, and see my discussion in Segal, *Days of Ruin*, 92–93nn60–62.

95. According to the list in appendix 6 in Braham, *The Politics of Genocide*, 2:1403–1405, twenty-eight trains carried around eighty-five thousand Jews from Ungvár (approximately seventeen thousand), Munkács (twenty-nine thousand), Beregszász (ten thousand), Huszt (eleven thousand), Nagyszőllős (ten thousand), Ökörmező (Mizhhirya; three thousand), Aknaszlatina (Solotvyno; thirty-five hundred), and Técső (two thousand). But the Hungarian perpetrators also placed Jews from Subcarpathian Rus' in the ghettos in Szeklence and Mátészalka. Some of the Jews from Rahó (Rakhiv), Nagybocskó, Kőrösmező (Iasynia), Bustyaháza (Bushtyno), Felsőapsa (Verkhnye Vodyane), and from several other small towns and villages in Máramaros County ended up in Mátészalka, and five thousand Jews from the region concentrated in Szeklence were moved there right before deportation. See the daily reports from the ghetto in Mátészalka, 3, 9, and 18 May, in Frojimovics and Molnár, *Makor*, 99–100; and Braham, *The Politics of Genocide*, 1:603 and 623n109.

96. Yeshayahu A. Jelinek, *The Carpathian Diaspora: The Jews of Subcarpathian Rus' and Mukachevo, 1848–1948* (New York: Columbia University Press, 2007), 298, 301, 315.

97. MMHSJ, H.ooo.UNGVA, B.8858. The mayor had turned to residents a month earlier (26 April) to help expunge books written by Jews and other publications deemed "anti-Axis" from schools, libraries, and various associations. See YVA, O.15H/60.

98. See the letter (3 June 1944), in YVA, JM/3759.

99. See the report of the captaincy of the army unit no. VIII, Munkács "K" office, to the army unit no. VIII command, Subcarpathian office of Department no. II, 27 June 1944, in YVA, JM/10963.

100. See the telegram from Veesenmayer to Ritter, 20 July 1944, NG-5613, in Braham, *The Destruction of Hungarian Jewry*, 2:625–627.

101. USC Shoah Foundation, 3721.

102. See the report of the Ungvár captaincy of the police to the lord lieutenant, 9 Oct. 1944, in GaZo, fond 45, opis 3, delo 1952.

103. Vozáry, *Így történt!* 33.

104. See László Ferenczy's report to the Minister of the Interior, 29 May 1944, in MMHSJ, H.ooo. MUNKA.

105. See the list in GaZo, fond 236, opis 1, delo 253.

106. See, e.g., the testimony of Ilona Raffael from Adács, in Donald Kenrick and Grattan Puxon, *Gypsies Under the Swastika* (Hatfield: University of Hertfordshire Press, 1995), 103–104. On the deportations of Roma from Hungary in fall 1944 see Katalin Katz, "Story,

History and Memory: A Case Study of the Roma at the Komarom Camp in Hungary," in *The Roma: A Minority in Europe*, ed. Roni Stauber and Raphael Vago (New York: Central European University Press, 2007), 74–87, who drew on testimonies of survivors. The article focuses on the camp in the fortress at Komárom, a town in northern Hungary on the border with Slovakia, from which Roma men were deported to German concentration and labor camps; women and children who survived in the camp until December 1944 were released. A collection camp operated in Mezőkövesd as well, also in northern Hungary. See Kenrick and Puxon, *Gypsies Under the Swastika*, 102–103.

107. USC Shoah Foundation, 36366.

108. Ibid., 37402.

109. Ibid., 43593.

110. Documents in MOL, K774-1944.

111. For instance, Ungvár was bombed four times in September. See the report of the town's police captaincy to the lord lieutenant, 9 Oct. 1944, in GaZo, fond 45, opis 3, delo 1952.

112. See Amos Rubin, "A Jewish Boy Alone in Munkács," in *Encyclopedia of the Jewish Diaspora*, vol. 7, *Karpatorus*, ed. Yehuda Erez (Hebrew) (Jerusalem: Encyclopedia of the Jewish Diaspora, 1959), 502.

113. Gordon J. Horwitz, *In the Shadow of Death: Living Outside the Gates of Mauthausen* (New York: Free Press, 1990).

114. Victoria J. Barnett, *Bystanders: Conscience and Complicity During the Holocaust* (Westport, CT: Greenwood Press, 1999); Ernesto Verdeja, "Moral Bystanders and Mass Violence," in *New Directions in Genocide Research*, ed. Adam Jones (London: Routledge, 2012), 153–168.

115. Tim Cole, "Writing 'Bystanders' into Holocaust History in More Active Ways: 'Non-Jewish' Engagement with Ghettoization, Hungary 1944," *Holocaust Studies: A Journal of Culture and History* 11, no. 1 (2005): 55–74. See also "Viewing Deportations: Photographs from Körmend, Kőszeg and Balatonfüred," in Tim Cole, *Traces of the Holocaust: Journeying In and Out of the Ghettos* (London: Continuum, 2011), 85–101.

116 . The dearth of research on the responses of Romanians in northern Transylvania and Serbs in the Délvidék to anti-Jewish violence is reflected in two sections (which address only Magyars) on bystanders in Hungary in Vági, Csősz, and Kádár, *The Holocaust in Hungary*, 279–306.

117. See Timothy Snyder, "Collaboration in the Bloodlands," his response in a review forum about his book *Bloodlands*, in *Journal of Genocide Research* 13, no. 3 (2011): 339–352, esp. 339–340.

118. Omer Bartov, "Wartime Lies and Other Testimonies: Jewish-Christian Relations in Buczacz, 1939–1944," *East European Politics and Societies* 25, no. 3 (2011): 7.

119. Joint testimony of eight female survivors, DEGOB, 129.

120. DEGOB, 1284.

121. USC Shoah Foundation, 19818.

122. Ibid., 21141.

123. DEGOB, 2342. See also Segal, *Days of Ruin*, 89–91.

124. On the link between resentment and Schadenfreude see N. T. Feather and Rebecca

Sherman, "Envy, Resentment, Schadenfreude, and Sympathy: Reactions to Deserved and Undeserved Achievement and Subsequent Failure," *Personality and Social Psychology Bulletin* 28, no. 7 (2002): 953–961. On gloating as signifying Schadenfreude see Russell Spears and Colin Wayne Leach, "Intergroup Schadenfreude: Conditions and Consequences," in *The Social Life of Emotions*, ed. Larissa Z. Tiedens and Colin Wayne Leach (Cambridge, UK: Cambridge University Press, 2004), 340. See also Colin Wayne Leach and Russell Spears, "'A Vengefulness of the Impotent': The Pain of In-Group Inferiority and Schadenfreude Toward Successful Out-Groups," *Journal of Personality and Social Psychology* 95, no. 6 (2008): 1383–1396.

125. Anton Weiss-Wendt and Uğur Ümit Üngör, "Collaboration in Genocide: The Ottoman Empire 1915–1916, the German-Occupied Baltic 1941–1944, and Rwanda 1994," *Holocaust and Genocide Studies* 25, no. 3 (2011): 404–437, esp. 426–427. They rely on Petersen, *Understanding Ethnic Violence*.

126. See Daniela Saxer's remarks in "Forum: History of Emotions," *German History* 28, no. 1 (2010): 67–80, 78.

127. See report no. 10.173/1944 VII. res. B.M. of the investigation department of the Hungarian gendarmerie to the head of the Department of Public Security in the Ministry of the Interior, 1 June 1944, about rumors among Carpatho-Ruthenians in Nagyszőllős and its area, according to which the Hungarian authorities would deport Carpatho-Ruthenians after the deportation of Jews. Whether or not such plans existed—most probably not— many Carpatho-Ruthenians found enough reason to fear. See MOL, K774-1944.

128. See testimonies of Samuel Muller, USC Shoah Foundation, 23869, from Alsókálinfalva (Kalyny), about four kilometers south of Dombó along the Teresva River; Herman Schonfeld, ibid., 18759, from Brusztura (Brustury [today's Lopukhiv]), some twenty kilometers north of Dombó.

129. USC Shoah Foundation, 1768.

130. See, e.g., the order (8 June 1944) of the gendarmerie unit of Tiszaújlak to the public notaries in the area to "announce via drumming 2–3 times, also in the native language of the population," that anyone providing shelter, money, food, or any other kind of support to "a partisan or the enemy" risked the death penalty. "Therefore, everybody is obliged to report to the authorities even his relative's contact with the enemy, conversation with partisans or collaboration with them." See GaZo, fond 293, opis 2, delo 36.

131. See, e.g., the testimony of Nicholas J. Babos, USC Shoah Foundation, 40452, a Jew from Budapest who was drafted to a forced labor battalion in the Hungarian army and stationed in Zdeneve, northeast of Ungvár and close to the Polish border, for a few months from late 1943 until after the German invasion. He reported on partisans in that area. See also the testimony of Samuel Moskowitz, ibid., 40835, who fled from his home in Kálnik right before the start of ghettoization. He found shelter with a few non-Jews in and around Kálnik and decided, in late summer 1944, to join partisans in the area, with whom he remained until the Soviet occupation. And see the telegrams of Veesenmayer to Ritter, 30 April and 16 May 1944, NG-5597 and NG-5607, in which he reported the struggle of the Hungarian gendarmerie against several groups of partisans (ranging in strength from two dozens to two hundred people) in the area of Munkács and Beregszász, which might have

received some supplies dropped by Soviet planes. See Braham, *The Destruction of Hungarian Jewry*, 2:562–563, 574–575.

132. A copy of the diary, three notebooks in Hungarian handwriting, is in my possession. Parts of it in English translation are in the Archives of the United States Holocaust Memorial Museum (USHMM), RG 02.008*01, and published as Gabriel Mermall and Norbert J. Yasharoff, *By the Grace of Strangers: Two Boys' Rescue During the Holocaust* (Jerusalem: Yad Vashem; New York: Holocaust Survivors' Memoirs Project, 2006), 87–148. The original diary includes a drawing of the route Ivan Gartner took when smuggling Gabriel and Thomas from the forest to his home.

For other accounts of hiding in the Carpathian Mountains see, e.g., testimony of Dalia Bar-David, YVA, O.3/9453. Her father, an influential doctor in the area of interwar Buština (Bushtyno), close to the Romanian border, where she grew up, managed to secure the help of several Carpatho-Ruthenian acquaintances, among them a Greek Catholic priest, in preparing a bunker in the forest and providing the family with food. After a month, however, locals discovered them, and her father bribed them to keep them from betraying the family. But staying there had become dangerous, and they moved to the attic of a barn, where another Carpatho-Ruthenian kept them for a few months until they continued to a third hiding place, the house of a Carpatho-Ruthenian couple. They stayed there until the Soviet occupation of the region.

Helen Comite was born in 1920 in Vel'ky Rakovec (Velikiy Rakovets), about fifteen kilometers northwest of Chust. Along with her parents, four sisters, and three brothers she fled to the forest after the town's mayor warned them of the impending ghettoization and even offered to take the children and provide them with forged identity papers. The family decided to remain together, however, and they wandered for five weeks in the forest, relying on local inhabitants for food, until they were caught in a barn. She remembered that in the forest they met many other Jews attempting to avoid the deportations. See her testimony in USC Shoah Foundation, 11620.

133. Paul Robert Magocsi, *The Shaping of a National Identity: Subcarpathian Rus', 1848–1948* (Cambridge, MA: Harvard University Press, 1978), 252–256. On the process of the Soviet takeover of Subcarpathian Rus' as witnessed and documented by the Czech representative in the region between October 1944 and January 1945, see František Němec, *The Soviet Seizure of Subcarpathian Ruthenia* (Westport, CT: Hyperion, 1981). See also Ivan Pop, "Transcarpathian Ukraine," in *Encyclopedia of Rusyn History and Culture*, ed. Paul Robert Magocsi and Ivan Pop, rev. and exp. ed. (Toronto: University of Toronto Press, 2005), 496–497, an entry on the "state" of Transcarpathian Ukraine (Zakarpats'ka Ukraïna), the name that the Soviet authorities gave the region between October 1944 and January 1946, when they demoted it in status to an administrative unit—*oblast*—in Soviet Ukraine.

134. On the persecution of the Greek Catholic church in the region, also meant to remove opposition to Soviet designs, see Magocsi, *Shaping of a National Identity*, 265–266; and Athanasius B. Pekar, *The History of the Church in Carpathian Rus'* (New York: Columbia University Press, 1992), 144–161.

135. Miklós Zelei, "Subcarpathia: Bridgehead or No-Man's Land," *Hungarian Quarterly*

38, no. 146 (1997): 38–50, esp. 41–43, 44–45, 46; Paul Robert Magocsi, "The Hungarians in Transcarpathia (Subcarpathian Rus')," *Nationalities Papers* 24, no. 3 (1996): 528. On the general policy against Magyars at the end of and immediately after World War II see Mark Kramer, introduction to *Redrawing Nations: Ethnic Cleansing in East-Central Europe, 1944–1948*, ed. Philipp Ther and Ana Siljak (Lanham, MD: Rowman and Littlefield, 2001), 14–15. On Magyars in the region under Soviet Ukrainian rule see Steven Bela Vardy, "Soviet Nationality Policy in Carpatho-Ukraine since World War II: The Hungarians of Sub-Carpathia," *Hungarian Studies Review* 16, no. 1–2 (1989): 67–91. Svalyava is about thirty kilometers northeast of Mukachevo.

136. Georg Melika, "Die Deportation der Deutschen aus Transkarpatien in den Jahren 1944–1946," *Jahrbuch für Deutsche und Osteuropäische Volkskunde* 38 (1995): 42–64.

137. USC Shoah Foundation, 6828.

138. See the testimony of József Strausz's wife, Margit Strausz, YVA, O.3/3147, 7; and Rubin, "A Jewish Boy Alone in Munkács," 497–502.

139. Testimony of Margit Strausz, YVA, O.3/3147, 8, 12.

140. Thomas Mermall, *Seeds of Grace: A Memoir*, unpublished manuscript, 37. Thomas Mermall shared this manuscript with me in 2009, and he passed away two years later. It has been published only in Spanish (Thomas Mermall was a retired professor of modern Spanish literature and culture): Thomas Mermall, *Semillas de gracia: Memorias de guerra, amor y amistad* (Valencia: Pre-Textos, 2011).

141. This estimate is based on the sources in note 148 below.

142. See the list in YVA, M.52/572 (although pages 15 to 45, which include the list numbers 858 to 1,797, are missing), originally in GaZo, fond 324, opis 1, delo 63; and see examples of application forms for relief, which provided the information (including, for each survivor, the name of the concentration camp where she or he was liberated and her or his tattoo number) to prepare the lists, in YVA, M.52/575 and 576, originally in GaZo, fond 324, opis 1, delo 1 and delo 2, and in PIL, 941/3, 24 ő.e.

For the relief and some Jewish communal activities in the region between fall 1944 and summer 1946, headed by survivors and supported by the JDC, see Mikhail Mitsel, "The Activity of 'The Joint' in Mukachevo in 1944–1945 and the Soviet Attitude Toward It in 1953," *Jews in Russia and Eastern Europe* 1 (2007): 5–39, 12–15.

143. While some Carpatho-Ruthenians managed to gain property and possessions owned by Jews during ghettoization and deportations, the struggle between the Hungarian authorities, the German occupiers, and the Magyar residents of the region left very little for Carpatho-Ruthenians. If we consider, furthermore, that the vast majority of Jews in Subcarpathian Rus' lived in poverty and that the war only made matters worse, it is clear that Carpatho-Ruthenians could not benefit substantially from the persecution and annihilation of their Jewish neighbors. In Bustyaháza, for instance, Magyars took possession of forty-five of the sixty-five apartments and houses previously owned by Jews, while Carpatho-Ruthenians, the majority of the town's population, acquired only twelve. See "Kimutatás: A bustyaházai elhagyott zsidók lakásokban ténylegesen beköltözésről" (Statement: Those who actually moved into the abandoned apartments of the Jews of Bustyaháza), 25 July 1944, PIL, 941/3, 28 ő.e. The town authorities took over eight of the apartments and houses,

turning one into a Hungarian preschool and kindergarten, one into a Carpatho-Ruthenian preschool and kindergarten, and one into a shelter for the poor.

In 1941, besides 994 Jews, 2,099 people of the Greek Catholic (1,258) and Christian Orthodox (841) religions lived in the town, the majority among them Carpatho-Ruthenians; the census recorded only 183 Roman Catholics, mostly Magyars. See *Kárpátalja Településeinek Vallási Adatai (1880–1941)* (Budapest: Központi Statisztikai Hivatal, 2000), 112.

144. See, e.g., testimonies of William Jacoby about his return to Belki, USC Shoah Foundation, 21589; Zvi Shafir on his return to Svalyava, YVA, O.3/11792, 7; Mordechai Berkowitch, *We Shall Remember: The Experiences of a Boy from Subcarpathian Rus' in the Period of the Holocaust* (Hebrew) (private publication, 2002), 136–145, on his return to Neresnytsya.

145. USC Shoah Foundation, 49876. In March 1945 George Zimmermann was transferred from Svalyava to Sanok in Poland, and he spent time in Soviet POW camps until August 1947, when Soviet authorities repatriated him to Hungary. For the fate of Jews in Hungarian labor battalions captured by the Soviet army and treated as POWs see Eugene Duschinsky, "Hungary," in Peter Meyer et al., *The Jews in the Soviet Satellites* (Syracuse, NY: Syracuse University Press, 1953), 393–395. According to very imprecise estimates there were twenty thousand to thirty thousand Jews among the six hundred thousand to seven hundred thousand Hungarian prisoners in the Soviet Union after the war. A large majority of them never returned from the Soviet prison camps. See Tamás Stark, *Hungarian Jews During the Holocaust and After the Second World War, 1939–1949: A Statistical Review* (New York: Columbia University Press, 2000), 45–56.

146. USC Shoah Foundation, 21141.

147. See, e.g., testimony of Katherine Bodek, USC Shoah Foundation, 13482, who decided not to return to her town, Poroshkovo, because of the danger of rape by Soviet soldiers. See also Shmuel Yitzhak Freilich, "The Jews of Subcarpathian Rus' After the World War," in *Encyclopedia of the Jewish Diaspora*, vol. 7, *Karpatorus*, 507–508.

148. Stark, *Hungarian Jews*, 107. Four thousand Jews left for Romania, eight thousand to ten thousand moved to Bohemia and Moravia, one thousand to Slovakia, and a few thousand to Hungary. See Yehuda Bauer, *Flight and Rescue: Bricha* (New York: Random House, 1970), 152–153; Peter Meyer, "Czechoslovakia," in Meyer et al., *Jews in the Soviet Satellites*, 64, 67; Stark, *Hungarian Jews*, 108–109; Erich Kulka, "The Annihilation of Czechoslovak Jewry," in *The Jews of Czechoslovakia: Historical Studies and Surveys*, vol. 3 (Philadelphia: Jewish Publication Society of America, 1984), 319.

149. Mark Levene, *The Crisis of Genocide*, vol. 2, *Annihilation: The European Rimlands, 1939–1953* (Oxford: Oxford University Press, 2013), in particular chaps. 5 and 6, 303–414.

150. This instance of mass violence in the southern border areas of Hungary, conceived as an "emergency measure" against Tito's partisans there, included a speedy process of ghettoization and internment, dispossession, and deportations of almost ten thousand Jews. See Braham, *The Politics of Genocide*, 1:604–605.

151. The numbers are based on table 19.1 in Braham, *The Politics of Genocide*, 1:674. See also Donald Bloxham, *The Final Solution: A Genocide* (New York: Oxford University Press, 2009), 246–249.

Conclusions, Comparisons, Implications

1. On the fate of Jewish sites after World War II see Michael Meng, *Shattered Spaces: Encountering Jewish Ruins in Postwar Germany and Poland* (Cambridge, MA: Harvard University Press, 2011).

2. Jenő Lévai, *Black Book on the Martyrdom of Hungarian Jewry* (Zurich: Central European Times Publication, 1948), 139–140.

3. Randolph L. Braham, *The Politics of Genocide: The Holocaust in Hungary*, 2 vols. (New York: Columbia University Press, 1994); Christian Gerlach and Götz Aly, *Das letzte Kapitel: Realpolitik, Ideologie und der Mord an den ungarischen Juden 1944/45* (Stuttgart: Deutsche Verlags-Anstalt, 2002).

4. On Hungary's occupation of these borderlands during World War II, see note 9 of my introduction.

5. On Transylvania see Rogers Brubaker, Margit Feischmidt, Jon Fox, and Liana Grancea, *Nationalist Politics and Everyday Ethnicity in a Transylvanian Town* (Princeton, NJ: Princeton University Press, 2006), 76–80; Holly Case, "The Holocaust and the Transylvanian Question in the Twentieth Century," in *The Holocaust in Hungary: Sixty Years Later*, ed. Randolph L. Braham and Chamberlain S. Brewster (New York: Columbia University Press, 2006), 17–40. On the Délvidék see Krisztián Ungváry, "Deportation, Population Exchange, and Certain Aspects of the Holocaust," in *The Holocaust in Hungary: A European Perspective*, ed. Judit Molnár (Budapest: Balassi Kiadó, 2005), 97–98; Yossef Lewinger, "The Holocaust in the Regions Occupied by Hungary," in *History of the Holocaust: Yugoslavia*, ed. Menachem Shelah (Hebrew) (Jerusalem: Yad Vashem, 1990), 341–368.

6. Gerlach and Aly, *Das letzte Kapitel*, 425–429, 430–433.

7. The number of Jewish victims of mass murder in Bessarabia and northern Bukovina in the summer of 1941, also killed by local Romanians and Ukrainians, amounted to sixty thousand people. The Romanian authorities initiated extremely violent death marches of another two hundred thousand Jews from those regions to Transnistria, where fewer than fifty thousand remained alive by November 1943. The Romanian occupation regime in Transnistria engaged in the mass murder of 180,000 of the 200,000 local Jews as well. See Jean Ancel, *History of the Holocaust: Romania*, vol. 2 (Hebrew) (Jerusalem: Yad Vashem, 2002), 1347–1403, esp. 1387–1389.

8. Vladimir Solonari, *Purifying the Nation: Population Exchange and Ethnic Cleansing in Nazi-Allied Romania* (Washington, DC: Woodrow Wilson Center Press; Baltimore: Johns Hopkins University Press, 2010). Solonari has also laid out his thesis in two articles: "An Important New Document on the Romanian Policy of Ethnic Cleansing During World War II," *Holocaust and Genocide Studies* 21, no. 2 (2007): 268–297; and "Model Province: Explaining the Holocaust of Bessarabian and Bukovinian Jewry," *Nationalities Papers* 34, no. 4 (2006): 471–500.

On the persecution of Roma in Romania and mass deportations of almost twenty-five thousand Roma—both nomadic and settled—to Transnistria, mostly in June and September of 1942, see M. Benjamin Thorne, "Assimilation, Invisibility, and the Eugenic Turn in the 'Gypsy Question' in Romanian Society, 1938–1943," *Romani Studies* 21, no. 2 (2011): 177–205. See also Marius Turda, "The Nation as Object: Race, Blood, and Biopolitics in

Interwar Romania," *Slavic Review* 66, no. 3 (2007): 413–444, on the combined political and academic efforts (in anthropology and serology) in Romania during the 1920s and 1930s to imagine a Romanian ethnonational collective in bio-political terms.

Previous research on Romania during World War II has treated the fate of Jews under the Antonescu regime without placing it within the broader ethnonational drive of the state. Despite its title, Radu Ioanid's *Holocaust in Romania* deals primarily with the destruction of Jews in Romania, devoting a chapter of twelve pages to the assault against Roma without looking at the connections between the policies against Jews and those that targeted Roma. See Radu Ioanid, *The Holocaust in Romania: The Destruction of Jews and Gypsies Under the Antonescu Regime, 1940–1944* (Chicago: Ivan R. Dee, 2000), 225–237. Dennis Deletant's biography of Antonescu explores the political and military conditions, events, and processes that framed Romanian policies between 1940 and 1944, but his narrative includes only passing comments on the persecution, deportation, and mass murder of Jews as part of Antonescu's broader political vision and its violent implications with regard to other groups. See Dennis Deletant, *Hitler's Forgotten Ally: Ion Antonescu and His Regime, Romania 1940–1944* (New York: Palgrave Macmillan, 2006). Finally, Ronit Fischer has written about the anti-Jewish violence in Romania in the frame of "ethnic cleansing" but not within the broader picture of mass violence in Romania during World War II. See Ronit Fischer, "Between Ethnic Cleansing and Genocide: An Alternative Analysis of the Holocaust of Romanian Jewry," *Yad Vashem Studies* 40 (2012): 157–196.

9. See Deletant, *Hitler's Forgotten Ally*, 205–229; and Ancel, *History of the Holocaust: Romania*, 2:1241–1297.

10. See Solonari, *Purifying the Nation*, chap. 18.

11. Solonari, "An Important New Document," 282–285, 282.

12. Ibid., 287.

13. Alexander Korb, *Im Shatten des Weltkrieges: Massengewalt der Ustaša gegen Serben, Juden und Roma in Kroatien, 1941–1945* (Hamburg: Hamburger Edition, 2013). See also Alexander Korb, "Understanding Ustaša Violence," *Journal of Genocide Research* 12, no. 1–2 (2010): 1–18; Dulić Tomislav, *Utopias of Nation: Local Mass Killings in Bosnia and Herzegovina, 1941–1942* (Uppsala: Uppsala University, 2005); Rory Yeomans, *Visions of Annihilation: The Ustasha Regime and the Cultural Politics of Fascism, 1941–1945* (Pittsburgh: University of Pittsburgh Press, 2013).

14. Menachem Shelah, "Croatia," in Shelah, *History of the Holocaust: Yugoslavia*, 164–226.

15. See Emily Greble Balić, "When Croatia Needed Serbs: Nationalism and Genocide in Sarajevo (1941–1942)," *Slavic Review* 68, no. 1 (2009): 116–138.

16. For summaries of the historical background that runs from the Eastern Crisis (1875–1878), the war between Russia and the Ottoman Empire in 1877 and 1878, through the two Balkan Wars in 1912 and 1913, to World War I and World War II, see Marshall Lee Miller, *Bulgaria During the Second World War* (Stanford: Stanford University Press, 1975), 2–3; Mark Biondich, *The Balkans: Revolution, War, and Political Violence since 1878* (New York: Oxford University Press, 2011), 28–31; Donald Bloxham, *The Final Solution: A Genocide* (New York: Oxford University Press, 2009), 58–61. On the persecution and

mass deportations of both Turkish-speaking and Bulgarian-speaking Muslims in Bulgaria during this history and after World War II until 1989, see Mary C. Neuburger, *The Orient Within: Muslim Minorities and the Negotiation of Nationhood in Modern Bulgaria* (Ithaca, NY: Cornell University Press, 2004).

17. Joseph Rothschild, *East Central Europe Between the Two World Wars* (Seattle: University of Washington Press, 1974), 323–326.

18. Theodora Dragostinova, "Speaking National: Nationalizing the Greeks of Bulgaria, 1900–1939," *Slavic Review* 67, no. 1 (2008): 154–181. For her expanded argument see Theodora Dragostinova, *Between Two Motherlands: Nationality and Emigration Among the Greeks of Bulgaria, 1900–1949* (Ithaca, NY: Cornell University Press, 2011).

19. Miller, *Bulgaria During the Second World War*, 126–130. See also Xanthippi Kotzageorgy-Zymari with Tassos Hadjianastassiou, "Memories of the Bulgarian Occupation of Eastern Macedonia: Three Generations," in *After the War Was Over: Reconstructing the Family, Nation, and State in Greece, 1943–1960*, ed. Mark Mazower (Princeton, NJ: Princeton University Press, 2000), 273–292.

20. Miller, *Bulgaria During the Second World War*, 126–130.

21. Raphael Lemkin, *Axis Rule in Occupied Europe* (Washington, DC: Carnegie Endowment for International Peace, 1944), 188–190, 188 (emphasis added), and see 264 (concerning Bulgarian occupation policies in Macedonia).

22. Kotzageorgy-Zymari with Hadjianastassiou, "Memories of the Bulgarian Occupation," 283–284, 283.

23. See Holly Case, "The Combined Legacies of the 'Jewish Question' and the 'Macedonian Question'," in *Bringing the Dark Past to Light: The Reception of the Holocaust in Postcommunist Europe*, ed. John-Paul Himka and Joanna Beata Michlic (Lincoln: University of Nebraska Press, 2013), 357.

24. Major examples include Frederick Chary, *The Bulgarian Jews and the Final Solution, 1940–1944* (Pittsburgh: University of Pittsburgh Press, 1972); Leni Yahil, *The Holocaust: The Fate of European Jewry, 1932–1945* (New York: Oxford University Press, 1991), 578–587; and Ethan J. Hollander, "The Final Solution in Bulgaria and Romania: A Comparative Perspective," *East European Politics and Societies* 22, no. 2 (2008): 203–248.

25. Holly Case has stated with regard to the accounts about Jews in Bulgaria during World War II that, for the most part, "the deportation of the Jews of Macedonia and Thrace is elided or deemphasized." See Case, "The Combined Legacies," 358, 369. Books that have placed rescue narratives at the heart of discussions on the fate of Jews in Bulgaria during World War II include Tzvetan Todorov, ed., *The Fragility of Goodness: Why Bulgaria's Jews Survived the Holocaust* (Princeton, NJ: Princeton University Press, 2001), a collection of primary sources with an introduction and commentary by the editor; and Michael Bar-Zohar, *Beyond Hitler's Grasp: The Heroic Rescue of Bulgaria's Jews* (Holbrook, MA: Adams Media, 1998).

26. For an analysis that concentrates on the social level rather than on the pressures and interests of the government, see Stephen Reicher et al., "Saving Bulgaria's Jews: An Analysis of Social Identity and the Mobilization of Social Solidarity," *European Journal of Social Psychology* 36, no. 1 (2006): 49–72.

27. On mass robbery see Mary C. Neuburger, *Balkan Smoke: Tobacco and the Making of Modern Bulgaria* (Ithaca, NY: Cornell University Press, 2013), chap. 5, esp. 159; and Yahil, *The Holocaust*, 586.

28. Historians Israel Bartal and Scott Ury explain the matter in the following words:
East European Jewry remains frozen and sacralized in a myth as the ultimate victim of Nazi policies. As such, it is particularly resistant to any attempts to problematize, theorize, or even humanize this past. Often it seems as if one slight adjustment to this paradigm of victimhood would lead to another catastrophe, the destruction of east European Jewry as the symbol of Jewish suffering and the subsequent collapse of the Jewish master narrative of the Holocaust, the twentieth century, and modern Jewish history and society. While these myths draw their strength from the realm of popular culture and the politics of community, where they are particularly well entrenched, they also maintain their influence in the hallowed corridors of academia. As a result, except for several recent studies of early modern Jewry, there are few attempts to create an alternative story of east European Jewry that do not revolve around powerlessness and victimhood and an accompanying Zionist postscript of rebirth and redemption.

See "Between Jews and Their Neighbors: Isolation, Confrontation, and Influence in Eastern Europe," in *Polin: Studies in Polish Jewry*, vol. 24, *Jews and Their Neighbors in Eastern Europe since 1750*, ed. Israel Bartal, Antony Polonsky, and Scott Ury (Oxford: Littman Library for Jewish Civilization, 2012): 3–30, 23.

29. For further discussion see Daniel Blatman, "Holocaust Scholarship: Towards a Post-Uniqueness Era," *Journal of Genocide Research* 17, no. 1 (2015): 21–43.

30. A. Dirk Moses, "Revisiting a Founding Assumption of Genocide Studies," *Genocide Studies and Prevention* 6, no. 3 (2011): 287–300.

31. Adam Jones, *The Scourge of Genocide: Essays and Reflections* (New York: Routledge, 2013).

32. Donald Bloxham and A. Dirk Moses, "Editors' Introduction: Changing Themes in the Study of Genocide," in *The Oxford Handbook of Genocide Studies* (New York: Oxford University Press, 2012), 8, emphasis in the text.

33. For the view of the Holocaust as a number of cases of genocide throughout Europe during World War II see Mark Levene, *The Crisis of Genocide*, vol. 2, *Annihilation: The European Rimlands, 1939–1953* (Oxford: Oxford University Press, 2013).

Selected Bibliography

Primary Sources

Hungary

Magyar Országos Levéltár (National Archives of Hungary), Budapest
Record Group K, especially K490; K429 (Miklós Kozma's files); and K774 (the papers of the Hungarian governors of the region).

Politikatörténeti Intézet Levéltár
(Archive of the Institute of Political History), Budapest
941/3: Ágnes Ságvári collection.

National Széchényi Library, Budapest
Unpublished manuscripts.

Israel

Yad Vashem Archives, Jerusalem
0.3: Testimonies of survivors from Subcarpathian Rus'.
JM/3732; 3734; 3759: Records of the Hungarian authorities concerning anti-Jewish persecution, ghettoization, and deportations in Kárpátalja (Subcarpathian Rus'), 1938–1944.
JM/10963: Papers of the Hungarian governors of Kárpátalja (Subcarpathian Rus'), 1941 and 1944.
M.52/570; 572; 575; 576; 732: Documents from the State Archives of the Transcarpathian Province in Berehovo, Ukraine.
M.72: Files from the Joint Distribution Committee (JDC) Archives in New York (JM/19639—Czechoslovakia; JM/19776—Hungary).
TR.2/JM/2020; 2023; 2026: German documents related to Subcarpathian Rus', 1938–1944.
0.15H/60; 77; 303; 378: Material from archives in Hungary.
0.41/310; 375; 479: Lists of Jews deported from towns and villages in Subcarpathian Rus'.

Archive of the Memorial Museum of Hungarian Speaking Jewry, Safed
H.472.21611 to H.472.21833: Lists pertaining to the mass robbery of Jews in Subcarpathian Rus', 1944.
Personal documents (letters, postcards, songs, etc.).

The following archives contain material on the activity of Zionist movements in Subcarpathian Rus', election campaigns in the region, and survivors' accounts: Central Archives for the History of the Jewish People, Jerusalem; The Central Zionist Archives, Jerusalem; Moreshet Archive, Givat Haviva; National Library of Israel, Hebrew University of Jerusalem; The Pinchas Lavon Institute, Tel Aviv.

Ukraine

Gosudarstvennyi arkhiv Zakarpatskoi oblasti
(State Archives of the Transcarpathian Province), Berehovo
Fonds pertaining to the following offices or places during Hungarian rule in World War II:
45; 281: Office of the Chief Constable of Ung County
67: Office of the Mayor of Beregszász
94: Office of the Mayor of Ungvár
185: Office of the Chief Constable of Beregszász
340: Office of the Chief Constable of the Huszt District
1553: Office of the Mayor of Munkács
47: Ungvár
118: Perecseny
129: Ungvár and Szerednye
144: Aknaszlatina
162; 357: Huszt
236: Nagyrákóci
259: Nagyszőllős
272: Nagyszőllős and Huszt
293: Tiszaújlak
576: Beregszász

United States

JDC (Joint Distribution Committee) Archives,
New York
File III: Hungary, 1914–1918.
Files 126, 127, 186, 192, 196: Czechoslovakia.

Archives of the United States Holocaust Memorial Museum
Memoirs and personal documents.

Private Collections

Meir Frankel, Brooklyn, NY.
Tuvia Klein, Ramat-Gan, Israel.

Yitzhak Livnat, Kiron, Israel.
Paul Robert Magocsi, University of Toronto.

Collections of Survivors' Testimonies and Memoirs

Testimonies from DEGOB (Deportáltakat Gondozó Országos Bizottság/National Committee for Attending Deportees), *www.degob.hu/*.

Memoirs from Prefaces to Rabbinical Literature, accessed through "The History of the Holocaust in Prefaces to Rabbinical Literature," software developed by the Center for Holocaust Research, Jerusalem College.

Testimonies from the Shoah Foundation Institute of Visual History and Education, University of Southern California.

Published Documents

Benoschofsky, Ilona, and Elek Karsai, eds. *Vádirat A Nácizmus Ellen: Dokumentumok a magyarországi zsidóüldözés történetéhez.* Vol. 1, *1944 március 19–1944 május 15: A német megszállástól a deportálás megkezdéséig.* Budapest: A Magyar Izraeliták Országos Képviselete Kiadása, 1958.

Braham, Randolph L. *The Destruction of Hungarian Jewry: A Documentary Account.* 2 vols. New York: Pro Arte for the World Federation of Hungarian Jews, 1963.

Frank, Menahem, and Yehiel Tenne, eds. *Hechalutz Hatzair in Subcarpathian Rus': A Collection* (Hebrew). Lohamei Haghettaot: Ghetto Fighters' House and Hakibbutz Hameuchad, 1984.

Frojimovics, Kinga, and Judit Molnár, eds. *Makor: Gettómagyarország 1944. A Központi Zsidó Tanács iratai.* Budapest: Magyar Zsidó Levéltár, 2002.

Mendelsohn, John, ed. *The Holocaust: Selected Documents in Eighteen Volumes.* Vol. 8. *Deportation of the Jews to the East: Stettin, 1940, to Hungary, 1944.* New York: Garland, 1982.

Netzer, Eli. *For a Better World: Life and Death of User Oszkár Eizikovics* (Hebrew). Kibbutz Dalia: Ma'arechet, 2005.

Communal and Individual Memoirs

Deutsch, Naftali. *A Holocaust Survivor: In the Footsteps of His Past: A Fascinating Chronicle of a Jewish Boy's Miraculous Survival from Five Concentration Camps* (Hebrew). Jerusalem: Yad Vashem, 2010.

Eden (Einczig), Joseph. *The Jews of Kaszony, Subcarpathia.* New York: published by the author, 1988.

Erez, Yehuda, ed. *Encyclopedia of the Jewish Diaspora.* Vol. 7. *Karpatorus* (Hebrew). Jerusalem: Encyclopedia of the Jewish Diaspora, 1959.

Fuchs, Avraham. *I Shall Talk and Testify: The History of the Karpatorus Community of Shandrif* (Hebrew). Jerusalem: private publication, 2001.

Gelb, David. *The History of Our Rabbi* (Hebrew). Mukačevo: Grafia, 1938.

Gerend, László. "Expelled from Our Town." In *The Holocaust in Hungary: An Anthology of Jewish Response,* edited by Andrew Handler, 91–109. Tuscaloosa: University of Alabama Press, 1982.

Gershuni, Yitzhak, ed. *Tapuach: A Collection of Names and Details on the History of the Jewish Community of Tetsh* (Hebrew). Private publication, 1994.
Greenwald, Yekutiel Yehuda. *Thousand Years of Jewish Life in Hungary* (Yiddish). New York: Farish Press, 1945.
Gross, S. Y., and Y. Joseph Hacohen, eds. *Maramorosh Book: One Hundred and Sixty Holy Communities in Their Life and Destruction* (Hebrew). Tel Aviv: Maramorosh House, 1983.
Henderson, Alexander. *Eyewitness in Czecho-Slovakia.* London: George G. Harrap, 1939.
Manshel, Zvi, ed. *The Jewish Community of Khust and Its Environs, Memorial Book* (Hebrew). Rehovot: Organization of the Khust Community and Its Environs, 2000.
Nagy, Milada, ed. *Nagyszőlős: A világ közepe.* Budapest: Aposztróf Kiadó, 2009.
Němec, František. *The Soviet Seizure of Subcarpathian Ruthenia.* Westport, CT: Hyperion, 1981.
Perényi, Eleanor. *More Was Lost.* New York: Helen Mark Books, 2001.
Schoenfeld, Eugen. *My Reconstructed Life.* Kennesaw, GA: Kennesaw State University Press, 2005.
Shandor, Vincent. *Carpatho-Ukraine in the Twentieth Century: A Political and Legal History.* Cambridge, MA: Harvard University Press, 1997.
Siegal, Aranka. *Upon the Head of the Goat: A Childhood in Hungary, 1939–1944.* London: J. M. Dent and Sons, 1981.
Spiegel, Yehuda. "Ungvar." In *Jewish Towns: An Inventory of Jewish Communities Destroyed by the Despots and the Impure in the Last World War.* Part 4. Edited by Y. L. Hacohen Maimon (Hebrew). Jerusalem: Mossad Harav Kook, 1949.
Stefan, Augustin. *From Carpatho-Ruthenia to Carpatho-Ukraine.* New York: Carpathian Star, 1954.
Vozáry, Aladár R. *Így történt! 1944. Március 19.–1945. Január 18.* Budapest: Halász Könyvkiadóvállalat, 1945.
Weingarten, Shmuel Hacohen, ed. *Memorial Book for the Jewish Community of Nagyszőllős and Its Surroundings* (Hebrew). Private publication, 1976.
Zelkovitz, Rose Pinkasovic. *From the Carpathian Mountains to the New Jersey Seashore: A Holocaust Survivor's Memoir.* Edited by Maryann McLoughlin. Galloway, NJ: Holocaust Resource Center, Richard Stockton College of New Jersey, 2004.

Books and Articles

Abramson, Henry. "Collective Memory and Collective Identity: Jews, Rusyns and the Holocaust." *Carpatho-Rusyn American* 17, no. 3 (1994): 4–7.
Agamben, Giorgio. *Homo Sacer: Sovereign Power and Bare Life.* Stanford: Stanford University Press, 1998.
Ahmed, Sara. *The Cultural Politics of Emotions.* New York: Routledge, 2004.
Applegate, Celia. "A Europe of Regions: Reflections on the Historiography of Sub-national Places in Modern Times." *American Historical Review* 104, no. 4 (1999): 1157–1182.
Arendt, Hannah. *The Origins of Totalitarianism.* New York: Harcourt, Brace and World, 1966.
Barnett, Victoria J. *Bystanders: Conscience and Complicity During the Holocaust.* Westport, CT: Greenwood Press, 1999.

Bar-On, Dan. "The Bystander in Relation to the Victim and Perpetrator: Today and During the Holocaust." *Social Justice Research* 14, no. 2 (2001): 125–148.
Baron, Salo W. "Ghetto and Emancipation: Shall We Revise the Traditional View?" *Menorah Journal* 14, no. 6 (1928): 515–526.
Bar-Tal, Daniel, Eran Halperin, and Joseph de Rivera. "Collective Emotions in Conflict Situations: Societal Implications." *Journal of Social Issues* 63, no. 2 (2007): 441–460.
Bartal, Israel, and Scott Ury. "Between Jews and Their Neighbors: Isolation, Confrontation, and Influence in Eastern Europe." In *Polin: Studies in Polish Jewry*. Vol. 24, *Jews and Their Neighbors in Eastern Europe since 1750*, edited by Israel Bartal, Antony Polonsky, and Scott Ury, 3–30. Oxford: Littman Library of Jewish Civilization, 2012.
Bartov, Omer. "Seeking the Roots of Modern Genocide: On the Macro- and Microhistory of Mass Murder." In *The Specter of Genocide: Mass Murder in Historical Perspective*, edited by Robert Gellately and Ben Kiernan, 75–96. Cambridge, UK: Cambridge University Press, 2003.
——— . "Wartime Lies and Other Testimonies: Jewish-Christian Relations in Buczacz, 1939–1944." *East European Politics and Societies* 25, no. 3 (2011): 486–511.
Bartov, Omer, and Eric D. Weitz, eds. *Shatterzone of Empires: Coexistence and Violence in the German, Habsburg, Russian, and Ottoman Borderlands*. Bloomington: Indiana University Press, 2013.
Bauer, Yehuda. *The Death of the Shtetl*. New Haven, CT: Yale University Press, 2009.
——— . *My Brother's Keeper: A History of the American Jewish Joint Distribution Committee, 1929–1939*. Philadelphia: Jewish Publication Society of America, 1974.
——— . *Rethinking the Holocaust*. New Haven, CT: Yale University Press, 2001.
Bergholz, Max. "Sudden Nationhood: The Microdynamics of Intercommunal Relations in Bosnia-Herzegovina After World War II." *American Historical Review* 118, no. 3 (2013): 679–707.
Bhabha, Homi. "Of Mimicry and Man: The Ambivalence of Colonial Discourse." *October* 8 (Spring 1984): 125–133.
Biondich, Mark. *The Balkans: Revolution, War, and Political Violence since 1878*. New York: Oxford University Press, 2011.
Bjork, James E. *Neither German nor Pole: Catholicism and National Indifference in a Central European Borderland*. Ann Arbor: University of Michigan Press, 2008.
Blatman, Daniel. "Holocaust Scholarship: Towards a Post-Uniqueness Era." *Journal of Genocide Research* 17, no. 1 (2015): 21–43.
Bloxham, Donald. *The Final Solution: A Genocide*. New York: Oxford University Press, 2009.
Bloxham, Donald, and A. Dirk Moses. "Editors' Introduction: Changing Themes in the Study of Genocide." In *The Oxford Handbook of Genocide Studies*, 1–17. New York: Oxford University Press, 2012.
Bogatyrëv, Pëtr. *Vampires in the Carpathians: Magical Acts, Rites, and Beliefs in Subcarpathian Rus'*. Translated by Stephen Reynolds and Patricia A. Krafcik. New York: Columbia University Press, 1998.
Bourke, Joanne. *Fear: A Cultural History*. London: Virago, 2005.

Braham, Randolph L. *The Politics of Genocide: The Holocaust in Hungary*. 2 vols. New York: Columbia University Press, 1994.

Braham, Randolph L., and Bela Vago, eds. *The Holocaust in Hungary: Forty Years Later*. New York: Columbia University Press, 1985.

Browning, Christopher R. *Collected Memories: Holocaust History and Postwar Testimony*. Madison: University of Wisconsin Press, 2003.

———. *Remembering Survival: Inside a Nazi Slave-Labor Camp*. New York: Norton, 2010.

Brubaker, Rogers. *Nationalism Reframed: Nationhood and the National Question in the New Europe*. Cambridge, UK: Cambridge University Press, 1996.

Brubaker, Rogers, and Frederick Cooper. "Beyond 'Identity'." *Theory and Society* 29, no. 1 (2000): 1–47.

Brubaker, Rogers, Margit Feischmidt, Jon Fox, and Liana Grancea. *Nationalist Politics and Everyday Ethnicity in a Transylvanian Town*. Princeton, NJ: Princeton University Press, 2006.

Calhoun, Cheshire, and Robert C. Solomon. *What Is an Emotion? Classic Readings in Philosophical Psychology*. Oxford: Oxford University Press, 1984.

Case, Holly. *Between States: The Transylvanian Question and the European Idea During World War II*. Stanford: Stanford University Press, 2009.

Cohen, Nathan. "Between the Pain of Survival and the Joy of Rescue: The History of Two Hungarian Rabbis During and After the Nazi Occupation" (Hebrew). *Dapim: Studies on the Shoah* 20 (2006): 113–124.

Cole, Tim. *Traces of the Holocaust: Journeying In and Out of the Ghettos*. London: Continuum, 2011.

———. "Writing 'Bystanders' into Holocaust History in More Active Ways: 'Non-Jewish' Engagement with Ghettoization, Hungary 1944." *Holocaust Studies: A Journal of Culture and History* 11, no. 1 (2005): 55–74.

Confino, Alon. "Why Did the Nazis Burn the Hebrew Bible? Nazi Germany, Representations of the Past, and the Holocaust." *Journal of Modern History* 84, no. 2 (2012): 369–400.

———. "A World Without Jews: Interpreting the Holocaust." *German History* 27, no. 4 (2009): 531–559.

———. *A World Without Jews: The Nazi Imagination from Persecution to Genocide*. New Haven, CT: Yale University Press, 2014.

Crowe, David M. *A History of the Gypsies of Eastern Europe and Russia*. New York: St. Martin's Griffin, 1996.

de Swaan, Abram. "Widening Circles of Disidentification: On the Psycho- and Sociogenesis of the Distant Hatred of Strangers—Reflections on Rwanda." *Theory, Culture and Society* 14, no. 2 (1997): 105–122.

Dicker, Herman. *Piety and Perseverance: Jews from the Carpathian Mountains*. New York: Sepher-Hermon Press, 1981.

Dinur, Dov. *Chapters in the History of Subcarpathian Rus' Jewry* (Hebrew). Jerusalem: Hebrew University, 1983.

———. *The Holocaust of Subcarpathian Rus' Jews: Uzhorod* (Hebrew). Jerusalem: Hebrew University, 1983.

Don, Yehuda, and George Magos. "The Demographic Development of Hungarian Jewry." *Jewish Social Studies* 45, no. 3–4 (1983): 189–216.

Dragostinova, Theodora. *Between Two Motherlands: Nationality and Emigration Among the Greeks of Bulgaria, 1900–1949*. Ithaca, NY: Cornell University Press, 2011.

———. "Speaking National: Nationalizing the Greeks of Bulgaria, 1900–1939." *Slavic Review* 67, no. 1 (2008): 154–181.

Dwork, Debórah. *Children with a Star: Jewish Youth in Nazi Europe*. New Haven, CT: Yale University Press, 1991.

Dwork, Debórah, and Robert Jan van Pelt. *Holocaust: A History*. New York: Norton, 2002.

Eisen, George, and Tamás Stark. "The 1941 Galician Deportation and the Kamenets-Podolsk Massacre: A Prologue to the Hungarian Holocaust." *Holocaust and Genocide Studies* 27, no. 2 (2013): 207–241.

Engel, David. "Away from a Definition of Antisemitism: An Essay in the Semantics of Historical Description." In *Rethinking European Jewish History*, edited by Jeremy Cohen and Moshe Rosman, 30–53. Oxford: Littman Library of Jewish Civilization, 2009.

———. *Historians of the Jews and the Holocaust*. Stanford: Stanford University Press, 2010.

Erez, Zvi. "The Beginning of the Slope in Hungary: The Deportations from Subcarpathian Rus' in 1941" (Hebrew). *Yalkut Moreshet: Holocaust Documentation and Research* 50 (1991): 159–173.

Farbstein, Esther. "Rabbinical Introductions as Historical Texts of the Holocaust: The Rabbi, the Boy, and the Refugees in Budapest, 1944" (Hebrew). *Dapim: Studies on the Shoah* 20 (2006): 81–111.

Fein, Helen. *Accounting for Genocide: National Responses and Jewish Victimization During the Holocaust*. New York: Free Press, 1979.

Fejes, Judit. "On the History of the Mass Deportations from Carpatho-Ruthenia in 1941." In *The Holocaust in Hungary: Fifty Years Later*, edited by Randolph L. Braham and Attila Pók, 305–328. New York: Columbia University Press, 1997.

Friedländer, Saul. *Nazi Germany and the Jews, 1939–1945: The Years of Extermination*. New York: HarperCollins, 2007.

———. *Nazi Germany and the Jews*. Vol. 1. *The Years of Persecution, 1933–1939*. New York: Harper Perennial, 1998.

Frojimovics, Kinga. *I Have Been a Stranger in a Strange Land: The Hungarian State and Jewish Refugees in Hungary, 1933–1945*. Jerusalem: Yad Vashem, 2007.

Gellately, Robert, and Ben Kiernan, eds. *The Specter of Genocide: Mass Murder in Historical Perspective*. Cambridge, UK: Cambridge University Press, 2003.

Gerlach, Christian, and Götz Aly. *Das letzte Kapitel: Realpolitik, Ideologie und der Mord an den ungarischen Juden, 1944/45*. Stuttgart: Deutsche Verlags-Anstalt, 2002.

Goldberg, Amos. *Trauma in First Person: Diary Writing During the Holocaust* (Hebrew). Or Yehuda: Kinneret, Zmora-Bitan, Dvir; Beer Sheva: Heksherim Institute, Ben-Gurion University of the Negev, 2012.

Gur, David. "Missions of the Zionist Youth Movements in Hungary to the Provincial Cities in 1944." *Yalkut Moreshet: Holocaust Documentation and Research* 2 (2004): 77–85.

Hanebrink, Paul A. *In Defense of Christian Hungary: Religion, Nationalism, and Antisemitism, 1890–1944*. Ithaca, NY: Cornell University Press, 2006.
Heimann, Mary. *Czechoslovakia: The State That Failed*. New Haven, CT: Yale University Press, 2007.
Hilberg, Raul. *The Destruction of European Jews*. New Haven, CT: Yale University Press, 2003.
———. *Perpetrators, Victims, Bystanders: The Jewish Catastrophe, 1933–1945*. New York: HarperCollins, 1992.
Himka, John-Paul. *Last Judgment Iconography in the Carpathians*. Toronto: University of Toronto Press, 2009.
Jelinek, Yeshayahu A. *The Carpathian Diaspora: The Jews of Subcarpathian Rus' and Mukachevo, 1848–1948*. New York: Columbia University Press, 2007.
The Jews of Czechoslovakia: Historical Studies and Surveys. 3 vols. Philadelphia: Jewish Publication Society of America, 1968, 1971, 1984.
Kádár, Gábor, and Zoltán Vági. *Self-Financing Genocide: The Gold Train, the Becher Case and the Wealth of Hungarian Jews*. Budapest: Central European University Press, 2004.
Karsai, László. "Jewish Deportations in Carpatho-Ruthenia in 1944." *Acta Historica* 101 (1995): 37–49.
Katzburg, Nathaniel. *Hungary and the Jews: Policy and Legislation, 1920–1943*. Ramat Gan: Bar-Ilan University Press, 1981.
Kerner, Robert J., ed. *Czechoslovakia: Twenty Years of Independence*. Berkeley: University of California Press, 1940.
King, Charles. "The Micropolitics of Social Violence." In *Extreme Politics: Nationalism, Violence, and the End of Eastern Europe*, 55–76. New York: Oxford University Press, 2010.
Kopstein, Jeffrey S., and Jason Wittenberg. "Beyond Dictatorship and Democracy: Rethinking National Minority Inclusion and Regime Type in Interwar Eastern Europe." *Comparative Political Studies* 43, no. 8/9 (2010): 1089–1118.
Korb, Alexander. "Understanding Ustaša Violence." *Journal of Genocide Research* 12, no. 1–2 (2010): 1–18.
Kramer, Mark. Introduction to *Redrawing Nations: Ethnic Cleansing in East-Central Europe, 1944–1948*," edited by Philipp Ther and Ana Siljak, 1–41. Lanham, MD: Rowman and Littlefield, 2001.
Krofta, Kamil. "Ruthenes, Czechs and Slovaks" (Parts 1 and 2). *Slavonic and East European Review* 13 (1934–1935): 363–371; 611–626.
Lévai, Jenő. *Black Book on the Martyrdom of Hungarian Jewry*. Zurich: Central European Times Publication, 1948.
Levene, Mark. *The Crisis of Genocide*. Vol. 1, *Devastation: The European Rimlands, 1912–1938*. Oxford: Oxford University Press, 2013.
———. *The Crisis of Genocide*. Vol. 2, *Annihilation: The European Rimlands, 1938–1953*. Oxford: Oxford University Press, 2013.
Lupovitch, Howard N. *Jews at the Crossroads: Tradition and Accommodation During the Golden Age of the Hungarian Nobility, 1729–1878*. New York: Central European University Press, 2007.

Lutz, Catherine, and Geoffrey M. White. "The Anthropology of Emotions." *Annual Review of Anthropology* 15 (1986): 405–436.

Macartney, C. A. *October Fifteenth: A History of Modern Hungary, 1929–1945*. Edinburgh: Edinburgh University Press, 1961.

———. "Ruthenia." In *Hungary and Her Successors: The Treaty of Trianon and Its Consequences, 1919–1937*, 200–250. London: Oxford University Press, 1937.

Mackie, Diane M., and Eliot R. Smith, eds. *From Prejudice to Intergroup Emotions: Differentiated Reactions to Social Groups*. New York: Psychology Press, 2003.

Magocsi, Paul Robert. *Historical Atlas of Central Europe*. Seattle: University of Washington Press, 2002.

———. "The Political Activity of Rusyn-American Immigrants in 1918." *East European Quarterly* 10, no. 3 (1976): 347–365.

———. *The Shaping of a National Identity: Subcarpathian Rus', 1848–1948*. Cambridge, MA: Harvard University Press, 1978.

Magocsi, Paul Robert, and Ivan Pop, eds. *Encyclopedia of Rusyn History and Culture*. Rev. and exp. ed. Toronto: University of Toronto Press, 2005.

Majsai, Tamás. "The Deportation of Jews from Csikszereda and Margit Slachta's Intervention on Their Behalf." In *Studies on the Holocaust in Hungary*, edited by Randolph L. Braham, 113–163. New York: Columbia University Press, 1990.

Mallmann, Klaus-Michael. "Der qualitative Sprung im Vernichtungsprozess: Das Massaker von Kamenez-Podolsk Ende August 1941." *Jahrbuch für Antisemitismusforschung* 10 (2001): 239–264.

Mamatey, Victor S., and Radomír Luža, eds. *A History of the Czechoslovak Republic, 1918–1948*. Princeton, NJ: Princeton University Press, 1973.

Marushiakova, Elena, and Vesselin Popov. "The Gypsy Court in Eastern Europe." *Romani Studies* 17, no. 1 (2007): 67–101.

Mazower, Mark. *Hitler's Empire: Nazi Rule in Occupied Europe*. London: Allen Lane, 2008.

———. "Violence and the State in the Twentieth Century." *American Historical Review* 107, no. 4 (2002): 1158–1178.

Mendelsohn, Ezra. *The Jews of East Central Europe Between the World Wars*. Bloomington: Indian University Press, 1983.

Molnár, Judit, ed. *The Holocaust in Hungary: A European Perspective*. Budapest: Balassi Kiadó, 2005.

———. "Two Cities, Two Policies, One Outcome: The De-Judaization of Pécs and Szeged in 1944." *Yad Vashem Studies* 32 (2004): 97–12.

Moses, A. Dirk. "Conceptual Blockages and Definitional Dilemmas in the 'Racial Century': Genocides of Indigenous People and the Holocaust." *Patterns of Prejudice* 36, no. 4 (2002): 7–36.

———, ed. *Empire, Colony, Genocide: Conquest, Occupation, and Subaltern Resistance in World History*. New York: Berghahn, 2008.

———. "Redemptive Antisemitism and the Imperialist Imaginary." In *Years of Persecution, Years of Extermination: Saul Friedländer and the Future of Holocaust Studies*, edited by Christian Wiese and Paul Betts, 233–254. London: Continuum, 2010.

———. "Revisiting a Founding Assumption of Genocide Studies." *Genocide Studies and Prevention* 6, no. 3 (2011): 287–300.
Nadler, Alan L. "The War on Modernity of R. Hayim Elazar Shapira of Munkacs." *Studia Judaica* 3 (1994): 91–123.
Newman, Leonard S., and Ralph Erber, eds. *Understanding Genocide: The Social Psychology of the Holocaust*. New York: Oxford University Press, 2002.
Olbracht, Ivan. *Nikola the Outlaw*. Translated by Marie K. Holeček. Evanston, IL: Northwestern University Press, 2001.
Ormos, Maria. *Egy magyar médiavezér: Kozma Miklós*. 2 vols. Budapest: PolgART, 2000.
Papp, Susan M. *Outcasts: A Love Story*. Toronto: Dundurn Press, 2009.
Patai, Raphael. *The Jews of Hungary: History, Culture, Psychology*. Detroit: Wayne State University Press, 1996.
Pekar, Athanasius B. *The History of the Church in Carpathian Rus'*. New York: Columbia University Press, 1992.
Petersen, Roger D. *Understanding Ethnic Violence: Fear, Hatred, and Resentment in Twentieth-Century Eastern Europe*. Cambridge, UK: Cambridge University Press, 2002.
Ravitzky, Aviezer. *Messianism, Zionism, and Jewish Religious Radicalism* (Hebrew). Tel Aviv: Am Oved, 2006.
Rosen, Ilana. "Hasidism Versus Zionism as Remembered by Carpatho-Russian Jews Between the Two World Wars." In *Jewishness: Expression, Identity, and Representation*, vol. 1, edited by Simon J. Bronner, 213–238. Oxford: Littman Library of Jewish Civilization, 2008.
———. *"In Auschwitz We Blew the Shofar": Carpatho-Russian Jews Remember the Holocaust* (Hebrew). Jerusalem: Yad Vashem and the Avraham Harman Institute of Contemporary Jewry at the Hebrew University, 2004.
Rosenwein, Barbara H. "Worrying About Emotions in History." *American Historical Review* 107, no. 3 (2002): 821–845.
Rothkirchen, Livia. "Deep-Rooted yet Alien: Some Aspects of the History of the Jews in Subcarpathian Ruthenia." *Yad Vashem Studies* 12 (1977): 147–191.
Rothschild, Joseph. *East Central Europe Between the Two World Wars*. Seattle: University of Washington Press, 1974.
Rusinko, Elaine. *Straddling Borders: Literature and Identity in Subcarpathian Rus'*. Toronto: University of Toronto Press, 2003.
Sajti, Enikő A. *Hungarians in the Voivodina, 1918–1947*. New York: Columbia University Press, 2003.
Schmidt, Mária. "Provincial Police Reports: New Insights into Hungarian Jewish History, 1941–1944." *Yad Vashem Studies* 19 (1988): 233–267.
Schmidt-Hartmann, Eva. "Tschechoslowakei." In *Dimension des Völkermords: Die Zahl der jüdischen Opfer des Nationalsozialismus*, edited by Wolfgang Benz, 353–379. München: R. Oldenburg, 1991.
Segal, Raz. "Becoming Bystanders: Carpatho-Ruthenians, Jews, and the Politics of Narcissism in Subcarpathian Rus'." *Holocaust Studies: A Journal of Culture and History* 16, no. 1–2 (2010): 129–156.

———. "Beyond Holocaust Studies: Rethinking the Holocaust in Hungary." *Journal of Genocide Research* 16, no. 1 (2014): 1–23.

———. *Days of Ruin: The Jews of Munkács During the Holocaust*. Jerusalem: Yad Vashem, 2013.

———. "Imported Violence: Carpatho-Ruthenians and Jews in Carpatho-Ukraine, October 1938–March 1939." In *Polin: Studies in Polish Jewry*. Vol. 26, *Jews and Ukrainians*, edited by Yohanan Petrovsky-Shtern and Antony Polonsky, 313–336. Oxford: Littman Library of Jewish Civilization, 2014.

———. "The Jews of Huszt Between the World Wars and in the Holocaust." *Yalkut Moreshet: Holocaust Documentation and Research* 4 (2006): 80–119.

Shumsky, Dimitry. *Between Prague and Jerusalem: The Idea of a Binational State in Palestine* (Hebrew). Jerusalem: Zalman Shazar Center and Leo Baeck Institute, 2010.

Silber, Michael K. "The Emergence of Ultra-Orthodoxy: The Invention of a Tradition." In *The Uses of Tradition: Jewish Continuity in the Modern Era*, edited by Jack Wertheimer, 23–84. New York: Jewish Theological Seminary of America, 1992.

———, ed. *Jews in the Hungarian Economy, 1760–1945*. Jerusalem: Magnes Press of the Hebrew University, 1992.

Sláma, Jiří. "Die Parlamentswahlen im Jahre 1935 in Karpatorussland." *Bohemia* 29 (1988): 34–49.

Snyder, Timothy. *Bloodlands: Europe Between Hitler and Stalin*. New York: Basic Books, 2010.

Solonari, Vladimir. "An Important New Document on the Romanian Policy of Ethnic Cleansing During World War II." *Holocaust and Genocide Studies* 21, no. 2 (2007): 268–297.

———. *Purifying the Nation: Population Exchange and Ethnic Cleansing in Nazi-Allied Romania*. Washington, DC: Woodrow Wilson Center Press; Baltimore: Johns Hopkins University Press, 2010.

Stark, Tamás. *Hungarian Jews During the Holocaust and After the Second World War, 1939–1949: A Statistical Review*. New York: Columbia University Press, 2000.

Staub, Ervin. *The Roots of Evil: The Origins of Genocide and Other Group Violence*. New York: Cambridge University Press, 1989.

Stearns, Peter N., and Carol Z. Stearns. "Emotionology: Clarifying the History of Emotions and Emotional Standards." *American Historical Review* 90, no. 4 (1985): 813–836.

Stone, Dan. *Histories of the Holocaust*. New York: Oxford University Press, 2010.

Suda, Zdenek L. *Zealots and Rebels: A History of the Communist Party of Czechoslovakia*. Stanford, CA: Hoover Institution Press, 1980.

Thorne, M. Benjamin. "Assimilation, Invisibility, and the Eugenic Turn in the 'Gypsy Question' in Romanian Society, 1938–1943." *Romani Studies* 21, no. 2 (2011): 177–205.

Tiedens, Larissa Z., and Colin Wayne Leach, eds. *The Social Life of Emotions*. Cambridge, UK: Cambridge University Press, 2004.

Tilkovszky, Loránt. *Revízió és Nemzetiségpolitika Magyarországon (1938–1941)*. Budapest: Akadémiai Kiadó, 1967.

Todorova, Maria. "The Trap of Backwardness: Modernity, Temporality, and the Study of Eastern European Nationalism." *Slavic Review* 64, no. 1 (2005): 140–164.

Tunstall, Graydon A. *Blood on the Snow: The Carpathian Winter War of 1915*. Lawrence: University Press of Kansas, 2011.

Vági, Zoltán, László Csősz, and Gábor Kádár. *The Holocaust in Hungary: Evolution of a Genocide*. Lanham, MD: AltaMira Press, in association with the United States Holocaust Memorial Museum, 2013.

Vago, Bela, and George L. Mosse, eds. *Jews and Non-Jews in Eastern Europe, 1918–1945*. Jerusalem: Israel Universities Press, 1974.

Varga, László. "Ungarn." In *Dimension des Völkermords: Die Zahl der jüdischen Opfer des Nationalsozialismus*, edited by Wolfgang Benz, 331–351. München: R. Oldenburg, 1991.

Verdeja, Ernesto. "Moral Bystanders and Mass Violence." In *New Directions in Genocide Research*, edited by Adam Jones, 153–168. New York: Routledge, 2012.

Vološin, Agustin. "Carpathian Ruthenia." *Slavonic and East European Review* 13 (1934–1935): 372–378.

Wolff, Larry. *Inventing Eastern Europe: The Map of Civilization on the Mind of the Enlightenment*. Stanford: Stanford University Press, 1994.

Yahil, Leni. *The Holocaust: The Fate of European Jewry*. Oxford: Oxford University Press, 1990.

Zahra, Tara. *Kidnapped Souls: National Indifference and the Battle for Children in the Bohemian Lands, 1900–1948*. Ithaca, NY: Cornell University Press, 2008.

Index

Primary entries for towns and villages in Subcarpathian Rus' appear in present-day forms in Ukrainian. Hungarian and Czech forms refer readers to present-day Ukrainian usage.

Agrarian Party (Czechoslovakia), 37, 39–40, 43, 68, 150n56
Agriculture, 24, 35, 41, 69
Ahmed, Sara, 49, 90
Allied powers, 30, 86, 89, 110
American National Council of Uhro-Rusyns, 29
Antisemitism, 18, 63, 87, 119; as explanatory concept, 9, 11–13, 17, 47, 63, 116–17; and Holocaust, 10, 17, 125; in Subcarpathian Rus', 12–13, 26, 47, 49, 52, 56, 74, 115; treatment in historical literature, 27, 33; in wartime Bulgaria, 124; in wartime Croatia, 122; in wartime Romania, 121
Antonescu, Ion, 121–22, 189–90n8
Applegate, Celia, 1, 18
Arrow Cross, 103, 171n82, 173n121
Auschwitz, 3, 7, 95, 97, 109, 120, 172–73n112, 182–83n93; and Adolf Eichmann, 89, 100
Austro-Hungarian Empire, 3, 28, 38, 141n26, 151n63, 155n123
Axis powers, 11, 18; and Hungary, 3, 81–82, 89, 102, 110, 120

Baky, László, 90, 93, 96
Bárdossy, László, 71–72
Bar-Tal, Daniel, 12, 49

Bereg (county), 2–3, 35, 67, 69, 78, 94, 144n58, 179n52
Berehovo, 2, 6, 53, 83, 142n45, 174–75n135, 154n104; and anti-Jewish policies, 67–69; deportations from, 91, 95, 100, 183n95; ghettoization in, 92, 94, 180n58; and Hungarian Soviet regime of Béla Kun, 28; and Roma, 78, 103; and sexual violence against Jews, 99; synagogue of, 113; testimonies from, 133n25
Beregszász. *See* Berehovo
Beskyd, Antonii, 30–31
Bessarabia, 121–22, 135n42, 189n7
Bíró, József (of Huszt), 80, 95–96
Birobidzhan, 39, 44
Borderlands, 1, 74, 85, 90, 100; and Bulgaria, 123–24; of eastern Europe, 1; and "Greater Hungary," 5, 66, 90, 101, 110; in historical literature, 1; and Holocaust, 15, 110, 119, 125; and Romania, 121; and social violence, 3; and Subcarpathian Rus', 1, 5–6, 19, 92, 100–101; and Transylvania, 3, 74, 120
Brodii, Andrei, 38, 52
Brubaker, Rogers, 55, 60
Budapest, 4–5, 80–81, 85–86, 89–92, 98, 117; Adolf Eichmann in, 17, 101; and control of Subcarpathian Rus' society, 76; flight

205

of Jews to, 100–101; in historical literature on Holocaust, 14; and Imre Kertész, 75; in interwar period, 28, 34, 65; Jewish leaders in, 73; perceptions of Jews in, of Subcarpathian Rus', 21–22; and Soviet occupation authorities, 109; Zionist movements in, 99
Bukovina, 2, 121–22, 130–31n10, 189n7
Bulgaria, 121, 123–24, 157n140
Bystanders, 9, 11–13, 18, 104–7, 111, 119

Carpathian Mountains, 6, 23–24, 44, 62, 83, 114; and deportations, 73, 92; flight of Jews to, 81; and interwar period, 16, 37, 57, 62; settlement of Jews near, 21; and Soviet occupation, 101, 108; and World War I, 27–28
Carpathian Sich, 54, 56–58, 60–61, 71, 159n8
Carpatho-Ruthenians, 2, 6–8, 11–15, 17–18; as bystanders, 104–6, 111, 119; changing relations with Jews, 12, 56–61, 63, 85, 114–16, 118; coexistence with Jewish neighbors, 19, 23–26, 46, 51, 114; and communist underground, 84; and competing national narratives, 37, 44, 47, 49, 55; and Czechoslovakia, 29–31, 33–34, 48; and deportations, 67, 70, 72, 76; and Greek Catholic priests, 21; and Hutsul Republic, 28; in interwar period, 33, 35, 38, 45, 48, 52–53; persecution under Hungarian control, 58–59, 65, 67, 71–72, 76–77, 82, 84–86, 116; and rescue of Jews, 107–8; and Roma, 87; schools of, 16, 45; and Soviet deportations, 109; and "Ukrainianism," 50, 52, 60–62, 84. See also Carpatho-Ukraine; Subcarpathian Rus'
Carpatho-Ukraine, 3, 44, 65, 67, 106, 115–16, 157n2, 164n1; rise and fall of, 16, 51–58; and "Ukrainianism," 59–63, 76, 87
Case, Holly, 3, 191n25
Central Rusyn National Council, 30. See also Avhustyn Voloshyn
Cholera, 24, 41
Chust. See Khust
Citizenship, 18, 37, 71–74, 117, 126
Cole, Tim, 11, 15, 104, 176n148, 178n27
Colonialism, 5, 48, 60, 62–63, 74–75
Communism, 28, 66, 68, 84, 96, 124, 129n1,

157n2; and interwar period, 38–39, 44–45, 163n55
Communist Party. See Czechoslovak Communist Party
Confino, Alon, 12, 66, 83, 155–56n125
Croatia, 11, 120, 122–23
Czechoslovakia, 1, 3, 5, 28, 53, 126; anti-Catholic positions in, 40; and Carpathian Sich, 57; and Carpatho-Ukraine, 52, 54, 58; dissolution of, 51; and Germany, 47; in interwar period, 16, 33–35; and land reform, 76; and Ministry of Education, 44; Orthodox Jews in, 41; political parties in, 16, 37–38; protectionist policies of, 35; Red Cross of, 35–36; relations with Jews, 48, 61, 115; and schools, 16; state-building by, 7, 14, 34–36; and Subcarpathian Rus', 13–14, 29–31, 34, 47, 60–61, 115–16, 118; trade relations with Hungary, 35; and Treaty of St. Germain-en-Laye, 30
Czechoslovak Communist Party, 38–39, 45, 84
Czechoslovak Jewish Party, 38–40, 46
Czechoslovak National Socialist Party, 38
Czech People's Party, 38

Délvidék, 74, 82, 100, 110, 120
Deportations, 5, 7, 17, 71, 183n95; and bystanders, 104; and Carpatho-Ukraine, 57; from the Délvidék, 74; from Dombó, 81; of ethnic Germans, 108, 120; from Huszt, 75, 97; from Kőrösmező, 73; from Nagyszőllős, 94–95; from Ungvár, 101; from southeast Europe, 123–24; from Transylvania, 80–81; and genocide, 86, 89; and ghettoization and violence, 65, 91, 93–97, 102, 105, 111; and "Greater Hungary," 67, 71–72, 76, 79, 102, 110; historical literature on, 15; of Roma, 65, 70–71, 76, 78, 103, 110; rumors of, among Jews of Subcarpathian Rus', 83, 100; by Soviets, 108–9; termination by German authorities, 117–18; and World War I, 36
de Rivera, Joseph, 12, 49
Dombó. See Dubove
Dragostinova, Theodora, 123
Dubove, 81–82, 95, 107

Eichmann, Adolf, 17, 89, 91, 100–101, 110
Endre, László, 90, 93

Engel, David, 9, 47, 132n19
Ethnic cleansing, 8, 122, 189–90n8

Felsőbisztra. *See* Verkhniy Bystryy
Fentsyk, Shtefan, 38, 52
Ferenczy, László, 91, 101–2
"final solution," 5, 18, 86, 89, 110, 124; and Miklós Kozma, 79; in Romania, 121
France, 30–31
Friedländer, Saul, 10

Galicia, 2, 35, 44, 56, 58, 115; communal violence against Jews in, 104, 106; and deportations from Subcarpathian Rus' (1941), 71, 73, 79, 117; in interwar period, 44; rise of modern Jewish Orthodox politics in, 151n63; settlement of Jews from in Subcarpathian Rus', 20; and World War I, 27, 42
Genocide, 13, 17–18, 27, 83, 89, 91, 98; and bystanders, 11, 105–6; definition by Raphael Lemkin, 86, 123; terminology of, 8, 125–26
Gerlach, Christian, 14, 100
Germany, 5, 10, 36, 119; alliance with Hungary, 3; antisemitism in, 26; attack on the Soviet Union, 71, 117; attack on Yugoslavia and Greece, 123; and Carpatho-Ukraine, 55; conflicts with wartime aims of Hungary, 97, 120; and Croatia, 122; deportations of Jews from Hungary, 73, 89, 101–2, 117–18; in historical literature, 11, 66, 121; and influence in Hungary, 69; in military retreat, 82, 122; plunder in Subcarpathian Rus', 97; refugees from, 36; and Subcarpathian Rus', 52
Gömbös, Gyula, 65–66
"Greater Hungary," 14, 18; and Carpatho-Ruthenians, 76, 86, 104; and collaboration, 120; conflict with "Greater Germany," 97, 120; defeat of, 103, 110; and deportations, 101; and German invasion, 87, 90; and Jews, 15, 17, 70, 86–87, 90–91, 111; and mass violence, 74, 76, 102; as political consensus, 5, 67, 117; in political imagination, 66–68, 70, 72, 83; and Roma, 86; and Subcarpathian Rus', 15, 17, 65, 67, 79, 112–13; and Trianon Treaty, 5
Greece, 66, 123–24

Greek Catholic (Uniate) Church, 6, 16, 40–41, 85, 180n58, 186n132; and "magyarization," 21, 139n12; in United States, 29
Greek Catholic Union of Rusyn Brotherhood, 29
Greenwald, Rabbi Moshe (of Huszt), 22, 56
Greenwald, Rabbi Yehoshua, 56, 58, 100
Greenwald, Rabbi Yekutiel Yehuda, 22, 56

Halperin, Eran, 12, 49
Hebrew Gymnasium (Mukačevo/Munkács), 36, 42–43
Hechalutz Hatzair, 39, 42–43, 99
Heimann, Mary, 52, 145n1
Hitler, Adolf, 10, 58, 80, 89, 91, 101
Holocaust: and antisemitism, 9–11, 125; and bystanders, 119; in historical literature, 5–6, 7–11, 13–15, 17, 49–50, 121, 125; in Hungary, 5, 7, 85, 100, 111, 119–20; in southeast Europe, 125; and Subcarpathian Rus', 18, 27; and testimonies by survivors, 9, 25, 45; terminology of, 8, 125–26
Hóman, Bálint, 66, 77
Horthy, Miklós, 65–66, 101
Hubay, Kálmán (mayor of Beregszász), 95–96
Hungary, 1–4, 10–11, 13, 86, 126; and aftermath of World War I, 28; and anti-Jewish violence after World War II, 109; and Arrow Cross, 103; and Axis powers, 3, 81–82, 89, 102, 110, 120; and borderlands, 3, 5, 66, 90, 101, 110; and bystanders, 104; and Carpatho-Ukraine, 52–53, 57, 63; and citizenship, 71, 74, 117; and collaboration, 120; defeat of, 112–13; and deportations, 70–76, 79–81, 100–101; ethnic Germans in, 120; German invasion of (1944), 3, 17, 89, 110, 118; and "Greater Hungary," 17, 65–67, 72, 87, 90–91, 110; in historical literature, 14–15, 85; and Holocaust, 7–8, 85, 100, 111, 119–21; irredentism of, 38; and Jews, 21–22, 41, 47, 69, 79, 93; and "magyarization," 66; and Nazi Germany, 100; post-World War I Soviet regime of Béla Kun in, 28; and Roma, 77; and SS, 92; and trade relations with Czechoslovakia, 35; Trianon Treaty, 5, 101; and United States, 29; and World War I, 31. *See also* Budapest; "Greater Hungary"
Huszt. *See* Khust

Hutsul Republic, 28, 60–61

Iasynia, 2, 28–30, 60–61, 73, 75, 183n95

Jaross, Andor, 90
Jedwabne (Poland), 11, 118
Jews, 7–8; and bystanders, 104–107; coexistence with Carpatho-Ruthenian neighbors, 23–27, 114; deportations of, 57, 70–76, 79–81, 100–101, 117, 183n95; destruction of in Subcarpathian Rus', 89–101, 113; and emancipation, 22; and ghettoization, 92–96, 110; and "Greater Hungary," 15, 17, 70, 86–87, 90–91, 111; and interwar Czechoslovakia, 33, 36–37, 45–50, 114–15; legal attack against, 67–70, 92–93; political activity in Subcarpathian Rus', 16, 37–40, 44; relations with Carpatho-Ruthenians, 11–12, 56–61, 63, 85, 114–16, 118; religious life in Subcarpathian Rus', 22–24, 40–42; and settlement in Subcarpathian Rus', 19–22; survivors from Subcarpathian Rus', 109; and World War I, 27–28; Zionism in Subcarpathian Rus', 42–45
Joint Distribution Committee (JDC), 27, 30, 35–36, 46, 69, 146–47n22

Kállay, Miklós, 86, 121
Kamenets-Podolsk, 76, 120
Kamins'kyi, Iosyf, 38, 45
Károlyi, Mihály, 28, 66
Karpatendeutschen, 6–7
KEOKH. *See* National Central Alien Control Office
Kertész, Imre, 75
Khust, 2, 6–7, 53–54, 56–57, 109; deportations of Jews from, 73, 75, 91, 101, 183n95; and formation of Czechoslovakia, 30; ghettoization and persecution of Jews in, 80, 91, 94–95, 97, 99–100, 105, 174n129; Hungarian gendarmes in, 83, 97; and Hungarian Race Protection Law, 69; and Hungarian fears of "Ukrainianism," 59; and Joint Distribution Committee (JDC), 35; rabbis of, 22–23, 41, 56; and Roma, 78
King, Charles, 3, 59
Kingdom of Serbs, Croats, and Slovenes, 30. *See also* Yugoslavia

Klympush, Dmytro. *See* Carpatho-Ukraine
Kőrösmező. *See* Iasynia
Kozma, Miklós, 58, 65, 71–72, 77, 79, 117
Kun, Béla, 28, 66

Lemkin, Raphael, 86, 123
Lipcse. *See* Lypcha
Lypcha, 74, 97

Macartney, Carlile A., 35, 40
Macedonia, 123–25, 157n140
Magocsi, Paul Robert, 2, 4, 13, 53, 131n12, 163n50, 170n69
Magyar Christian Socialist Party, 38
Magyarkomját. *See* Velikiye Komyaty
Magyar National Party, 38
Máramaros (county), 2–3, 6–7, 35, 56, 74, 117, 164n1, 183n95; and underground network of Carpatho-Ruthenians, 107
Máramarossziget, 2, 4, 21, 28, 80
Marxism, 23, 42, 158n5
Masaryk, Tomáš G., 29, 46
Mass violence, 1, 6, 9, 15; and bystanders, 105–6; and emotions, 12–13; and "Greater Hungary," 17, 76, 102; in historical literature, 7–9, 15, 105, 119; and Holocaust, 8, 10, 18, 119, 126; in Hungarian borderlands, 74, 120; against Jews in Hungary, 75, 79, 81, 85–86, 98, 107, 111, 117–18; against Roma, 63, 65, 71, 76, 102–3, 110–11, 116–18, 121–22; in southeast Europe, 121, 125; by Soviet authorities, 108, 112–13; in Subcarpathian Rus', 5–6, 11, 63, 87, 116–17, 119; and World War I, 28
Mauthausen, 104
Megay, László (mayor of Ungvár), 93, 102
Moldavia, 121–22
Mukačevo. *See* Mukachevo
Mukachevo, 2, 4, 6, 82, 103, 107, 131n11, 146–47n22; and Carpathian Sich, 54; and Carpatho-Ukraine, 53, 57, 59; and deportations, 101, 183n95; ethnic Germans in, 7; and expulsions, ghettoization, and robbery, 91–95, 97–99, 102, 105; and "Greater Hungary," 67; and interwar period, 35, 45–46; Jews of, 20–22, 24–25, 43, 75, 142n45; and Joint Distribution Committee (JDC), 36; and legal measures against Jews, 69; old Jewish cemetery of, 113–14; and post-

Index   209

World War II period, 113; and railways, 26; and Royal Hungarian Gendarmerie, 83, 91; schools in, 36, 42, 44; and Shapira, Rabbi Chaim Elazar, 39, 41–42, 152n77; Soviet occupation of, 103, 108–9; and World War I, 28, 30; and Zionism, 39, 42–43
Munich Pact (1938), 52
Munkács. *See* Mukachevo

Nagyszőllős. *See* Vynohradovo
National Central Alien Control Office (KEOKH), 70, 72–73, 86
Nazi Germany. *See* Germany

Olbracht, Ivan, 51
Operation Margarethe I, 89
Orthodox Christians, 6, 15–16, 21, 40–41
Orthodox Mukačevo-Prešov Eparchy, 41

Palestine, 37, 39, 41–44, 109, 122, 124, 164n4
Paris Peace Conference (1919), 30
Party of Autonomy (Autochtonpartei), 46
Perényi, Baron Zsigmond, 28, 65
Petersen, Roger, 12, 90
Poland, 53; and anti-Jewish violence after World War II, 109, 118; and Carpatho-Ukraine, 52, 54; deportations to, 70; and Galicia, 35; German occupation of, 10; and Isaiah Trunk, 49; and Jedwabne pogrom, 11, 118; partitions of, 20; refugees from, 31, 83; and Zionism, 41–42
Prešov, 2, 4, 30, 41, 53

Race laws, 69, 93
Radvánc. *See* Radvanka
Radvanka, 70–71
Railways, 26, 97, 101, 183n95
Relations between Jews and Carpatho-Ruthenians, 6–9, 12–14, 17–19, 84–85, 111, 118–19, 131n11; and bystanders, 104–8; and rise of political resentments, 45–52, 55–63, 114–16; and shared beliefs, 23–26
Roma, 63, 120–122; expulsions, deportations, and violence against, 70–72, 76–78, 103, 116–18; and "Greater Hungary," 17, 65, 67, 86–87, 102, 110–11, 113; and interwar period, 36–37; school in Užhorod, 37; in Subcarpathian Rus', 6–7; testimonies of, 9
Romania, 2, 7, 11, 53, 124, 189n7; and anti-Jewish violence after World War II, 109, 118; flight of Jews to, 99, 108–10; frontier with Czechoslovakia, 35; and "Greater Hungary," 5; and "Greater Romania," 121–22; and Little Entente, 30; and Nazi Germany's Axis alliance, 3, 89; ultra-Orthodox Jews in, 41; World War I aftermath, 28–29, 66
Rongyos Gárda, 54, 58, 65
Royal Hungarian Gendarmerie, 59; and deportations, 72–73, 91, 105; and violence against Jews, 67–69, 83, 93–97, 99, 174n129; and violence against Roma, 77–78, 102–3
Russia, 2, 87, 113; and Bolshevik Revolution, 29; influence in Subcarpathian Rus', 6, 21, 40, 44–45, 87; refugees from, 31; and World War I, 27–28. *See also* Soviet Union
Russian National Autonomist Party, 38

Serbia, 74, 81, 123
Serbs, 15, 67, 74, 82, 120, 122–23, 139n13
Shapira, Rabbi Chaim Elazar, 39–43
Shtefan, Avhustyn, 44–45
Sighet. *See* Máramarossziget
Siménfalvy, Árpád, 72, 78–81, 91, 177n9
Siménfalvy, Sándor, 72
Sisters of Social Service, 80–81
Slachta, Margit. *See* Sisters of Social Service
Slovakia, 34, 39, 42, 53, 81, 99, 159n16, 188n148; deportations to, 57; Jewish Orthodox communities in, 39; and Munich Pact, 52; refugees from, 83; and Zionism, 42
Snyder, Timothy, 11, 104
Solonari, Vladimir, 121–22
Soviet Ukraine, 3, 108, 113, 186n133
Soviet Union, 87; advance of armies into Hungary, 81, 89, 103, 111; annexation of Subcarpathian Rus', 3, 110; and Battle of Stalingrad, 81; and Birobidzhan, 39, 44; flight to, 72, 84; German attack and occupation of, 10, 17, 71; invasion of Romania, 121; occupation of Subcarpathian Rus', 3, 102, 108–9, 111–12, 116; and partisans, 107; targeting of Magyars and ethnic Germans, 113; and violence against Jews, 109

Subcarpathian Rus': and antisemitism, 12–13, 26, 47, 49, 52, 56, 74, 115; as a borderland, 1, 5–6, 19, 92, 100–101; and Budapest, 21–22, 76; and Czechoslovakia, 13–14, 29–31, 34, 47, 60–61, 115–16, 118; destruction of Jews in, 7, 74, 89–101, 111; and Germany, 52, 97; and "Greater Hungary," 15, 17, 65, 67, 79, 112–13; and Jewish survivors, 109; and Jews and World War I, 22, 68, 114; mass violence in, 5–6, 11, 56–58, 63, 70–76, 87, 116–17, 119; political activity of Jews in, 16, 37–40, 44; relations between Jews and Carpatho-Ruthenians in, 6–9, 12–14, 17–19, 84–85, 111, 118–19, 131n11; religious life of Jews in, 22–24, 40–42; and Roma, 6–7; and Russia, 21, 40, 44–45, 87; settlement of Jews in, 19–22; and Soviet Union, 3, 102, 108–12, 116; and World War I, 25–27, 31, 47–48, 50–51, 115; and World War II, 6–8, 14, 18–19, 111; Zionism in, 42–45

Svalyava, 2, 39, 45–46, 108–9
Svalava. *See* Svalyava
Synagogues: in Berehovo, 113; demolition by Hungarian Ministry of Interior, 102; in Munkács/Mukačevo, 20, 41–42; in Nagyszőllős, 94; use in expulsions and ghettoization, 94–95, 180n65

Timber, 20, 24, 35
Tisza River, 6, 28, 162n39
Todorova, Maria, 62
Tomcsányi, Vilmos Pál, 91, 93
Transcarpathian (Zakarpats'ka) oblast. *See* Subcarpathian Rus'
Transylvania, 3, 93, 121, 164n1, 165n17; deportations from, 100–101; and "Greater Hungary," 5, 67, 74, 77, 120; and Jews of, 80
Treaty of St. Germain-en-Laye, 30, 115
Trianon Treaty (1920), 5, 14–15, 66, 73, 85, 101

Ugocsa (county), 2–3, 67, 78, 91, 164n1
Ukraine, 6, 29, 114, 158n5. *See also* Carpatho-Ukraine; Soviet Ukraine; "Ukrainianism"; Western Ukrainian Republic
"Ukrainianism," 6, 16, 44–45, 50, 53, 55, 59–63, 77
Ukrainian Studies, 13–14, 136n52
Ung (county), 2–3, 72, 74, 78, 91, 93, 177n9

Ungvár. *See* Uzhhorod
United Jewish Party. *See* Czechoslovak Jewish Party
United States, 26, 29–31; immigration to, 136n52, 143n50
Uzhhorod, 2, 4, 6, 46, 53, 108, 113, 129n2; and Árpád Siménfalvy, 72, 78–79, 91; and deportations, ghettoization, and persecution, 70, 76, 91–94, 101, 183n95; Jewish survivors from, 109; legal measures against Jews, 69, 102; mass robbery in, 96–97; and national councils, 30; political parties in interwar period, 37–39; and Roma, 37, 103; schools in, 44; settlement of Jews in, 22, 26, 142n45; and "Ukrainianism," 59; and World War I, 27
Užhorod. *See* Uzhhorod

Veesenmayer, Edmund, 100–101, 176n1
Velikiye Komyaty, 25, 46, 75, 95
Velké Komjaty. *See* Velikiye Komyaty
Verkhniy Bystryy, 46, 67, 82
Verdeja, Ernesto, 11, 104
Voloshyn, Avhustyn, 30, 52, 54, 60
Voronezh, 81, 86
Vozáry, Aladár, 91, 94, 102
Vynohradovo, 2, 6, 65, 78, 83, 99–100, 142n45; and Árpád Siménfalvy, 72, 91; deportations from, 94–95, 183n95; ghettoization in, 92–93, 98, 102; and Hungarian Race Protection Law, 69; and World War I, 28
Vyšný Bystrý. *See* Verkhniy Bystryy

Werth, Henrik, 67, 77
Western Ukrainian Republic, 29, 60, 144n58
Wilson, Woodrow, 29
World War I, 3, 7, 18–20, 29, 44, 60; and Austro-Hungarian army, 38; and collapse of Central Powers, 28; Hungarian defeat in, 5, 66, 72, 85; and hunger, 30; and Jews of Subcarpathian Rus', 68, 114; and promises of autonomy for Carpatho-Ruthenians, 13; and refugees, 27, 31, 36, 42, 71; and rise of ethnonational nation-state, 23; and southeast Europe, 124; as turning point for Subcarpatian Rus', 25–27, 31, 47–48, 50–51, 115; and Zionism, 42

World War II, 1, 3, 27, 63, 85, 108, 119, 163n50; and antisemitism, 13, 52, 117; and bystanders, 104; communal violence during, 11; and destruction of Jewish communities of Subcarpathian Rus', 7, 74, 92–101, 111; and destruction of Roma, 9; in historical literature, 10–11, 104, 125; and Holocaust, 120–22, 125–26; and Hungarian borderlands, 74, 119; and Hungarian occupation of Subcarpathian Rus', 18; and mass deportations, 74, 79; in southeast Europe, 121–23, 125–26; and Subcarpathian Rus' prior to, 6, 8, 14, 16, 19; and subsequent anti-Jewish violence, 109; and testimonies of survivors, 9, 25

Yad Vashem, 25
Yiddish, 3, 20, 25, 75–76, 113, 149n51
Yugoslavia, 5, 30, 123, 125

Zhatkovych, Gregory I., 29, 31, 36
Zionism, 16, 36–37, 39–45, 47, 99

The authorized representative in the EU for product safety and compliance is:
Mare Nostrum Group
B.V Doelen 72
4831 GR Breda
The Netherlands